THE DUEL

THE DUEL

Its Rise and Fall
In Early Modern France

FRANÇOIS BILLACOIS

Edited and translated by
Trista Selous

Yale University Press
New Haven and London 1990

Set in Linotron Bembo by Best-set Typesetter Ltd., Hong Kong and
printed and bound at The Bath Press, Avon, Great Britain

Library of Congress Catalog Card No: 90-70103
ISBN 0-300-04028-8

Contents

Note on the English Text

The present text is a condensed version of François Billacois's extensively researched, immensely detailed and comprehensive study. The French edition includes footnote references for all quotations, a number of documents, tables and engravings reproduced as appendices and a very full bibliography giving details of Billacois's many manuscript and printed sources as well as other works consulted. In preparing the condensed version I have taken out most of the footnotes and all the appendices and greatly shortened the bibliography, giving English translations of texts where possible. I have also condensed the main text by about a third, largely by cutting details of Billacois's research procedure, but also by removing a number of tables and quotations. In so doing I hope to have left intact the development of Billacois's arguments and also to have retained the flavour of his text. Specialist readers seeking further documentary or bibliographical details will doubtless find what they require in the French edition.

Although I have occasionally found it necessary to rearrange some sections, I have very seldom had to resume or rewrite in order to condense. The present version therefore consists almost entirely of my rendition of Billacois's words. All translations of previously untranslated texts or those for which a french title is quoted in the Bibliography are also mine. On this point, I am greatly indebted to the author for his clarification of certain points and to Peter James, from whose attention to detail and many helpful suggestions this translation has benefitted enormously.

T. S.

Introduction

This aim of this study is to describe one of those human practices which Marcel Mauss has termed 'total social phenomena'. The duel is a total social phenomenon by virtue of the richness of its meanings and implications. It is a judicial institution, a factor in social differentiation, a political manifestation, a work of art and a religious (and/or ungodly) ritual. It has also been thought to have demographic significance. The only dimension it lacks is the economic, although the phenomenon could be interpreted as a form of compensation or revenge on the part of extra-economic forces in regard to purely material powers. This is a historical study, which aims to describe for a given period (the first two centuries of what are called 'modern' times) and for a defined area (the kingdom of France) the establishment over time of the phenomenon's constitutive elements and the stages of its decline, in terms of the social groups and ideological imperatives which maintained or countered it. It also attempts to analyse the particular duration of the practice of duelling seen as a resistance to official norms, a resistance which withstood both prohibition and propaganda, those two weapons of centralised authority.

The duel is a touchstone. For the author of the present work, and (I hope) for his reader, it is an aid to the identification and understanding of a particular period, society and political system, with its moral and aesthetic sensibilities and metaphysical and spiritual background.

This subject and the tangle of problems which it suggests or raises has led me to study a great number of heterogeneous sources which are sometimes very rich but never lend themselves to simple and repetitive treatment. There are theoretical writings (codes of honour and moral refutations) and concrete testimonies (fulsome or laconic anecdotes, not necessarily in agreement on the same example of single combat), legislative texts and jurisprudence and records of actual legal proceedings, the analyses of Catholic casuists and the beautified or highly charged images of the poets, songwriters or

engravers. Whenever a homogeneous group of sources has allowed,
I have attempted a quantitative study (*La Gazette*, confession manuals). But elsewhere such a study is impossible, even where one would
expect it to be most possible. The judicial sources are above all rich
in silences on this subject, by no means all of which are imputable to
gaps in documentary series. These silences are meaningful, but they
obviously do not lend themselves to quantitative study.

Often the subject – both as a real phenomenon and as an ideal
image – the nature of the sources and the present state of research
in the field of the history of mentalities have led me to choose a
qualitative approach. This is why I have so often presented a 'close-
up', a detailed description and minute study of a person, an episode
or a text. Taking a particular and eloquently documented case, I ask
myself to what extent it makes explicit that which is implicit in the
extensive but laconic and even deliberately silent sources.

When I tell the story of Jarnac's duel or Bouteville's trial, it
is because I am concerned with a field of the history of mentalities
in which the *exemplum* has a major and irreplaceable value. I have
therefore tried to give events which stand as examples their proper
place: they prefigure, crystallise and symbolise more durable possibi-
lities.

Lastly, I have done my utmost not to confound the profusion of
contemporary interpretations with the profusion of reality. But the
interpretations of the period are in themselves also a reality and the
historian's task here is to establish what mediates the connexion
between these two degrees of reality. Or rather to suggest personal
interpretations, whose sole value lies in the degree to which they can
honestly establish some coherence between these two degrees of
reality.

The first three parts of this study trace the chronological progress
of the duel as a phenomenon: first its origins in time, space and
human needs, secondly the more or less virulent phases of its maturity, and thirdly its resistible decline. A fourth part, which is less historical and therefore more fragile and personal, sketches, in a series
of pictures, some of the constituent themes of the duel as a concept: it
is to some extent a predella which has its place under the chronological triptych and signifies that the phenomenon of the duel has a
history outside which it is nothing, but that it is more than its
history.

PART I

The Sixteenth Century:
Early Stages of the French Duel

Chapter 1
The Word Duel

This is the excellence of Court: take away the ladies, duels
and ballets and I would not want to live there.
(A. d'Aubigné, *Baron de Foeneste*, II, 17)

Leprosy and incurable sickness rooted in our guts.
(C. Joly, *Antiduel*, 1612, p. 1)

Outlining a sociology of the duel at the end of the nineteenth
century, La Grasserie defined it as the 'clash of two parties who both
claim to be in the right, a trial by strength taking the place of the legal
form in the absence of a common judgement ... a trial which
decides no more than a war who is right, but simply who will win'.

To this definition, interesting in its comparison of duel and war,
we shall add two others. The first we owe to Muzio, the sixteenth-
century Italian theoretician, who was quickly translated and became
famous in France: '[The duel] is nothing other than a battle fought
hand to hand, to prove the truth; when I say hand to hand, I do not
mean it is limited only to two.' The other is taken from one of
François I's patents, which permits two gentlemen to 'fight each
other in a closed field and to prove themselves one against the other
for the justification of the honour of him with whom the victory will
rest'.

Starting from these three definitions, we shall here call duel a fight
between two or several individuals (but always with equal numbers
on either side), equally armed, for the purpose of proving either the
truth of a disputed question or the valour, courage and honour of
each combatant. The encounter must be decided or accepted jointly
by both parties and must respect certain formal rules, be they tacit,
oral or written, which will give it the weight of a legal proceeding, at
least in the eyes of the two adversaries.

Duels can therefore be distinguished from brawls and private
wars. They can also be distinguished from jousts or tournaments.
We should add that classically a distinction is made between a *judicial
duel*, a formal affair presided over by the sovereign prince, who

proclaimed the victor, and an *extra-judicial duel*, which was private, or concerned a point of honour, and where the combatants had no spectators or judge but themselves. It is this latter type which is the real object of this study, although chronologically speaking it grew out of the former, and the two were never completely separated in sixteenth- and seventeenth-century minds.

The word *duel* entered French vocabulary late, with the practice being established some time before its conceptualisation. The diary written by L'Estoile describes instances of single combat between 1578 and 1611, but they are called *duels* only after 1599, while we find the first use of the word *duelliste* to mean a participant in single combat in 1614. Looking at the word in its setting among other words in contemporary sentences and at the other (related or antithetic) notions associated with it, we find three series of words or themes.

The first series consists of the following; *courage, défi, démenti, querelle, réputation, satisfaction, valeur* (courage, challenge, accusation of lying, quarrel, reputation, satisfaction, value). This is only to be expected, as are the concrete words designating the material and other conditions of combat: *arme, épée, pré, second, sang* (weapon, sword, field, second, blood). This series of expressions simply develops the definition of the duel, and makes a factual account of events possible. Moreover, we find it primarily in narrative and anecdotal sources.

A second series places the duel among the different actions that may lead to violent death: *assassinat, suicide, sacrifice humain, exécution capitale, joute, tournoi, guerre civile, étrangère* or *sainte* (murder, suicide, human sacrifice, execution, joust, tournament, civil, foreign or holy war). This series is more often, but not exclusively, found in the work of lay or ecclesiastical moralists: jurists or theologians. It reflects a concerted effort to classify the duel as a species of the genus homicide. It shows an awareness that this phenomenon is linked to a particular ethical judgement about the value of human life.

The third series interests us even more. The word associations and links made between *duellistes* and other social types, and between their fights and other activities that were generally disapproved of, clearly express a value judgement. They shows us the horizon on which the duel appeared in the minds of a certain section of society, which at the least comprised the authors we quote and the readers they convinced, but was quite probably very large, since we find here all types of writings and authors with all kinds of allegiances. For all these people the duel was inseparable from the celebrations and splendours of the life of the gentleman, of life at Court. But at the same time, it was related to the activities of marginal, inassimilable or unavowable layers of society: the dregs and slums of the cities. And above all it was related to various forms of ungodliness, particularly blasphemy, and was thus a direct affront to God.

So this notion, which took almost a century to become emancipated, was thus criticised even before it reached adulthood, and was attacked on both social and religious grounds. A brief look at the qualifiers linked to the word *duel* confirms this. In a minority of cases the duel is presented as an exploit worthy of admiration: 'an act of honour', 'a brave act ... that enhances one's reputation'; in this frame of mind a gentleman invites people to his duel as he would to his wedding. But far more often the qualifiers are pejorative. The duel is a regrettable aspect of social custom: 'unhappy custom', 'misfortune and labyrinth', 'accursed practice'. For society it is seen as an almost inexorable public calamity: 'this precipice', this Greek fire', this 'horrifying monster', cause of 'universal consternation' is 'a disaster that tarnishes the candid freshness of our lilies!' For the individual, it is a guilty passion: 'like the passion of love, both of them in thrall to a vain and superficial beauty'; it is a 'damnable vice', which engenders 'misbehaviour' and 'horrible frolicking', it is 'a species of despair'. It also appears as a contagious disease, striking the nobility and gentry and even the entire population of France: 'plague', 'gangrene', 'rabies', 'pernicious disease', 'disease which has long been inveterate among the bravest men'. Lastly, the duel appears as a collective madness, a 'national mania', a 'public frenzy', a 'gigantic frenzy', a 'continual frenzy', a 'bloody and more than soldierly frenzy'. It reduces Christian, civilised man to the level of the idolatrous savage, even to that of unreasoning animals: the 'savage opinions that preoccupy and imbue your minds' are 'barbarisms'.

Though slow to come to prominence and reach its final shape, the duel was a phenomenon that aroused passions and caused division between people.

Chapter 2
Description

After considering explicit and implicit definitions, one way of getting to know the phenomenon we are looking at is to describe the chronological unfolding of a duel, to follow the account given of it by contemporary witnesses and to compare it to other duels and to a theoretical description, in order to arrive at an image which is valid overall.

Let us take, for example, the combat at Moulins on 17 February 1538, in which Lion de Barbençois, Sieur de Sarzay, confronted François de Saint-Julien, Sieur de Véniers, both of whom were gentlemen from Berry. We find an account of the affair in a small volume published immediately after the event, some memoirs of the period mention it and, a century later, Vulson de La Colombière gives it a place in his *True Theatre of Honour*. In addition, we have the texts of two royal statements relating to it.

The contemporary volume, devoted to descriptions of spectacle and prowess, neglects to relate the events preceding the morning of the combat. However, a duel is inseparable from the quarrel of which it is the logical, often fatal, outcome. In this case – and curiously – the quarrel had lasted many years and at the outset had brought Sieur de Sarzay into dispute not with Véniers, his opponent in the Moulins fight, but with a third person, Sieur de La Tour-Landry. Sarzay stated that La Tour-Landry had fled like a coward during the battle of Pavia in 1525. La Tour-Landry took offence at this and asked Sarzay for the source of his information. Sarzay (who was not at Pavia) said he had got it from a certain Gaucourt, and then from Véniers (who was not at Pavia either). 'Véniers denied having said it to the said Sarzay, and gave him the lie.' From this point on, Véniers adopted the position of the opponent, and La Tour-Landry was out of the picture. The duel took place not to wipe out an accusation of betrayal on the field of battle, but to dispel the suspicion of a lie – a lie which, according to present-day criteria, would be nothing more than a piece of malicious gossip. This example illustrates particularly well the kind of affront which would lead to a

The injured party is not the gentleman accused of cowardice in the field of battle, it is the man of honour suspected of having uttered a lie. In a duel, the offended party is the man accused of having said something that he asserts he did not say.

The accusation of lying was called *le démenti* and was the essential act which set in motion the duel procedure. Montaigne, who calls a chapter of the 1580 edition of his *Essays* 'On giving the lie' ('Du démentir'), states that 'the worst insult we can be given in words is to accuse us of lying'. Usage fairly rapidly codified expressions which distinguished the *démenti* from a simple denial. To say 'That is not true' was not to touch someone's honour; to say 'You're lying' and above all 'You're lying from your own throat' ('Vous en avez menti par la gorge') was an invitation to slit each other's throats in single combat. Later generations refined the subtleties of the *démenti*: at the beginning of the seventeenth century, the words 'You do not know what you are doing' were frequently considered to commit one to a duel. But the classic formula remained the one employing the verb 'to lie'. This was the one that François I used to challenge Charles V to a duel: the Emperor denounced the King of France as a traitor for violating clauses of a treaty he had signed; it was enough for the King to reply that this accusation was a lie to take the debate out of the sphere of diplomatic integrity and into that of aristocratic honour: 'As we have never done a thing that a gentleman who loves his honour should not do, we say that you are lying from your own throat and that, each time that you say it, you will be lying!'

He who has been given the lie – Sarzay in our example – is the offended party. It is up to him to give the challenge, to invite his opponent to a duel, to 'call' (*appeler*) him. He may be described variously as the 'appellant', the 'assailant', the 'actor' or the 'petitioner' (*demandeur*). His opponent is the 'called' (*appelé*) or the 'defender'. The sources concerning Sarzay and Véniers do not even mention the call. In this first half of the sixteenth century, the challenge in which a glove, dagger or some other 'battle pledge' was thrown down at the feet of one's opponent was no longer practised as it had been in medieval times. The call was given orally, in front of witnesses, or preferably in writing, by cartel. 'Just as in a civil court case one proceeds by issuing a writ to the parties who must respond, so for combat (which we take to be a form of legal proceeding) one must call one's enemy by a cartel on which the matter of the quarrel should be put as briefly as can be done.'

But more important in the procedure than the cartel (which was, after all, only the obligatory response to a *démenti*) was the request for a field (*demande du camp* or *demande du champ*). The offended party would ask the King for permission to settle the quarrel by force of arms. The King, if he accepted, would decide where and when the combat would take place, the form it would take and who was to preside over it, either alongside the King or in his place, to ensure correct procedure. We have the texts of the letters patent by which François I gave the field to Sarzay and Véniers. The King summarises the quarrel, after both parties have been questioned 'by the knights and captains we have appointed as our deputies'; after a meeting of the Privy Council 'and deliberation by several princes, lords and knight captains', he decides with his 'full power and royal authority' to call the two parties to fight in his presence, 'or in that of another whom we will appoint'.

There could be no duel between equals that was not in a circumscribed space, 'conceded' to this end by a sovereign prince, of whom the duellists were not necessarily subjects, but who possessed the two superior attributes of political authority over a territory and power as a supreme judge. The reason invoked by certain theoreticians to explain why a king could not accept a challenge was that there was no superior power on earth who could grant the field to a soverign. A few decades later, this custom of granting the field fell into disuse; but many duellists looked back to it with nostalgia – linked to a certain traditional image of arbitration by the King– dispenser of justice. In 1621 the Duc de Nevers requested a field from Louis XIII, as did Châteauvillain in 1624 and Malherbe in 1627. During the Fronde, Gaston d'Orléans was ready to grant a field to the Duc de Beaufort in the name of the young Louis XIV.

For Sarzay and Véniers François I chose the courtyard of the château at Moulins, a town close to the residences of both gentlemen. Any open space could be the right place for a duel. It would then be roped or fenced off, or even delimited with large stones or a wall of snow. At the beginning of the seventeenth century, when the closed field was no more than a memory, authors were still seriously discussing its ideal dimensions. Through force of habit, certain frequently chosen places became favourite sites for duels, permanent closed fields, such as the 'battlefield' in Pau, at one end of the bridge over the Gave, or the bridge over the Po, 'a place expressly designated for it' by the Prince of Melfi for the army under his command in Piedmont. The places chosen, château courtyards, town squares, esplanades under fortifications, or crossroads and stopping-places, were always very busy spots where a large number of spectators could be accommodated. To grant a field to a pair of opponents was to make their confrontation public.

While the Prince would choose the place of combat, the combatants chose their own weapons and equipment, the only rule being that the champions had to be identically armed. The man who had received the challenge was generally recognised as having the privilege of proposing the weapons, it being understood that the appellant could dispute his choice until they reached an agreement. This is what happened in our Moulins duel, where Véniers, the defender, chose to wear 'a corslet with long tassets, mail sleeves and gauntlets'. This same Véniers, on his arrival in the field, declared in front of the King that he 'wanted to fight with two naked swords, one in each hand for the first fight. And for the second, a sword in one hand and a dagger in the other. The two swords went to the assailant and were also placed in the hands of the defender.'

Sometimes the combatants would fight on foot, more often on horseback. They were usually protected by a helmet and frequently by armour and would carry two offensive weapons (one in each hand): often a sword and a dagger.

The entry of the champions into the field would be accompanied by an indispensable ceremonial, more or less elaborate according to the case. The King's role was passive until the end of the fight. But his presence, or that of his personal delegate, was essential in the imaginary sphere of the society of the time: engravings of the period giving more or less schematic depictions of a duel never fail to show the King with his crown on his head, or indeed the royal couple, to the extent of making him stand for the entire audience if there is not enough space.

The active presidency went to the Constable or to a marshal who was 'master of the field'. For the fight between Véniers and Sarzay, the Constable was flanked by the Comte de Nevers, the Comte de Saint-Pol and Marshal d'Annebault, 'each one carrying a helberd and all dressed the same, in velvet with facings', gold for the Constable and the Comte de Nevers, silver for the others.

On the 'scaffolds' surrounding the lists would sit the most select group of spectators, among whom ladies of all ages were never absent, and lastly four heralds, who were responsible for proclamations. At first the lists would be empty. Then the two champions would enter them, each flanked by a 'godfather' (*parrain*), Captain Bonneval for Véniers and Sieur de Villebon, Provost of Paris, for Sarzay. The godfathers were both moral support for their godsons and guarantors to all that the combat would be correctly conducted.

According to custom, the actor arrived first, 'before the hour of midday', in response to a cry from the heralds: 'Come to the field to do your duty!' In fact Sarzay arrived at dawn, 'led and accompanied by the King's tabors and fifes, and by his godfather with a large company of his gentlemen relatives'. Then it was the turn of the defender, similarly accompanied. After the proclamation of their identity and of the royal decree, each went to the tent allotted to him in one of two opposite corners of the area. These tents, or pavilions, were in fact 'thrones . . . covered in cloth in such a way that they did not have to see each other if they did not want to'.

Then would come the final procedures before the fight began.

The master of the field would forbid the spectators to do anything that might disturb the combat and be to the advantage of one of the opponents: 'to move or make signs with their feet or hands or to speak or cough, or to blow their noses or spit, on pain of having a hand cut off'.

The godfathers and people appointed by the master of the field would 'feel [to ensure that the combatants had] neither weapons nor charms under their clothing'. Recourse to magic that might distort equality to the advantage of one of the duellists was still, in the sixteenth century, almost as greatly feared as it had been in medieval ordeals. And the more demanding were only partially satisfied by the godfathers' 'visit' to the champions. Certainly it enabled them to find relics, talismans or 'blank parchments given by some magician or sorcerer', but there were more subtle charms: 'And I know that words of enchantment are written on to the naked flesh the night before entering the field, and, if my sources are correct, there are other words that knights mutter through their teeth as they walk side by side, looking their enemy in the eye. . . .'

Then the master of the field would hear the opponents' oaths. These oaths seem to have been a minor element of the ritual in the duel of Véniers and Sarzay. Is this not a sign that the oath was becoming anachronistic and that the fight itself was taking over the role of the oath in duels, those last avatars of the ordeal?

'Let the valiant fighters go!': with this thrice-repeated cry the heralds set the opponents against each other. From this point they were left to themselves and to the 'fate of arms'. No brake was set against their ardour, and only the 'extremity' of the combat could distinguish the victor from the vanquished. In the normal run of things, therefore, the fight between Véniers and Sarzay would have finished when one of them died, or was at least wounded sufficiently seriously to render him incapable of continuing the struggle. The sovereign or his representative would have intervened only to proclaim that the cause of the loser was bad and that he had lost his honour as well as the fight. François I, when he authorised their combat, explicitly stated 'that the said weapons of the loser will be dragged away and reviled and those of the victor will be exalted, and the said loser, be he dead or alive, will be punished at the discretion of the King'. The victor could kill his fallen opponent, or he could appropriate his weapons and 'drag his enemy off the field still alive.

He could also choose to show generosity and not claim all his due. In so doing he would enhance his reputation and humiliate the loser a little more, by placing him in his debt: the unfortunate who thus survived the sentence of arms then had no possible way out apart from a second duel ending in the death of one or the other. Royal justice would be content – except in the always possible case of clemency – to confirm the punishment manifested in the outcome of the conflict. 'Let it be known that when one of the champions is defeated on his surrender or death, he must be sent to the gibbet and punished as fits the case.'

If the fight's outcome was still uncertain by nightfall, the master of the field would put an end to it and name the appellant as victor. Indeed, the rule was that the duel began 'after the rising of the sun' and could not go on after dusk, nor be restarted the next day. One aspect of its public nature was that it had to take place out of doors, in daylight and lit by the sun alone.

Finally, a fight which remained undecided could be stopped on the King's initiative. This is what happened in our Moulins duel. Véniers and Sarzay fought with more courage than skill. The defender received a serious cut on his heel, which bled profusely. 'The King, seeing this, called out to them to stop and threw down a baton, which he had with him in the field.' The guards went into the arena and separated the two opponents. And François I, who had wanted this conflict to be settled by force of arms, ended it with a speech: 'the King confirmed that he had seen [La Tour-Landry] on the day of the battle [of Pavia] doing his duty at his side'. He 'declared that there was neither winner nor loser, called them both men of honour and gentlemen, said that he was pleased with them and forbade them to assault each other further'. Soon afterwards he gave each of them five hundred écus as a token of his esteem and in recompense for their bravery.

It is not our concern here to discuss François I's apparent illogicality in accepting that an argument relating to an event which he had seen and which the two parties knew of only by hearsay should be settled by force of arms. For the moment we merely wish to understand the unfolding of a duel. The King who conceded the field, who in some sense abstracted this closed space from his jurisdiction, and who wanted only to be a mute witness to the confrontation, a guarantor content with ratifying a decision – the victory – which was not his, this King could, at any time, take up his sovereign prerogative once more. He had only to throw the baton or sceptre he was holding down into the field and this gesture would end the fight, suspend the spilling of blood and avoid the necessity for naming a winner and a loser. However, because the confrontation had taken place, the honour of both parties would emerge complete (intact or restored) from the trial.

This description of a duel taking place about a third of the way through the sixteenth century shows it as an official and formal procedure. It was motivated by the accusation that one party was a liar, this being the supreme stain for a man of honour, for a gentleman. The duel condemned the loser and dishonoured him. As far as the actual proceedings were concerned, public opinion was more interested in the majesty of the spectacle than in the skill and bravery of the combatants: *The Order of Combat*, a pamphlet with 138 lines of text, dismisses the confrontation and exchange of blows between Sarzay and Véniers in only six. To make it a public event, the duel needed the ritual of ceremonial, the presence of spectators and even a particular choice of place and time of day for its staging. It also needed the authorisation of the King, who 'granted the field'; by this action the sovereign limited his power, restricting himself to a passive role, to being at most the executor of a verdict coming from elsewhere. But he could always take back the initiative and suspend the fight by throwing down his baton. The Prince's function was thus indispensable, but ambiguous.

Chapter 3

The Origins of the Duel in France

The duel might have been a new phenomenon in sixteenth century French vocabulary, but in practice it was a continuation of very old traditions.

One can see the duel for a point of honour as having a double root: in medieval Franco-Burgundy and the Italian Renaissance.

The duel is a form of ordeal or judgement of God. It is well known that in the early Middle Ages trials by such things as water, red-hot iron or boiling oil were made widespread by 'barbaric' laws. Those defendants who survived such an experience unscathed (as Daniel came out of the lions' den, or the three Hebrews from the fiery furnace) demonstrated their innocence, or that they had truth on their side, or more precisely that their cause had been chosen by God. The trial proved it, and served as both sentence and punishment.

The ordeal was not a practice exclusive to Germanic peoples of the early Middle Ages. It had existed, among other places, in ancient Greece. In a Christianised form, or at least called a 'judgement of God', it runs right through the history of the medieval West. The Church disapproved of this trivial procedure, worthy only of the inferior classes of society (called *probatio vulgaris* or 'popular proof'), and increased its condemnations, without success. Long after the Middle Ages lay magistrates returned to the ordeal in trials where the supernatural was inextricably linked to the natural: as late as 1601, the Paris Parliament had to make a decree forbidding trials by immersion (or proof by water) in sorcery cases.

The oath, which often took over from trials by ordeal, is simply a more abstract form of judgement of God and judicial combat was itself another, although it perhaps appeared later than the unilateral ordeal, in which a single defendant was tried using a material element. Judicial combat seems to have been specific to Western Christendom, being unknown in Byzantium and the Muslim countries, while the Normans took it to Sicily and the Crusaders to Cyprus. In medieval society, the great supporters of such procedures (in principal open to all) were the knights, who were fanatically keen on combat and had been prevented from fighting in private wars by the birth of states. While the bourgeoisie in the towns were dispensing with ordeals in their franchise charters, the nobility imposed on Philippe le Bel, and then on his sons, the re-establishment of 'battle pledges', which had been forbidden by Louis IX, known as St. Louis.

The period of the Hundred Years War and of the House of Burgundy at the end of the Middle Ages seems to have been the golden age of judicial duels or battle pledges. These were regular legal proceedings, fixed by the monarch or by a supreme court (in France this was one of the privileges of the Paris Parliament). They were also pageants, always formal and sometimes magnificent; the ladies were greedy for them and kings enjoyed them to the point where they would interrupt wars to attend a duel. The procedure did not alter after this time and was the same as that described for the sixteenth century in the preceding chapter.

A phenomenon akin to the duel, that of single combat between the champions of two armies or two sides, or indeed between two sovereigns, also flourished in the fourteenth and fifteenth centuries. The ritual was the same for both types of combat, which their contemporaries tend to combine in descriptions full of wonder.

Another related phenomenon which aroused great passions among the gentry and nobility at the end of the Middle Ages was the tournament. Tournaments were pure pageantry and sport, and in principal carried no judicial or judgemental weight. But they were lethal sport and the Church condemned them in the same breath as duels. Their pageantry was almost liturgical, with identical formal procedure to that of the battle pledge. As military exercises and warlike displays, they exalted the personal bravery of the winner, covering the warrior who showed cowardice, weakness or lack of skill in shame and ignominy. Such was their role as early as 1170, when the Comte de Flandres and his knights held tournaments 'for the honour of his lands and the training of the soldiers', and it was the same four centuries later, on the field of the Cloth of Gold, where eight French gentlemen challenged eight Englishmen 'who wish to attain honour'. It was a short step from the revelation of bravery in a tournament to the affirmation of honour through the duel.

Tournaments, single combat and judicial duels were aristocratic phenomena. The chronicles composed for the glory and entertainment of nobles and princes by Froissart, Monstrelet, Chastellain or La Marche are bejewelled with accounts of them. The anecdotal literature of the chronicles is paralleled by juridico-formal literature on combat. A Provençal monk, Honoré Bonet, made himself its theoretician towards 1387. A whole section of the treatise of war which he wrote under the title of *Trees of Battle* is devoted to 'combats to the death'. Bonet recalls the ecclesiastical condemna-

tions, states that 'often . . . he who was in the right nevertheless lost
the battle', but affirms that custom in France runs counter to these
considerations. He enumerates sixteen cases where, following Lombard laws, the battle pledge is permitted, and finally devotes nine
short chapters to the elucidation of points of procedure (enclosure,
oaths, the use of champions, and so on). This book, produced in
sumptuous manuscript form right through the fifteenth century, was
in the library of patron–princes such as René d'Anjou, Jean de Berry,
Charles d'Orléans and Philippe le Bon. It was printed very early and
did well: six editions prior to 1505 are known.

Jean de Villiers de L'Isle Adam (who died in 1437) also wrote a
treatise on the battle pledge, which he dedicated to the Duke of
Burgundy. Then Olivier de La Marche wrote one at the end of the
fifteenth century, and dedicated it to Philippe le Bel. These two
treatises exist in many copies, which bear witness to their success.

But let us not be misled by the word 'success'! The importance of
combat in a closed field as a cultural theme does not necessarily
correspond to its actual frequency. The sovereign or Parliament did
not automatically grant the battle pledge to anyone who asked for it.
As for duels between princes, many were anounced and some were
actually prepared at great expense, but none ever took place. One
may, with Huizinga, ask oneself 'if all that wasn't just a fine
pretence, or if the champions really expected to fight'.

Moreover, in the last decades of the fifteenth century, Olivier de
La Marche confessed: 'Few people living today have seen a battle
pledge carried out, and it is more than seventy years since such work
was done between two noblemen under this house of Burgundy.
And I, who have lived in this noble house nearly sixty years, I have
never in my life seen a battle pledge. . . .'

So judicial duels, like single combat in closed fields, were – even
according to a choice and particularly benevolent witness – extremely rare and rather outdated phenomena in the fifteenth century. It
seems to us that the duel (like the Crusade) must be considered on
two different levels. At the level of actual experience it was nothing
but a paltry relic, something exceptional and artificial. On the level
of the imagination, the duel was an essential anchoring point for
aristocratic attitudes.

This was a time when wars were being won by artillery and
rank-and-file soldiers. It was a time when the wheel of fortune was
raising the bourgeois Coeurs and Médicis to the highest levels; the
traditional nobility and gentry felt obscurely that they were on the
defensive. It was also the time when, in all the Christian monarchies
(and even around St Peter's throne) there were conflicts between
rival contenders, each claiming to be legitimate. There was a more

pressing desire for miracles, for the judgement of God to put an end to the distressing uncertainty. In this context, the duel's orchestrated sounds and codified furies were constantly present, like an obsessional fantasy.

So at the end of the Middle Ages the formal battle pledge was declining in practice but intensely alive in the imaginary sphere. This explains both its disappearance at the end of the sixteenth century and the strong genealogical link which then united it with the duel for a point of honour. We can see this link reflected in the following facts. The judicial duel disappeared only very slowly from customary law: 1539 in Brittany, 1583 in Normandy, 1789 in Béarn (despite a revision of Custom in 1552). The Paris Parliament protected its traditional prerogatives regarding 'combat' at the time of a *lit de justice*, or session of the King in Parliament, held by Henri II in 1549: exactly two years after the King had granted a closed field to Jarnac and La Châtaigneraye (the last formal duel authorised in the kingdom and, according to Morel, the last formally judicial duel). The 'opinions' of Olivier de La Marche and Villiers de L'Isle Adam were published in 1586 in an edition that included the cartels exchanged by François I and Charles V, under the significant title: *Treatises and Opinions of Some French Gentlemen on Duels and Battle Pledges*.

Philippe le Bel's legislation was ceaselessly used, cited and even published in its entirety by all those who, at the beginning of the seventeenth century, were writing polemics for or against the duel. Up until the middle of the century, the kings maintained the fiction that they were prepared to grant a closed field if they judged such a proceeding to be necessary, and occasionally some gentleman who had little interest in actually fighting, or who was nostalgic for the good old days, would ask his sovereign for a field.

So the relation between the combat of the Middle Ages and the duels of the sixteenth and seventeenth centuries is incontestable. On the level of practice, the transitions are imperceptible and the breaks neither total nor definitive. At the level of attitudes the link is even more visible, with a deliberate desire on the part of the nobility and gentry to keep within the tradition of their medieval ancestors.

Although gentlemen of the sixteenth and seventeenth centuries who were partisans of duelling were aware that they were continuing a tradition of the French Middle Ages, they were also convinced that they had to learn from the Italians in order to fight correctly and effectively. Following Charles VIII's cavalcades into the peninsula, and after more than a century of intensive migration and exchange in both directions across the Alps, Italy gave French gentlemen two things: a technique for single combat (fencing) and a juridico–ethical corpus (*scienza cavalleresca*).

'We go to Italy to learn to fence,' says Montaigne, who, when in Padua, visited 'the schools of fencing, dancing and horseriding, where there were more than a hundred French gentlemen'. His contemporary, Brantôme, boasts of having spent a month in Milan 'partly to see the town ... and partly to learn the use of arms from the great Tappe, who was then a very great master of arms'. The high nobility, who did not have the time to take a course in Italy but who had the means, would take on an Italian master; Pompeio came to France for Charles IX and his brothers, Salvio for Henri de Navarre, and 'the excellent' Cavalcabo for Louis XII and Gaston d'Orléans. Henri III owned a manuscript treatise on fencing which Lovino of Milan had written for him, illustrated with sixty-six magnificent miniatures.

For less princely students, certain Italians opened schools of arms in France, such as that of Faldoni in Lyons. Others commissioned or permitted the translation of their fencing manuals: Cavalcabo of Bologna was published at least four times in France between 1595 and 1617, Giganti of Venice was translated in 1619. Until the middle of the seventeenth century fencing manuals written by Frenchmen were comparatively few, the fact that copies surviving till our day are extremely rare is proof that the public attached little value to them, and many of these authors like the oldest-known writer, Henri de Saint Didier, contented themselves with cribbing the Italian masters.

The influence of the mentors of Italian chivalric science had different effects from that of the technical literature. The first Italian theoretician published and translated in France was the 'famous Alciat'. For Alciat the duel was something forbidden by ecclesiastical and civil law, but perfectly valid in terms of customary law. He defines 'this combat of which God is the judge' as 'a type of trial' and concludes ambiguously, describing the splendours of the victor's triumph and recalling how Diogenes incited champions to renounce illusory rewards and to devote themselves only to philosophy.

Possevino, who followed Alciat in the chronological sequence of publications, had much less effect than the latter. His *Dialogues of Honour* appeared in five books, the first four containing a hotchpotch of metaphysics and ethics. The fifth book is concerned with duels, but is of the same type as the other four, consisting of a series of laudatory definitions of aristocratic honour, virtue, the *démenti* and the duel itself. The author rejects the assertion that the duel is 'something bad ... against all reason'. It is 'naturally fair' and 'when it involves homicide, it is by accident'.

Muzio's (or Mutio's) *Combat*, which ran to three editions in Antoine Chappuys's translation, is above all a moralising work written by one of the men of letters of the Tridentine Church. Muzio recalls that 'trial by the sword is uncertain, in contrast to civil trial'. He condemns magic practices, criticises those who fight without an audience and without a defensive weapon and maintains that a duel does not have to be fatal to be honourable. But the book, written with a lyricism that can only be described as baroque, can easily be read as an apology for duelling. It exalts honour as a kind of universal motor force, and the word of honour as the very seal of human dignity. It follows that the supreme sin is to lie and, in consequence, 'those who wish to be valued in the exercise of arms and for their chivalry ... when they are accused of lying, cannot justify themselves in any other way, they have to unburden themselves with the sword'. Finally, any duel that is fought from neither hatred nor revenge, but as 'an instrument which eternal majesty wishes to use to carry out its justice', appears as right and praiseworthy.

These three authors weigh heavily in the bibliographical arsenal of French duellists of the sixteenth century. Until the last decade of the sixteenth century, Frenchmen undoubtedly learned the theory of the duel from Italy, more so even than the practice of fencing. Nevertheless, Champier's chapter and the late (and unique) edition of La Marche and other 'French gentlemen' of the preceding century discreetly but surely prove that the duel – an aspect of Italian society – was also felt to be an authentic French traditioin.

Chapter 4

A French Phenomenon

This is ... what I have heard and learned from the great
Italian captains, who in times gone by were the first
founders of these combats and their niceties and knew the
theory and practice very well. The Spanish too, but not so
much. Today our brave Frenchmen are the best masters, as
much for theory as for practice.

(Brantôme, *Discourse on Duels*, p. 376)

Not only the Germans, Spanish and Italians, who are our
neighbours and have the same faith as we do, but also the
Turks, Persians and Abyssinians ... all joke about French
laws of honour.

(V. d'Audiguier, *The True and
Ancient Practice of Duels* 1617, p. 6)

Moralists who denounced the practice of single combat often used a
comparative argument: that the duel was unknown among the
pagans of Antiquity and did not exist among the Infidels, Moors and
Turks, while other peoples of Christendom practised it only in
moderation. It was therefore shameful to France, the Church's Eldest
Daughter, and to her nobility and gentry, the offspring of the
Crusaders, to create such carnage with their own blood.

Is there a concrete observation underlying these rhetorical developments? Was the phenomenon particularly virulent in France
and did it take on particular and original forms? To answer this
question, it is necessary to examine France's most important neighbouring countries, those with which there might have been a reciprocal exchange of cultural influences. So before returning to France
in full possession of the facts, we shall take a rapid look at the
situation in four other close cultural spaces: the Germanic world, the
kingdoms of England and Spain and the states of Italy.

The Empire

The duel had such an important place in the military circles and
student world of the nineteenth century (even of the twentieth) that

many German historians have considered it to be a phenomenon native to Germany, established without a break at least from the time of the barbaric laws of the early Middle Ages, if not from the time of the Germans described by Tacitus. Other authors, belonging to the evangelistic current, have tried to demonstrate that the duel is too barbaric a custom to be authentically Germanic, and have declared it to be a foreign import that arrived with all the other problems during the Thirty Years War. Supporters of both sides have gone through many sources and show a great deal of erudition; their work allows us to pose the problems which conern us here: the link between the duel and medieval judicial combat, the dates and places at which the duel for a point of honour first appeared, and its relations with the French duel and comparisons between them.

Formal judicial combat was known in the late Middle Ages in Germany. Certain localities were traditionally renowned for such proceedings, which were upheld by legislation – Würzburg in Franconia, Onspach near Nuremberg and above all in Schwäbisch-Hall. Gentlemen who had a quarrel went to this latter town, where the Senate would try to reconcile them. If it was unsuccessful, it would make available to them a town square where they fought 'for honour and dignity' (*um eere und glimpf*). These details were given in 1537 by the town clerk, Maternus Wurzelmann. They bring the duel very close to the point of honour, even if we agree with the historian Below that the world *eere* had a much wider and vaguer sense than the modern *Ehre* ('honour'). But was Wurzelmann describing a living reality of his time, or a tradition which had fallen, or was falling, into disuse? Two generations later, in 1609, the town council of Schwäbisch-Hall formally stated that this famous right of combat was no longer in use. But just a few years after Wurzelmann, Sebastien Münster had already testified to this. In his *Universal Cosmography* he describes the procedure of a combat at great length, but all his verbs are in the past tense. His directions end with a list of four fights, the first dated 1005, the three others undated, and the last being moreover resolved before the actual confrontation by a reconciliation reached by the Senate. So Wurzelmann is talking about an 'antique', which was just an archaeological relic at the end of the Middle Ages in his town of Schwäbisch-Hall.

Even a generation with so chivalric an imagination as that of Maximilian did not revive the judicial duel. It is remarkable from this point of view that Goldast's collection of the Empire's laws contains no text relating to the *Kampfrecht* after the first years of the sixteenth century, while the nearest forerunner to this text itself dates from the beginning of the fifteenth century. On another point, the collection contains no law relating to extra-judicial duels. There is therefore a gap between these two forms of duel on the chronological level and doubtless also on the logical one.

At the time when Goldast was gathering his collection of texts and after his death (1635), the territories of the Empire passed laws forbidding and punishing the practice of the challenge and the duel for a point of honour. These laws set fines and sometimes prison as punishment, with the death penalty solely for cases of murder. Out of forty-two of these laws, only three were passed in the sixteenth century (a sixteenth century which starts in 1572). Three-quarters of them were passed in the second half of the seventeenth century and of the whole a quarter came in the period 1650–5. It seems that suppression began late, died down curiously between 1583 and 1609, was at its most intense in the fifteen years following the Treaty of Westphalia, and remained significant until the end of the seventeenth century, suggesting that duels were at their peak close to the time of the Thirty Years War. Certainly alliances and rivalries between gentlemen and warriors throughout Europe must have contributed to the acclimatisation of this cultural element in the Germanic countries; but the duel came into its full social importance only when the war was over. This statement leads us to an important question: is this chronological sequence more or less coincidental, or does it signify a deeper link?

Moving from legal to narrative sources, one gains a similar impression. At the beginning of the sixteenth century the *Story of Knight Wilwolt von Schaumburg* is full of disputes and brawls between mercenary foot soldiers, but no duels. The same thing can be seen in the autobiography of the knight Hans von Schweinichen, which covers the years 1568–1602. In a cosmopolitan university town like Strasbourg, where challenges were banned relatively early (1583), chroniclers mention a few affairs of honour. Osias Schad notes the first in 1602: it was a challenge not followed by a duel, a conflict between a man from Lorraine and a Frenchman. In 1613 a duel took place, this time between two men from Strasbourg. They stopped at the first scratch and paid a fine of fifty guilders. There was another affair in 1628, between two Parisians. It was only after 1650 that duels became more frequent and were fought between natives. Below cites a duel in the imperial army in which a Czech fought a German; this was in 1646. At Tübingen the first actual prosecution of duellists took place in 1657: two students were imprisoned for a week and sentenced to pay six Thalers to their seconds. The first death in a duel indicated in the material consulted was that of a young man of nineteen, killed in Hamburg in 1652.

So the duel penetrated late, and became of serious concern to public opinion only after the middle of the seventeenth century. In

Strasbourg, where, as we have seen, duels became established earlier than in the rest of the Empire, and where the magistrate began to worry about them in 1583, the ecclesiastical ordinances do not mention them in 1598, nor in 1604, nor even in 1670. It was in 1635 that the Strasbourg presses printed the first sermon against duels: twenty pages in Johann Schmidt's *Christliche Weisheit*. On the Catholic side the struggle was no more intense and began no earlier than that of the Protestants. *A Theological Debate on War and Duels* between Riepel and Schober was printed in 1600. However, it was a real exception. It was published at Ingolstadt and testifies above all to the Jesuits' vigilance and level of information concerning all the dangers which faith and society might face, including those less urgent in the present. Far more revealing, in our opinion, as far as the Germanic situation is concerned, is the attitude of the region's casuists. We have studied three: Binsfeld, Busenbaum and Laymann; on the duel, their treatises (none of which predates the 1620s) are lacking in originality in comparison with their foreign colleagues. Binsfeld only gives the duel a kind of appendix to his paragraph devoted to what we would call conscientious objection (the soldier's right to refuse to fight an unjust war) and in a highly revealing parenthesis Laymann states that, for a reason which he does not elucidate, 'the Germans and other Nordic peoples seem to be exempt from the excommunications' with which the Council of Trent and Pope Clement VIII had smitten duellists and their accomplices. In the Churches as in the German states, suppression began late and was slow, and not very severe, until far into the seventeenth century.

Before making a definitive decision about whether or not the duel was an imported phenomenon, we must look at the question of which social groups were the first to welcome the duel and in which did it become most firmly established. In 1615 the lawyer Matthias Berlich spoke of parasitic gentlemen and knights errant who gate-crashed banquets, where they picked quarrels and 'challenged [people] to fights and duels'. This milieu of the gentry and petty nobility, poor, rootless and aggressive, was the one which provided officers for both sides in the Thirty Years War.

Another group touched early by the duel, in the west as in the east, in north and south, was the small world of the universities. In its Latin constitution of 1546, the Königsberg academy warned its students against challenging others to fight and against accepting such challenges. *Studiosen* figure among those targeted by the edict of the magistrate of Strasbourg in 1583. Eight of the forty-two anti-duel laws we have recorded originate from academic authorities. A pamphlet by Fritsch on the subject of duels between students was published in Ratisbon in 1686 and a second edition appeared three years later in Leipzig. The importance of duels between students in the seventeenth century and even before can therefore not be denied. But can one place these duels between students in the same category as those duels between students that occurred in Germany in later centuries? It would seem not. The historian Klüpfel has very carefully gone through the registers of the academic senate at Tübingen and, although they show students causing commotions and committing murders all through the sixteenth century, it is not until the seventeenth century that a challenge is given or a duel fought. In 1628 the Senate stated that these practices had been established for some years, but the first decree banning duels did not appear until 1654 and first punishment (as we saw above) in 1657. So there was not such a big gap between the world of the university and Germanic society in general, in terms of either the period or the virulence of duelling. It is just that students were more receptive to the duel than others because they were grouped together away from the frameworks and constraints of their families and homes, at an age when they were turbulent and curious. It was also because places like Wittenberg or Ingolstadt were international centres, meeting points for the whole of Lutheran or Catholic Europe, where the fact that everyone was of the same faith made it easier to transmit more specific cultural elements. It was only late in the eighteenth century that student bodies fixed their rules and took up a 'medieval' pose, when the students' duel or *Mensur* became a ritual. At the time that concerns us here, students practised the duel not because they were living in a closed world but, on the contrary, because they represented a world that was particularly open to external influences. We should add that many of them were gentlemen, and therefore belonged to the same social group as the disruptive guests criticised by Berlich. Duels between students – which were very fashionable in the seventeenth and, in pockets, in the sixteenth centuries – reveal that rather than being places where Germanic traditions were preserved, the universities of the Empire were places where foreign influences were embraced.

So the duel penetrated Germany through two milieux on the fringes of society – these being the two milieux which were then most open to the unusual and which later strangely turned their attention inwards and became almost secret societies, those traditional bastions of the duel until our own twentieth century, the army and the universities.

The duel for a point of honour was perceived as an exotic product in the Germanic countries. Until the end of the seventeenth century it is never designated by the autochthonous word *Zweikamp*, but by the word *Duell*. The few lawyers and rare theologians who discuss it (usually in Latin) borrow their arguments from Roman and canon law and plagiarise Spanish, Italian and French authors. Let us take an example from the very end of the seventeenth century, when Caspar Thurmann produced an erudite dissertation in Latin and a bibliographical list on the question: *Duellica*. The work begins with a page of 'Declamations and exclamations against duels', consisting of quotations borrowed from three authors: a German, Ziegler, and two Frenchmen, Fenouillet Bishop of Montpellier, and 'magnus quidam praesul in Gallia'. The proportion of foreigners in his sources is even more massive: among the twenty-one lawyers that he quotes, only five are German. When he enumerates the causes of duels, he cites *bagatelle* and *reputation*, in French in the text, and the German summary which he gives his book is also peppered with French words. As this example indicates, German contemporaries of Louis XIV borrowed the vocabulary of duels and honour from French. Among technical or ritual terms at the end of the century, Klüpfel and Fritsch found the following: *Rencontre, Satisfaction, Comment-Comment?, Avantage, Contrahage, Touche, Maltratationen, secondieren, renomieren, chargieren*. But in 1615 Berlich was already writing, '*provocieren* zu Kämpfen und Duellen', employing a corruption of the French *provoquer*, 'to challenge'.

The vocabulary of duelling was French and the duel itself was perceived as French. The satirist Moscherosch makes this clear in his *Philander vom Sittewalt* (1643). Using the word *reculieren*, he explains that it is a bit of jargon used by 'duel fanatics'. In another passage he pities a German gentleman who has agreed to second a Frenchman, and declares the duel to be 'a wrong deed which has become commonplace in France. . . . Now it is equally practised by a section of the German nobility and gentry: they settle their quarrels at the point of a rapier, and no longer, as our venerated ancestors did, with their fists or daggers.'

So the duel, which penetrated slowly during the first half of the century, and massively after the Peace of Westphalia, was certainly an exotic commodity and one which entered under the French flag.

England

The welcome given to the duel in England was very different from that which it received in the continental mass of the Empire. England was certainly an island kingdom, but it was at the centre of the great currents of change in Western Europe. The problems were posed in a particular way there, and even in their irreducible aspects they help us grasp the issues in France.

First, the links between private and judicial duels were more tenuous and ambiguous in England than in the Germanic countries.

Formal combat in the presence of the sovereign was still a reality for the English of the sixteenth and even of the seventeenth centuries. The procedure was used as late as 1571 in a legal dispute over land between two lords in the country of Kent. Queen Elizabeth, who presided, suspended the fight before anyone was hurt and reconciled them through a negotiated settlement. In the neighbouring kingdom of Scotland, the King authorised a fight as late as 1631. After that the judicial duel ceased to be practised, without becoming outmoded. Bills aiming to end 'all trial by battle' were unsuccessfully submitted to the House of Commons in 1620, 1625, 1629, 1640, 1641 and then again in 1770 and 1774. The procedure was called upon again in a trial in 1817 and was not prohibited by law until the following year. The judicial duel may not have remained alive in practice, but it remained so in the letter and spirit of the law and in the collective consciousness. Anyone who needs convincing need only think of the historical narratives of fifteenth-century England, which were almost myths for a contemporary of Elizabeth I or the first Stuarts, or recall the splendid apology for judicial combat, for God's combat, which is Shakespeare's *Richard II*. Such things would have led people to think of the ritual duel before judges as a normal procedure and would have prevented recognition of the value of a duel which rolls judge, litigant, witness, sentence and execution into one.

How did the informal duel, which did not replace or succeed the judicial duel, become an English practice? A brief history of the word 'duel' will allow us to answer this, by marking out the progress of the adoption of the phenomenon. Shakespeare, who exalts the judicial duel in his history plays, was as far as we know the first to give a place to the extra-judicial duel, in this case in his exotic comedies. In fact the word makes its first appearance in *Love's Labour's Lost* (published around 1595), in the form 'duello'. At about the same time the word 'dualist' appears, this time in *Romeo and Juliet*. The context, peppered with Italian words, presents the duel as a bizarre and unassimilated novelty: 'The *passado* hee respects not, the *Duello* hee regards not', or 'The very butcher of a silk button, a *Dualist*, a *Dualist*, a gentleman.... Ah, the immortal *passado*, the *punto reverso*, the Hai....'

In 1606 Bryskett wrote the word in its latin form: *duellum*. He used it to designate a fashionable phenomenon and a traditionally accepted procedure (confused with the judicial duel): 'This kind of challenging and fighting man to man, under the name of *duellum* which is used now a day among soldiers and men of honour and by long custome authorized to discharge a man of an injury received.' But Selden was still using the form 'duello' in 1610 (*The duello, or single combat*) and Overbury in 1613 (*A Wife*). A seventeenth-century manuscript gives the form 'dewel'. However, the spelling 'duell' makes its entry in 1611 with Coryat's *Crudities*. Recounting an episode from his stay in France, he writes, 'They fought a duell,' but feels the need to define the thing he has named at once, 'that is a single combat in a field.'

In 1632 D'Espagne was still hesitating between 'Duello' (which he used in the title of a work) and 'duell' (which he used in the body of the text). So the duel did not figure in the collective awareness of the English until the very end of the sixteenth century and was seen as something imported and strange for a long time. It took at least twenty years for it to become acclimatised.

It was Italian in origin, but France took it over and the French influence was soon seen as the most important. The first school for arms in London was opened at Blackfriars in 1576 by Rocco Bonetti, and until 1600 fencing masters and manuals were all Italian. But by 1640 it was to the French academies that the English nobility and gentry were sending their sons to learn the use of arms. And from the beginning of the seventeenth century the French appear as authorities on the code of honour. Just as Shakespeare mixed Italian words into his English, so Selden weaves typical French expressions into his essay on duels: '. . . *Fame* impeached, *Body* wronged, or *Curtesy* taxed (*qu'on a diffamé l'honneur des dames*, as on saies) . . .', 'private combat, *seul à seul*'. Apart from a few references to Norman customs, this author mainly cites two Italians, Alciat and Muzio, and one contemporary Frenchman, La Béraudière. Selden is one of the three English authors we know of who published a work on duels between the reigns of Elizabeth and Charles I. Three other works appeared in the same period on these issues: two were translations of French books, and the last was the work of a Protestant minister from Dauphiné who was living in London. Those who found this literature insufficient had to supplement it on the continent, as did Lord North, who procured a *Book of Duels* in Rouen in 1605.

This rapid investigation of the vocabulary of publications confirms the impression of the seventeenth-century English: it was the French more than the Italians who were responsible for the epidemic of duels which broke out in England. Bacon mentions French and Italian publications, but incriminates France above all, 'whence this folly seemeth chiefly to have flowne', and King François I, 'source of this new doctrine'. Beaumont and Fletcher share his opinion in 1616 and a century later John Cockburn makes the same judgement, regretting that, to England's shame, it has taken France as its model and learned its lessons there.

So there is a chronological gap between England and France, with England adopting a receptive attitude, the position of a more or less reticent disciple. Does this mean that there were fewer duels in

England or that, as in the Empire, they grew in number only when they were in decline in France? Because of the lack of documentary series, it is no more possible to draw up annual statistics for challenges and fights in England than for those in France. But at least there are some indices of tendencies. Lawrence Stone, the historian to whom we owe this century's most penetrating analysis of the phenomenon in question, surveyed all the duels mentioned in all the letters and narrative sources that he went through for his *Crisis of the Aristocracy*. He gives us figures for the decades between 1580 and 1620 and we can compare them to similar figures we have obtained for France. Our figures are no more exhaustive than Stone's, but it is possible to draw a few conclusions from a comparison of the two sets.

In England, as in France, there was a progressive increase in the number of duels between 1580 and 1620, but their quantity (if not their exemplary value) does not appear to have been greater in France than in its island neighbour until around 1600. The disparity becomes obvious only in the decade 1610–20, when France goes clearly into the lead. Stone does not continue his figures after 1620; however, we can concur with him in saying that the phenomenon declined fairly rapidly in England after that. In France, on the contrary, the high level of the 1610s did not lessen until at least a third of the way, if not halfway, through the century.

A few indices suggest that there was a resurgence before and during the English Civil War. Stone himself invites us to think this by prudently restricting his conclusions on the decline of duels in the seventeenth century. Cockburn's anecdotal work, *The History of Duels*, recounts several fights at the time of Charles I. Cromwell banned them in 1654. Finally in 1659, Pestel, a former chaplain to Charles I, published a *Treatise on Duels*. So we can sketch out the following chronology: appearance of duels around 1590, increase until around 1620, then a very sharp decline, interrupted by a revival around 1645–55.

How are these rises and falls to be explained? The Elizabethan taste for things Italian has something to do with the beginnings of the infatuation. And the practice of the 'grand tour' on the continent, made possible by the Peace of Vervins (1598), has a part to play, as Stone notes. Then the French fashion, current everywhere in Europe at the time of Louis XIV and reinforced at Court by queens, foreign favourites and the exile of the Stuarts in Ile de France, explains why the duel never disappeared and why, at the same time, it kept its foreign flavour.

The upsurge we discern in the middle of the century is linked to the political and religious crisis that the country was going through at the time. When a king's authority is no longer unanimously respected, knights revert to aristocratic values. This was the period when, as Leo Strauss so clearly saw, Hobbes was exalting the virtue of honour and saw the duel as a manifestation of this political virtue. However, those who opposed the royal prerogative were certainly also tempted by the duel, for it was a way of proclaiming and realising equality between the gentry of the Commons and the Lords of the Upper House. And a deeper analysis would doubtless reveal something we find in France in similar circumstances, that is that when the monarchial model blurs, when the model of a deliberating assembly, a parliament in the most etymological sense of the word, takes over, both oratorical jousting and single combat flourish simultaneously. But this upsurge was only an Indian summer. In the Puritan Commonwealth, duellists faced a much stronger monarchial authority than that of Charles I, that of the Lord Protector, not to mention the Lord of Hosts.

Although they do not explain it, the measures taken to ban duels by the political and religious authorities at least give us indices of this revival of duelling towards 1620 and again after the Civil War. There was only one edict against duels before Cromwell's, that of James I in 1613. Except for cases where a man was killed, the punishment for duellists was banishment from the presence of the King, 'source of all honour'. To make an example, Bacon prosecuted two obscure gentlemen before the Star Chamber. The lack of insistence and firmness on the part of the lay powers contrasts with the rigour of the religious authorities. D'Espagne's *Antiduello* is a long refutation of those scriptural arguments sometimes used in favour of duels. The Christian cannot be responsible for his own justice, he says, it is the business of judges established by God to pass sentence. The only exception, and even here the author has reservations, is possibly that of duels between kings, for the sole reason that there are no judges above kings. The theologian Ames, whose moral teaching is often very close to Roman tradition, breaks firmly with his Catholic contempories in his *De conscientia* (1631) as soon as the issue of duelling is broached. He decides that all the cases of duels he discusses are illicit, even those fought in defence of God's honour. During the Restoration, the Anglican casuist Baxter was still more categoric: duelling does not appear as such in his *Christian Directory*, but it is implicitly condemned with the right to defend one's honour by force. Like the discreetness of civil law, the strictness of ecclesiastical law indicates that in England the duel never took on the dimensions of a social issue, or a political problem.

At this point a question arises: why, despite its fairly vigorous beginnings at the turn of the sixteenth century, and despite the fact that it found undeniable and lasting favour in aristocratic circles, did the duel have so little resonance in England?

Contemporary writers were preoccupied with this question, and their explanations, although in themselves unsatisfactory for us, provide food for thought. To Dallington, who accompanied the English Ambassador to Henri IV's France, the question was one of national temperament: whereas the spirit of vengeance drives the Frenchman to fight without stopping to think, 'the English gentleman, with mature deliberation ... judiciously determineth his maner of satisfaction according to the quality of the offence'. In the same period François de La Noue, the French nobleman and author of *Political and Military Discourses*, suggested that those sado-ludic tendencies which expressed themselves in France through quarrels and duels were satisfied in England by the spectacle of fights between animals. This remark deserves greater consideration (taking Dallington's opinion into account). As well as animal fights, the Elizabethan theatre of 'blood, voluptuousness and death' and judicial combat, which could be potentially if not actually watched, in some way sublimated the appetite for vengeance and the attraction of blood within ceremonial institutions. At a time when France was a prey to duels and collective revenge, its theatre gave only a minor place to the theme of revenge; in England, which escaped these convulsions of social sensibility, the theatre was dominated until 1620 by the theme of vengeance, by the Revenge Tragedy. Can this be simply coincidence?

The judicial duel diverted people from the private duel because it was a spectacle (even if only potential) and also, as we have seen above, because it was a legal procedure. Sir Robert Cotton was certainly not writing an erudite work unconnected to his time when he wrote a discourse on 'the lawfulness of Combats to be performed in the King's presence', in which he condemns in the name of Magna Carta any sentence which does not arise from the deliberations of a jury or from the laws of the country. Magistrates and laws are two notions which hold the key to English political thinking from the time of the Tudors onwards. Gentry, nobility and Crown were perceived, both by themselves and by those they governed, as public responsibilities and functions of the state. And the state was so distinct from those who held power within it that Charles I could be tried and convicted of High Treason. In England the King was recognised more as a magistrate than as the first among gentlemen. The 'fashion' of duels did not develop under Elizabeth and James I; there was no failing of public authority nor climate of anarchy as there was in France during the Wars of Religion. And although there was an upsurge of duels to coincide with Charles I's attempts at absolutism, as with those of Louis XIII, in England this was a manifestation on the part of the King's own supporters and not a protest against the new order. The later revolutionaries, the Parliamentarians, had too much of a sense of the state, law and public order really to be in favour of duels. Bacon gives magnificent expression to this sense, more or less confusedly felt by his compatriots, when he proclaims against those who, by fighting duels, 'presume to give law to themselves.... It bringeth calamity on private men, perill upon the State, and contempt upon the law.' Returning to the subject a few years later, the Chancellor declared the duel to be 'a direct affront of law and tends to the dissolution of magistracy'. 'Whosoever doth send a challenge to a man doth send a challenge to the law.'

This sense of the state was above all a sense of the social whole. For Bacon duellists were wrong because they were anarchistic and he readily compared them to the Anabaptists. In France, a Catholic country profoundly disturbed by the Reformation, which had suffered civil wars followed by absolutism, and where the gentlemen lorded it over the bourgoisie, the aspirations of individuals wishing to exercise their free will in its social aspects played themselves out in duelling. In England, where Puritanism, capitalism, free enterprise and freedom of thought were important in a society which was otherwise very hierarchical, only isolated and more or less anti-social individuals felt the need to fight duels. The English revolutionaries were not duellists because duellists are rebels.

Let us propose one final reason. The youngest son of a great house, who had gone into commerce, had the nerve to refuse a challenge, saying that he had a wife and six children to support. In England, where the middle class rose to power early, and where strictly economic arguments were listened to, the duel appeared as too great a risk to profit: honour which could not be converted into another asset was not worth a human life. In France the duel's enemies implored their contemporaries not to waste their blood; but this was so that they could save it for the service of the King in war, or better still, spill it for God in the Crusade. French gentlemen thought in terms of destructive potlatches: to sacrifice one's life was to manifest, to impose one's power. The reasoning of English gentlemen followed the precept of 'do ut des' and they conducted themselves like accountants. Again, Bacon gives the most lucid expression to this way of proceeding, which remained foreign to the French until late into the seventeenth century: 'It is in expense of blood as it is in expense of mony. It is no liberality to make a profusion of mony upon every vaine occasion, not noe more it is fortitude to make effusion of blood except the cause bee of worth.'

The duel did not become as widespread in England as its beginnings suggested it would because in that country there were bloody displays, because its people had a profound sense of the state and the social corpus and finally because they saw blood as money.

Spain

The image of Spain that its religious, artistic, literary and military creations give us is one of a country where the hidalgos had a strict sense of their identity, life was felt to be tragic, there was an intellectual intoxication with chivalric romance, an obsession with women's honour and a morbid anxiety about purity of blood. Such an image might lead us to assume that, from an early date and for a long period, Spain would have been a paradise for single combat.

Let us look more closely. Analysis of documents shows us that although the duel's place in the Spanish world was not as great as a certain traditional idea of the 'essence' of Spain might lead us to believe, it took a highly original form.

Particular characteristics can already be found at the level of vocabulary. Legal documents and literary sources – like the everyday language of today – do not use the word *duelo* a great deal, preferring *desafío*, which places the accent less on the symmetricality of the fight and more on the provocative words addressed by One to the Other. The French word *honneur*, which can be seen as a vague crossroads where women's honour, valour in battle, a good reputation in society and even honour in business meet, corresponds in Castilian to two words with different meanings, *honor* and *honra*. To these two words should be added a third, *hombra*. These simple lexical facts point to the richness of the conceptual complex surrounding the fact of the duel.

The particular characteristics of the duel in Spain are also discernible in the laws applying to it. In a juridical synthesis written at the end of Charles V's reign, Hugo de Celso devoted an article to *desafiar* which summarises chivalric jurisprudence at the end of the Middle Ages. It is a sort of Castilian equivalent of Olivier de La Marche's treatise on battle pledges, but had a greater effect, since it was integrated into royal legislation. Thirty years later, by order of Philip II, the famous collection of laws called *Recopilación de las leyes* was published and became the standard reference book for generations of jurists. The *Recopilación* contains no fewer than eleven texts governing the formal duel. None of them was the work of the 'prudent King', or of his father. The most recent (1480) was exactly a century old when the book was published; it was one of the laws of the Catholic kings condemning spontaneous duels that were not authorised by a sovereign and the sending of godfathers or cartels, and decreeing the punishment for a duel in which a man was killed to be death or exile for life.

If we are to believe Don Martin de Ulloa, a scholar of the Enlightenment, it was not until two hundred years later, during the reign of a sovereign of French origin, that the next legislative measure was passed. This was the Pragmatic Sanction of 1716, which which Philip V renewed the orders of his distant predecessors and also excluded those who contravened the law from pensions and public responsibilities and functions (including military orders).

This long gap, which corresponds very closely to the period under scrutiny, is something peculiar to Spain. Should we see it as indulgence or indifference on the part of the Habsburg dynasty? Or is it that, whether or not as a result of the law of the Catholic kings, the duel for a point of honour, which came into being very early, had stopped playing a real role in the social life of the peninsula by the beginning of the sixteenth century?

To answer this question would require an investigation of the judiciary archives, and other documentation. We will content ourselves here with a few indications gleaned at random during our research.

During the years 1517–19, two men from Navarre, followed by two Catalonians and then a Valencian and a Tuscan, took advantage of a brief period of peace in Béarn to go to the sovereign of Pau to 'ask for a field'. In one of these cases it is known that the opponents had first made a similar approach to their 'natural lord', Charles V. It was because this request was fruitless that they addressed themselves to Albert d'Albret. For those men at least, it seems that a duel had to be formal and authorised (although for a point of honour) and that their sovereign did not think fit to give them this authorisation.

In his *Discourse on Duels* (a polemical text addressed by a Frenchman to his compatriots, but generally well informed), La Noue portrays Philip II's Spain as a country with a sustained policy of sanctions against the perpetrators of unauthorised duels, and a consistent, subtle and energetic attitude which contrasted sharply with the incompetence of the Valois: 'some are ordered to be imprisoned in châteaux, others are banished for a certain time; some are also condemned to go to fight the Moors in Barbary. Sometimes they are made to make reparations in public. And when the deed is serious, it carries the penalty of confiscation of property or death.'

In 1566 Jeronimo Jimenes de Urrea, a Spanish Grandee and Viceroy of Apulia, published a *Dialogue on Real Military Honour*. In it he portrays a Spanish gentleman who, having just returned to his country, declares that he is obliged to leave once more for the army in Italy since, he says, 'if it should happen that some bold impertinent insults me or wrongs me in some way, the barbaric laws of Castile prevent me from challenging him publicly and showing by means of arms to God and the world that I am better than he, or killing him for this quarrel'.

In the middle of the following century, Father Alonso de Andradès tells the story of how, following a fatal duel, a presidio captain in Africa had to become a renegade in order to flee the justice of his country.

Two conclusions can be drawn on the basis of these few indications. First, without ever banning formal duels, the public authorities turned against them very early and, it would seem, stopped authorising them in practice. Also, at an early period, action was taken against those who practised private duels. It seems that there were sufficiently few who broke the law in this way for the renewal of the general ban to be unnecessary, and for the law to be applied without meeting resistance.

As a counter-proof, let us place the analysis at another level, that of the writings which were circulated on the theme of duels. Besides the manuscript of a contemporary of Charles V, we have been able to locate six sixteenth-century books and one that appeared in 1642. Only one of these books is a real code of honour, and allows for duelling as long as it takes place according to the rules and in a just cause. This is the jurisconsult Diego del Castillo's *Tracatus de duello*. But when this Latin work appeared in Castilian (1525), it was under a title which gave it a very restricted interpretation: *Remedio de desafíos*.

There are two other works, written on the occasion of the unfought duel between François I and Charles V. The aim of the highly unofficial humanist Alfonso de Valdès in his *Dialogue between Mercury and Charon* was merely to present an 'official report' of the quarrel between the two sovereign knights. In it he portrays François I as a megalomaniacal criminal, in contrast to the wise Habsburg monarch, who resembles Rabelais' Grandgousier faced with Picrochole. The duel is clearly not the main point of the debate. However, the *Dialogue's* author incidentally recognises that the opponent whose cause is just can only win and that therefore the duel could put an end to Christendom's internal wars.

In the other text, commissioned by the Emperor, the jurisconsult Ercilla also aims simply to gather documentation on the unfought duel of the sovereigns. But he goes beyond this project to give a theory of the general legitimacy of single combat. According to him this sort of combat is judicial in name only, because in it force carries more weight than the law and the winner is not always the best man. Justice belongs to God alone, only He can dispose of human lives, and if He permits the death of one of the combatants it may be as punishment for previous sins unconnected to the affair which the challenge is supposed to settle. Natural law, the law of men and canon law all oppose the duel and the *appelé* is no less guilty than the appellant.

Ercilla had read the theologians and quotes them; he had also read some 'doctors of duels', Baldo, Paris de Puteo, Giovanni da Legnano. So for this Spaniard the Italians were the authorities on duels. Muzio, the Italian author of the Counter-Reformation, was happy to quote Urrea's *Dialogue*. This work had a great influence in Spain, where it ran to several editions, and later authors frequently referred to it. It was, moreover, the only Spanish treatise which reached a French readership. Although qualified, as the genre of dialogue would tend to make it, the book is the opposite of an apology for duels. Certainly Urrea judges as a gentleman in cases involving honour, but at the same time, as a Catholic, he judges in line with the Council of Trent. The conclusion of the first part gives us the tone of the whole, where the noble Altamira declares to Franco: 'You have spoken to me prudently and as a Catholic, and so I have decided to reform and correct my vain propositions and to place myself at the bidding and discretion of reason and justice: for certainly the man who leaves these two things behind is, as you have already said, almost a beast, and very close to the bestial state.'

After Urrea authors merely give the death blow to the duel, which is by now a fallen enemy. Captain de Eguiluz sees it as a 'false procedure of bad intent', Count Sastago sees it as an unpardonable sin against the Holy Spirit, while Father de Andradès gives anecdotal illustrations of the eternal abandonment to which the duellist condemns himself.

Is this a victory of the Counter-Reformation supported by Philip II, against a former penchant of the nobility and gentry? To conclude in this way would be to simplify to the point of nonsense. We have seen that serious reservations were already being expressed during the previous reign. More importantly, in 1537 a Franciscan monk who was very close to Court, Antonio de Guevara, wrote a long epistle aimed at persuading a gentleman involved in an affair of honour not to fight a duel. This piece testifies to an active vigilance in which Guevara prefigures St Charles Borromeo, the Bishop of Milan. In Spain, religious opposition to the duel was not one of the battles of a Counter-Reformation imported from Trent; it was perhaps one of the victories of the humanist spirit that was ingested very early by the peninsula's intellectual elite.

The duel never really had a properly native existence in the Iberian peninsula. Whatever the Italian historian Benedetto Croce might have thought, it was not the Spanish who passed the sickness of single combat on to the Neapolitans. On the contrary, it was the Italians who, at the beginning of the sixteenth century, provided the Spanish with 'doctors of duels', masters of arms and often closed fields. And it was the French in the entourages of the Bourbon kings who, at the very end of the seventeenth century, began to revive the dying practice of duelling. France itself took no lessons from Spain in this area, except those from the moralising and in no way encouraging pens of Urrea and the casuists.

So the duel was not the dungeon in the Spanish aristocracy's castle of the soul. A sense of honour and a taste for challenges certainly allowed an early flowering of formal duels and judicial jousts; but during the golden age these were able to develop to their highest forms without the support of the duel for a point of honour, which soon faded.

We still have to consider the reasons for this early and rapid decline.

The most obvious reason is the same one that gave the country moral unity and put it in conflict with the France of the Valois, the England of the Stuarts and the German states with or without the Habsburgs, that is the politico-religious ambience of the Catholic kingdom. The Church of Spain carried out its humanist reformation very early and from the top. Its authority had a strong material base and was never afterwards seriously challenged. After the first third of the sixteenth century the authority of the sovereign (particularly in Castile) was as undisputed as that of the Church. Loyalism and obedience were such that subjects and believers had completely interiorised the ban on duels and had no feeling that it was a constraint imposed form outside.

Another reason can be added to the first. As in late-sixteenth-century England, and doubtless to a greater degree, those drives which elsewhere found satisfaction in duels were here resolved in the formal and official spectacles of jousts and animal fights. Cane fencing and javelin competitions (and, at the beginning of the sixteenth century, French-style tournaments) were both ludic and agonistic events. They were sporting trials and moments of moral truth, which were highly prized by Spanish gentlemen. The aristocracy went to bullfights just as commoners did and often practised this type of combat. 'The fashion for this lordly exercise extends throughout the entire peninsula . . . kings themselves, until Philip V, grandson of Louis XIV, had to undergo this test of knighthood.' When the Pope wanted to prevent this murderous sport with canonical sanctions, Philip II protested 'against the great violence this would do to his kingdom', and Rome had to give in.

The practice or the possibility of openly, officially and formally practising cane fencing or bullfights took away a great deal of the interest that a duel fought in secret might arouse. In his epistle against duels, cited above, Guevara clearly sensed the relationship between these two phenomena. He devotes two pages of his nine-page work to vituperations against the corrida, almost without transition, and mainly because he sees it as a 'pleasure coloured with blood' and a place where women lose all modesty. The associative complex of pleasure plus spilt blood plus attack on feminine honour highlights the elements that duels and bullfights have in common, and demonstrates that for Castilian society the one could be a substitute for the other.

With the notion of feminine honour, we have touched upon even more profound reasons for the paradoxical lack of interest in duels in Spain. As in all Mediterranean societies, there existed in Spain an obsessive anxiety about feminine virtue. In the 'cloak and sword drama' of the period, the hero's honour depends on the conduct of his wife, his daughter or his sister much more than on his own courage, merits or titles. 'A man cannot uphold his honour through his own virtues – he has to abandon this care to his wife.' Similarly, a slap, an insult or even a *démenti*, which were all motives for duels in France, appeared in Spain to be much less serious than the merest suspicion of a stain on a woman's virtue or reputation (whether or not she consented was unimportant). Urrea stated clearly: 'The worst dishonour that can happen to a man is the adultery of his wife, for if a man says I am lying and denies me rightness and truth, he can give them back to me, but my wife can take away my honour and can never return it to me.' When Madame d'Aulnoy visited Spain a good century after Urrea, she did not perceive this hierarchy of affronts, but she did notice its logical consequence:

> Murder is quite normal in this country on several grounds which are even authorised by custom.... These things can only be avenged by killing. They say the reason is that after such insults it would not be just to risk one's life in single combat with equal arms, where the offended party might die at the hand of the aggressor; and they will wait twenty years for vengeance if they cannot carry it out before then.

And she adds a few lines further on: 'To carry out these evil deeds men from Valencia are usually called in.... There are no crimes they will not resolutely undertake for money....' A murder, carried out if necessary by hired killers, was the required revenge for a woman's dishonour. This did not exclude duels, but rendered them secondary for gentlemen who had lost touch with both the subtleties of chivalric codes and the techniques of the fencing schools. In a country where honour was not a conquest in which a man had to be recognised by his *fellow*, his equal, against whom he measured himself, but was instead a family treasure, an inheritance exclusively and passively held by women, which could be taken away at any moment by an *other*, someone irreducibly foreign, reparation was no longer a matter of duels, but of vendettas.

In a kind of psychoanalysis of Spanish society at the time of the 'cloak and sword drama', Americo Castro has brilliantly shown that anxiety about feminine honour was a mask covering a more tenacious anxiety, that of the purity of Old Christian blood. One needs to reach down to this underlying anxiety, this deep and fundamental stratum of Hispanic mentality in the sixteenth and seventeenth centuries, to be able to synthesise and go beyond the reasons that we have found for the duel's lack of attraction for a society which was nevertheless intoxicated with a sense of honour. In France, duels flourished when society was breaking up into rival groups of Catholics and Protestants. Over the same period in Spain, the duel was fading away in a society desperately searching for unity by rejecting that which was not totally and essentially itself in fearful investigations of purity of blood.

This is certainly more than a coincidence. For a French Catholic gentleman, facing a Huguenot meant clashing with his double, his symmetrical complement, his negative, or rather his negator. This false image had to disappear to ensure the existence of him whom it merely reflected. To overcome my opponent, the so-called reformed Christian, is to force him to recognise me; and I can force him to do this only if I risk being overcome by him, if I put my own existence at stake. To drive the New Christian or the Moor from one's land, one's house and one's genealogy is to declare that they do not exist, it is to refuse to recognise them, to refuse to recognise oneself in them, to be recognised by them; taken to the extreme, it is to find one's identity only in self-mutilation.

In the duel as in the Wars of Religion, the Frenchman risked his existence to prove his essence. In investigations of pure blood, the Spanish risked their essence if it were proved by public opinion, independently of themselves, that one of their ancestors was not an Old Christian; and that was so no matter what their own merits, virtues and titles.

This requirement was plebeian in origin but it spread to the whole society, including the gentry and nobility, and by the end of the Middle Ages much of the nobility had allied itself to rich and powerful Jewish families. At a time when the gentlemen were always liable to find themselves on trial before the court of the people, they had more important things to do than go searching for recognition by measuring themselves against their equals with swords in their hands.

'I am one of the Old Christians, and that's enough to be a count!' says Sancho Panza; and his master replies: 'Too much, even!' This is because the madness of Don Quixote lies in the fact that he believes himself to be a knight, while his sanity lies in the fact that he is not sure of it, so that he needs to affirm himself, to have himself recognised, constantly to challenge other knights, his peers, his fellows, his rivals. But he does not – and herein lies his drama – meet knights. He meets only windmills or convicts. The knight of the sad countenance gives out challenges and receives punches. He cannot confront himself; and so he realises that he is a knight who does not exist.

Quixote's aristocratic madness saves him from the real anxiety about purity of blood which gripped actual aristocrats. This collective anxiety spread because of the religious and political unanimity of the Catholic monarchy. Within a nobility and gentry thirsting after honour and heroism, it was able to dispel, or at least to reduce almost to nothing, the desire for recognition through the death of the Other in single combat.

Italy

In England, Spain and France, the duel was seen essentially as a product imported from the Italian states. One must therefore go to Italy to find a valid comparison with the French duel in terms of the virulence and development of the phenomenon.

The important place of the duel in Italy is suggested to historians from the outset by the mass of manuscripts and printed documents which they come across and by a certain number of scholarly works which mark out their trail.

A first barometer of the importance of duels is offered by the works of chivalric science (*scienza cavalleresca*), the writings of those whom their readers called 'doctors of duels' or 'professors of honour'. These works form a continuous corpus from the 1360s (Giovanni da Legnano) until around 1560 (Muzio, Possevino), and their circulation was at its peak in the middle of the sixteenth century. Latin treatises on the duel were translated into the vernacular at this time and new editions followed in quick succession: at least six of Alciat between 1544 and 1552, six of Muzio between 1550 and 1563, five of Possevino between 1533 and 1564. They were only occasionally reprinted after this and, although others continued to refer to them right through the seventeenth century, had practically no new editions after 1590.

In fact after the second half of the sixteenth century, *scienza cavalleresca* underwent a profound transformation. The word 'duel' in treatise titles was replaced by that of 'honour' or, more rarely, 'reconciliation'. Perhaps the most typical of these writings is *Three Books on Honour*, an unfinished work by Giambattista Guarini. This is a long, subtle and rhetorical dissertation on the abstract notion of honour; in the pages in which it is discussed, the duel itself appears buried between that which, logically speaking, precedes it (the insult) and that which follows it (the reconciliation).

Only one treatise stands out from its contemporaries, in both title and content. This is *On the Duel*, written in 1572 by Giovanni Vendramin, a poet and soldier of Venetian origin who spent his life in the service of the Emperor. The argument of the treatise is traditional, but its analyses and presentation are original. Taking the form of a dialogue between some Milanese gentlemen who have been trapped by bad weather in a hunting lodge, it offers an autumnal, virile, Lombard counterpart to the springlike, gallant and courtly dialogue that Baldassare Castiglione set in motion half a century earlier in the castle of Urbino. In an accomplished way it treats the great themes of a society which was starting to decline before renewing itself. This work, which was something of an oddity in post-Lepanto Italy, has remained unpublished until today.

To sum up, it would appear that, at the level of the theoretical literature at least, the Italian duel had an unrivalled reputation. It was at its height in the middle years of the sixteenth century, but its subsequent decline was very rapid.

What was the situation at the concrete level of affairs of honour?

For Urbino we have Vendramin as witness: 'The most illustrious François-Maria della Rovere, Duke of Urbino of glorious memory, was held in his time to be a true oracle in terms of the practice of honour. All the professors of honour bowed to his infalliable judgement in disputed affairs, and entirely submitted to his pronouncements as if they came from God.' For Ferrara we have something even better: the archives of the court of honour, which was presided over by the princes of the Este family.

The dossiers of 123 affairs of honour covering the sixteenth and seventeenth centuries are gathered into four bundles at the Archivo di Stato at Modena. It is thus a rich collection, but the individual documents vary greatly in nature, from challenges and replies to authorisations for combat in a closed field, *pareri** and manifestos. So in many cases it is hard to tell whether or not the duel took place, and

---

*Literally 'opinions', given by a gentleman regarded as an authority on matters of duelling. (Ed.)

what its outcome was. We should add that the protagonists had very different geographical origins, from Piedmont to Sicily – not to mention a few Frenchmen and Spaniards and one German – and although their duels usually took place in Ferrara, Modena or Mantua, they might just as easily have occurred in Carinthia or Flanders. The only unifying element to this whole, allowing us to use it for more than just anecdotes, is that all the dossiers are addressed to the Duke of Este, or proceed from him. It is the jurisprudence of a chivalric law court whose sphere of influence went far beyond the boundaries of the Duchy of Ferrara–Modena.

Classifying these dossiers chronologically, one can discern the reflection of an overall evolution in the practice of duels. Between the Alps and the Apennines, fatal duels were always rare. After the middle of the sixteenth century, duels to even the first blood became almost non-existent (the two mentioned for the seventeenth century took place in Swiss and imperial territories respectively). Interest in affairs of honour was much less in the seventeenth than in the sixteenth century and, listing the affairs by decade, one finds that after a peak around 1550 there was a very rapid decline over the last thirty years of the sixteenth century.

If the Modena bundles are anything to go by, the practice of duelling was, like chivalric literature, very widespread in the first half of the sixteenth century, reaching its peak in the last years of Emperor Charles V's reign, after which it collapsed very quickly. Our work therefore merely confirms the impression of the most clear-sighted contemporaries. Alciat contrasts the moderation of the French with Italian readiness to accuse each other of lying and to arrange a duel. A generation later the protagonists of Vendramin's dialogue recall that golden age when the duel was 'more practised in Italy than anywhere else in Europe' and when renowned closed fields welcomed any man with an affair of honour to settle; but 'today, the duel is no longer practised in this way'.

Vendramin looks for the causes of this rapid decline. Before seeking them in our turn, we should ask ourselves whether what we have seen really represents a decline of duelling in Italy, or rather, as in other countries, a transfer from formal duels, which were banned from that time, to duels *alla macchia* (that is, private duels, fought in the countryside). Some contemporary authors think the latter to be the case; but there is no evidence of anyone begging sovereigns or the Pope to reinstate the closed field as a remedy against massacres brought about by duels *alla macchia*, as they did in France. If one form of combat did indeed take over from the other, it was only to a marginal degree compared to a general irreversible dissaffection with regard to duelling.

To convince ourselves of this, we need only look at what happened in the home country of duels *alla macchia*: Naples. According to Croce, duelling was rampant in the kingdom during the seventeenth century. However, when looked at closely, most of the anecdotes he presents tell less of duels than of vendettas between important families, with pitched battles, ambushes and recourse to hired killers. The Neapolitan historian was 'intoxicated' with the speeches of his gentlemen compatriots, who talked all the more of duels *alla macchia* as their desire actually to carry them out waned. We would do better to listen to the testimony of a Frenchman, Bouchard, who stayed in Naples in 1632, concerning the kingdom's gentry and nobility: 'Their valour consists in beating some poor lout, but when faced with an equal or a stronger man they are deuced cowards. They insult each other majestically and with extraordinary eloquence, but very rarely come to blows, for during my stay of eight months I heard nothing about any quarrels or duels, near or far, although they say they often fight them.' A similar attitude is to be found almost a century later from the pen of an Italian: gentlemen both great and small 'make declamations about duels and denounce present-day softness, but if they are offered the opportunity for a duel, they dodge it with some subtlety taken from chivalric science, a science which they have turned into a state secret'. In Naples as elsewhere in Italy, and more than elsewhere after 1650, duels were much discussed, but seldom fought, and men died in them even less often.

Why this sudden change halfway through the century? It is tempting to link it to a change of attitude at the time of the Counter-Reformation. F. R. Bryson, who has made a thematic study of the works of *scienza cavalleresca*, thinks this is right, and cites the decision of the Council of Trent 'entirely banning from all of Christendom the detestable custom of duels' (1563), while Vendramin had already seen the Council's ban as the principal cause of decline. The primary documents largely prove them right. In Rome itself a duel was authorised before St Peter's as late as 1550, and a winning duellist made a triumphant entry in 1557. But in 1582 two Roman gentlemen had to leave the Papal States to fight a duel and in all other states of the peninsula they were preceded by a letter from St Charles Borromeo imploring the Prince to prevent them fighting out of respect for the Council's decision and for the good of their souls. The Modena archives allow us to follow the evolution of one man's attitude, that of Alphonso II, Duke of Ferrara. As late as 1559, he presided over a duel for which he had given 'field licence' in the main square of his capital; the report specifies that 'more than a thousand people attended this spectacle'. One of the combatants, a soldier whom the Duke valued, died in this duel and 'the lord Duke was very sad that this had happened'. Two years later Count Stabile asked the same Alphonso II 'for a field' for one of his protégés. Alphonso, although 'desirous above everything to satisfy him', did not grant it; not without embarrassment, he begged the supplicant to excuse him, 'considering the decision of His Holiness to excommunicate anyone who grants a field'. In 1565, his scruples went even further. He refused even to put his *parere* on a cartel 'because the Council forbids us to become involved in such matters'. Late dukes of Este gave many *pareri* on 'questions of honour' but never again on cartels of challenge. This is a formal but very significant distinction: it expresses submission to pontifical and Council decisions and an opposition to bloodshed.

The role of the Council of Trent, and more generally that of the Counter-Reformation, is undeniable in the reduction in the number of duels during the second half of the sixteenth century. Perhaps this statement should be modified with regard to more distant lands, less subject to the temporal power of the Pope than St Peter's Patrimony or the Duchy of Ferrara, which was liable to be annexed.

However, it remains the case that the Counter-Reformation, even supported by the secular arm, was able to obtain this result only because the general climate of the society favoured it. It seems to us here that the virulence of duels was to some extent dampened by the qualitative and quantitative strength of the very literature that was devoted to it.

The concern with theory and the scruple not to perform a duel that did not conform to the writings of the best authors made more than one quarrel into a controversy rather than a fight. Just as for today's bridge player a game of cards is less important than the bidding procedure and its possible analysis, so for Italian men of honour a bloody combat was less important than arguments about the conformity of its potential execution with chivalric science. This explains the importance of *pareri*, which flourished more than ever when the duel was fading at the end of the sixteenth century and throughout the seventeenth century. These were consultations provided by competent gentlemen or sovereign princes on disputes submitted to them by men of honour and were, in a sense, the practical manifestations of treatises of honour. In these dossiers the issues include who has insulted whom, who should give the challenge and who should make the first steps towards a reconciliation. Sometimes gentlemen who were not satisfied with a response referred their problem to several authorities, or to all the 'knights of honour', even 'to the world', posting manifestos in the streets and distributing handwritten or printed diatribes. In every case the duel itself was eclipsed, replaced in practice by interminable preliminary quibbling, which both parties were sometimes happy to continue for years.

Given this, it is not surprising that so many fights were 'play duels', such as the one complacently recounted by its hero, Ariosto, in 1618. He had a most correctly conducted quarrel with Alessandro Guarino over a banal question of common windows; they executed a couple of fencing figures, but 'no one was touched because people ran to separate them . . . and so the story ended'.

It is not surprising either that so many duellists had the comfort of learning before the fight that their procedure was inadmissible for this or that error of form. Take, for example, the two characters who were declared improper opponents because one was a 'mercenary officer' for the Archduke of Austria, while the other, as a Venetian nobleman, was a member of the corps of the Republic, and therefore assimilated to a person of royal essence. Another example is that of the character in a *Dialogue* by Guazzo who makes this cynically commonsense declaration on the gentleman's use of the sword: 'It will doubtless be lawful for you as a knight to give the world some sign of your generous intentions, but as a Christian it would not be lawful for you to carry them out.' Christian morality and chivalric science were visibly two complementary alibis for saving one's face without losing one's life. As early as the beginning of the sixteenth century Castiglione criticised those who 'lack swiftness and courage . . . turn the affair into disputes over fine points and who, when they have the choice of weapons, choose those which neither cut nor prick'. So what took the fatal character out of Italian duels was, according to a phrase of the time, that they were 'more duels with pens than encounters with swords'.

A counter-proof of the case we are advancing is provided by examination of the repressive measures generated by single combat. We have done this for two states, aristocratic and landowning Ferrara and patrician and extraverted Venice. The latter first passed legislation in 1541, a time when it was publishing the greatest number of treatises on chivalric science, while Ferrara waited until 1573. But Ferrara renewed its edict in 1578, whereas Venice left it until 1632 to pass a second measure. The Estes then passed a third and last one in 1627, while in Venice this did not occur until 1739. Here then, with local variations in their spacing, are two sets of legislation which were repeated sufficiently rarely to convince us that they were not overtaken by the gallop of infractions. In Venice this spacing contrasts eloquently with that of measures taken against brawls and murders by 'bravi' (five *parti prese* by the Council of Ten in the last quarter of the sixteenth century alone). And the set punishments for those who contravened laws against duelling were fines and banishment, but never death.

The duel in Italy did not really fit into the category of criminality. Proofs of this abound. For example, the alphabetical list of judiciary matters at the beginning of the eighteenth century does not include an article entitled *duellum*, there is an absence of writings by lawyers on this subject in a centre of law studies such as Padua, and, for those who have read the French authors, there is an even more revealing absence of the term 'crime' in all the texts we have studied, the duel being called only an 'abuse'. These absences and indulgences could signify that duels were too frequent to be considered anything but normal, and this may be true of the period of the Wars of Italy. But we believe that what they signify above all is that after that time duels were seldom fatal, to the extent that the Counter-Reformation's ban on duels did not meet any serious obstacles in a country where combat, even it frequent, was rarely tragic. It was as if the duel had been devitalised.

So Italy, which gave Europe codes of honour, treatises on fencing and masters of arms, did not experience the murderous frenzy of duels. As in Spain, but considerably less so, a sense of honour attached to feminine virtue came into play, expressing itself in vengeful murder carried out, if necessary, by hired killers. But most important in its effects was the phenomenon of a cultivated aristocracy, a society where the 'art of conferring' was so subtle and so agile that dialogues rarely became stuck in one of those stalemates where all that can be done is to clear the way for an exchange of blows. The pen and the sword, those antithetical values in the symbolic world of the Renaissance, were not mutually exclusive in Italy. This is why, without losing his honour, a gentleman could choose 'duels with pens instead of encounters with swords'. Hence a keenness to publish, print and post cartels and manifestos without a sword being drawn. In a sense Italy sublimated duels by writing about them, producing theories where other cultural spaces took action.

So at the end of this rapid journey through the neighbouring countries, we have to conclude that after the third quarter of the sixteenth century 'only the French' – as a contemporary put it – 'recklessly engaged in duels', or at least engaged in them with an ardour which had no equivalent elsewhere. The accounts given by foreigners are the best proof of this. We must therefore take as a pertinent observation and not as boasting the affirmation by French authors that their compatriots surpassed their Italian masters and that the duel, which was brought back from Naples by Charles VIII's army, found its most favourable territory in France – as already witnessed by the character of the ancient Gauls. For it was not enough to state that duelling was a chiefly French phenomenon. This fact was justified and interpreted with all sorts of arguments which we can classify as natural and supernatural.

According to the supernatural arguments, the French aptitude, and indeed vocation, for single combat was beyond all rational explanation, except perhaps for that of the astrologers. It had been announced, and therefore imposed, by the most ancient and venerable prophecies, ranging from a vision which King Chilperic had at the dawn of French history to one of David's psalms or Nebuchadnezzar's dream in Holy Writ itself. So the French were duellists because of a mysterious and divine decision.

According to the natural arguments, the arguments of the 'naturalists', the French were 'full of blood', their complexion was 'generous' and 'heat' was the basis of 'the Gallic temperament'. So the French were duellists because of their national character.

Obviously such explanations do not explain the phenomenon for us, but they have an interest which goes beyond anecdotal curiosity. These explanations, formulated and disseminated at the time, helped to consolidate the phenomenon and reinforce its durability. For if it were destiny, be it biological, astrological or providential, which forced the French, commoners included, to fight duels, then it was pointless to try to resist. The acceptance that it is the nature or fate of a nation to adopt a certain social attitude constitutes an invitation to all individuals to conform to the image imposed on them by the collectivity. Where morality condemns this social attitude, it is a guarantee that individuals are not responsible for the unfortunate consequences of their actions. The stereotype of the *furia francese*, of the hot-blooded people, justified and reinforced the duel's strength in France.

For the twentieth-century historian the reasons for this French specificity of the duel and its durability will gradually appear, we hope, in the course of the present work. Some are emerging now in contrast to our observations regarding neighbouring countries (notably England and Spain) in the political and religious domains. There was a long occultation of royal power and the personal prestige of the sovereign in France, beginning halfway through the sixteenth century with the last of the Valois and prolonged by uncertainties over the legitimacy of the House of Bourbon and the two minorities of Louis XIII and Louis XIV. Through a constant but sometimes nostalgic desire for a unique and unanimously recognised authority, the nobility were led to dispense their own justice. The splitting of the country between two faiths, deepened by civil wars and their sequels, and made official by the Edict of Nantes, created an egalitarian antagonism within the same loyalism: the need to destroy one's fellow or be destroyed oneself in order to be recognised, the model for single combat on the field. The French path to absolute monarchy and the experience of religious dualism are two roots of the duel's vigour in the Most Christian Kingdom.

Chapter 5

A Crucial Collective Trial: Jarnac's Duel, 1547

All that was pure and proud in the provincial gentry, all that was indefatigable and nobly poor, was freed from that night, going forward lustily, no longer weighed down by the fascination with royalty that the late king had exerted. . . .

Such a serious revolution was made with three formless lines, unsigned, at the bottom of a challenge slip. Still it carried the words: made in Royal Council. And it was signed Laubespin (Secretary of State).

(J. Michelet, *History of France* 1856, vol. 9, pp. 5 and 32).

The event described by the present chapter was, without a doubt, the most famous duel of the whole sixteenth century in France. It even gave rise to an expression which has remained proverbial to this day: *le coup de Jarnac*, 'Jarnac's stroke', meaning 'a stab in the back'.

If it were only a heroic and/or villainous episode involving a clever sword stroke, it would be of little interest to us. But it stimulated so many and such varied accounts by contemporaries and their immediate successors that we have to look at it in greater depth. For them it was a sort of miracle whose fame spread like wildfire. Such an event is an occasion when collective attitudes become set for a long time. Its consequences reach far beyond the individuals involved or even its indirect protagonists.

We shall start by recalling the origin of the quarrel. Jarnac was the brother-in-law of the Duchesse d'Etampes, young mistress of the old King François I. La Châtaigneraye was a familiar of the Dauphin Henri and his old mistress, Diane de Poitiers. Both men were from Poitou, but the former had not yet won either glory, reputation or high office, while the latter was ten years his senior and had proved his courage by distinguishing himself at the battle of Cérisoles in 1544. The future King's confidence and the support of the House of Lorraine promised him a fine future. Both men were living the high life and it seems to have been Madame d'Etampes who funded Jarnac's expenditure. Tongues wagged in the clan hostile to the old King's favourite. One day the Dauphin declared that Jarnac was kept by his father's second wife. 'To keep' (*entretenir*) was an equivocal term which Diane, Henri and also La Châtaigneraye and all their friends were quick to interpret in the sense of more or less incestuous relations.

With his honour thus accused, Jarnac could only reply with a *démenti*, saying it was a lie. But who could he accuse of lying? Not a woman, nor a future king, for their positions would be too unequal for them to be able to fight a duel. So La Châtaigneraye took on the role of Henri's unofficial champion, maintaining that Jarnac had expressly told him that he had a liaison with his stepmother. Jarnac gave him the lie. La Châtaigneraye requested the field, but François I refused and judicial proceedings were set in motion for defamation concerning Madame de Jarnac. Then François I died and his successor granted the field. The whole Court took sides, the Guise family for La Châtaigneraye, Montmorency and the Bourbons for Jarnac. A crowd of gentlemen and commoners gathered at Saint-Germain to watch the fight. Contrary to all expectations it was Jarnac who killed La Châtaigneraye.

This victory seems to have been a big surprise to everyone, hence the meaning of 'Jarnac's stroke'. In his *Discourse on Duels*, La Châtaigneraye's nephew Brantôme endlessly discusses the unequal chances of victory attributed to each of the protagonists. According to him, La Châtaigneraye was 'big, brave and valiant ... one of the strongest and most skilful men ... with all weapons and techniques ... and as a fighter, because besides his strength he had great skill', while Jarnac was 'in no way his equal in strength or prowess ... afraid that it would come to a fight'. Perhaps this is just a nephew extolling his uncle's merits. But how else can we explain François I's refusal to expose the Duchesse d'Etampes' protégé to a duel and Henri II's rush to do so three weeks after his accession? How also do we explain Jarnac's numerous dilatory manoeuvres? He arranged for the period set for reconciliation to start from 14 June and not 25 April, he chose numerous weapons which were expensive and difficult to procure and two weeks before the duel his stepmother was still trying to have proceedings for defamation restarted. Above all, he practised his fencing and learned the famous thrust to the back of the knee which was to put his opponent out of action. His hesitation and the moderation with which he exploited the advantage which he gained from the beginning of the fight reflect his surprise as much as his fear of displeasing the King. Jarnac's victory was all the more astounding for being swift and, all things considered, easy.

These things said, how do we explain them? Remarkably enough, no one, not even the smug Brantôme, lingers over the *coup de Jarnac*, or disputes its legitimacy. The fight followed form; the King proclaimed the winner; there is no question of anyone appealing against the judgement of the fight. The consensus is quite amazing. The very paradox of the defeat of the stronger man prohibits any doubts as to the value of the result. Some think La Châtaigneraye died because he fought 'against his conscience', or 'against right and equity'. Here we see the old idea (still intact in the middle of the sixteenth century) of the combat-trial, the confrontation destined to reveal the truth.

Others, who are less convinced of the purity of Jarnac's life, or too firmly entrenched in the opposing faction, see the thing entirely in terms of the modern idea of honour; but they also think La Châtaigneraye's defeat was justified, because he had an insolent confidence in himself alone and was defeated in his arrogance. Had he not had a sumptuous banquet prepared beforehand to celebrate the victory he was convinced would be his? 'And this supper was entirely taken by the Swiss and the Court lackeys.' Had he not disdained the help of the Master of the world as much as that of the master of arms? He 'was little concerned with pleading with his God and calling on Him for help' at a time when his opponent was humbly performing extensive devotions. His death was the punishment for his pride. It was the condemnation of his hubris.

This kind of explanation of an unexpected (not to say absurd) fact led directly to a supernatural interpretation. To people of the time it was plain that in this duel 'God was ... witness and judge.' Vieilleville, who was hostile to La Châtaigneraye, affirms this: 'God, who was waiting for him, transformed him from winner in his imagination into loser in fact.' And Brantôme, who was hostile to Jarnac, agrees: 'God, taking the side of the weaker man, did not allow the victory to go to the valiant one, but gave it to the weaker, who could not take it himself but only from God. ... God is the righteous judge of everything.' Jacques de Thou, writing the story of his time fifty years later, argued no differently: 'the outcome of this fight showed plainly that victory does not depend on bodily strength or skill, nor on the favour of princes, but solely on God's will'. So the accounts are unanimous: the duel between Jarnac and La Châtaigneraye was decided by God. Not that in it God sanctioned courage, skill or strength, nor even that he used it as a trial to show which side was right by giving it victory. But it was a formidable and mysterious affirmation of the absolutism of the All Powerful.

This interpretation of the notion of God's judgement as an expression of the ineffable, as an affirmation of the hidden God, has two consequences on the human level: on the one hand, the loser in a duel is not necessarily discredited; on the other hand, the role of the sovereign must be reconsidered.

The Loser Is Not Discredited

Certainly the winner comes out of such a fight with an enhanced reputation. Ronsard, the 'prince of poets', celebrated Jarnac in one of his odes and did not hesitate to identify the renown of the duellist with the glory of France itself. However, Ronsard was alone in covering Jarnac with flattering epithets. In an anonymous popular song there is no word of either exaltation or disparagement for either of the opponents. The winner offers the loser's weapons to the King, 'who does not notice'. Vendôme (future King of Navarre) accepts them, promises to accept Jarnac's services, and then suggests he return to his estates, which Jarnac does at once.

This song (which may or may not have been composed at the time of the event) seems more closely to reflect the dominant feeling of the time than does Ronsard's ode. Jarnac's spectacular success did not open up a brilliant career for him. Although his subsequent destiny was less obscure than Michelet maintains, nothing suggests that it deviated in any way from that which any gentleman of his rank and generation might have expected.

And although when it happened Jarnac's victory did not bring down the rage of a king vexed at the loss of his favourite, it did not generate a wave of enthusiasm in his favour either. He did not take advantage of the traditionally recognised prerogatives of the winner. Constable de Montmorency, who was judge of the field, declared that he should 'parade round the field in triumph, with trumpets sounding and tabors beating' and the flexible King 'more or less followed what this judge said'. Nevertheless, Jarnac declined these honours, as his godfather and Vendôme himself were against them. They were afraid that young gentlemen on La Châtaigneraye's side and dressed in his livery would come down into the lists to avenge him and that the brawl would soon become a riot. A little later, Jarnac wanted to hang his trophy in 'a great church of this kingdom, but he was dissuaded by some of his friends'.

So Jarnac was the undisputed winner, but without gaining much prestige. And La Châtaigneraye lost without being condemned. Certainly Montluc said that death in a closed field brought dishonour on the proud gentleman, but this was an oral judgement, which has no echo in his written *Commentaries*. Against this isolated opinion, Brantôme maintains that he 'lost his life there, but not his honour'. This point of view dissociates defeat and loss of honour 'because no one loses in this game unless he surrenders like a coward to save his life'.

A death he has not sought to flee transforms the loser into a hero. It could almost be said that it did not matter whether or not a duellist lost, as long as he proved his courage. His death raised him up above the common run of mortals. This is how the Duc de Guise understood it when he had a Latin epitaph, a 'tomb after the ancient Roman fashion', written to exalt for the benefit of posterity the virtue of La Châtaigneraye, his unfortunate champion in the 1547 duel. 'Defeated when fully armed ... he was invincible unarmed.' And the eulogy ends thus: 'A great prince of Lorraine and France, and most excellent knight, greatly saddened and vexed at such an unexpected occurrence, has dedicated this tomb to the merits of this brave and valiant knight of Poitou.'

The Role of the Sovereign Reconsidered

During his lifetime François I had maintained the attitude of an arbiter in the quarrel between La Châtaigneraye and Jarnac. Whatever his personal preferences, or the preferences of those close to him, he remained aloof, as he had done at the time of the duel between Sarzay and Véniers and as the logic of trial on the closed field had traditionally required of the sovereign.

Henri II did not display the same serenity. His contemporaries held this against him. Montluc reproached him for his weakness in allowing tittle-tattle to turn into an affair of state and a tragedy. 'The King should have silenced the women who took it upon themselves to talk about his court.... Gossip caused the death of M. de La Châtaigneraye.... The King should have ordered them to mind their own business.' Vieilleville denounced his complicity: 'for he was partly responsible for the fight since he himself interpreted the word "keep" in too bad a way'. Brantôme goes further, writing of 'the King himself, for whom my uncle was in part fighting ...'. This is the main accusation. Henri II was not just negligent or biased, he descended into the closed field by procuration. Everyone knew that La Châtaigneraye was not just his favourite; he was his representative, he was the King's champion against Jarnac.

Unlike his father, Henri II threw himself into the fray, with a haste that the chronology clearly shows. The two gentlemen's quarrel had been dragging on for more than a year when the Dauphin became king. Three weeks later, Henri sent Guyenne the herald to notify Jarnac of La Châtaigneraye's call. Vieilleville, and doubtless many others, saw this as the first initiative of the new reign: 'for His Majesty wanted to see the outcome before having himself crowned'. Two weeks after watching the duel in Saint-Germain, Henri II was crowned in Rheims.

It is highly likely that Henri saw this duel as a prelude to the coronation. If, as expected, La Châtaigneraye had been victorious, the fight would have signified the defeat of the group who had ruled around the old King and the coming to power of a new regime. With the Guise family and their friends clearly siding with the King's champion, while Navarre and the Châtillon family did not conceal their preference for his opponent, La Châtaigneraye's victory would have signified a kind of investiture of one of the two factions into which not only Court aristocracy but all the politico-religious strata of French society were split. The new King, intoxicated by chivalric romances and perhaps by ancient memories, inaugurated his reign with a bloody ritual, an initiatory trial and founding sacrifice, in which he was to win his crown instead of passively inheriting it, and to sacrifice the old King without committing parricide.

Unfortunately for him, the luck of arms took an unexpected turn. He lost the prestige and authority which he had staked on this duel and, when he realised that his champion was coming off worst, his attitude only aggravated his own disaster. Awed by this ordeal, which he had wanted and which was escaping his control, he did not dare interrupt the fight once La Châtaigneraye was seriously wounded. Jarnac, prudent and somewhat sobered by his too-swift success, gave him plenty of opportunity to do so. Eye-witness accounts report that he went three times to the foot of the platform to beg the King to restore his honour and to put an end to the duel. But Henri II remained silent, as if prostrate, for a long time, during which La Châtaigneraye lost a great deal of blood. Finally he 'threw down the baton, but too late'.

By not daring to intervene in this fight, Henri II declared himself in some sense incompetent as a judge of the field. He abdicated one of his essential prerogatives, that of dispenser of justice, a prerogative which, as we have seen, was merely suspended by the granting of a field. When he came to himself again, it was too late. He had given the impression that the prince had no role in a duel, that everything happened and was decided between the opponents alone, or else between them and the mysterious and enigmatic power of God.

This duel, which Henri II had certainly intended to be a presage and a political symbol, did in fact become these things, but unfavourably for him. Michelet stresses this, not without a little lyrical exaggeration, when he says that spectators of the combat 'and many men who had been wavering until then began to take sides . . . [and that from that day on] many felt themselves to be Protestants without even knowing what Protestantism was'. But he is quite right when he calls Jarnac's stroke the 'defeat of royalty'.

There was a crowd of onlookers: the entire Court, foreign ambassadors (including the Grand Turk's representative), young nobles from both sides, the 'hundred or six score gentlemen' who had not left La Châtaigneraye's side for over a month, accompanying him with 'stompings of impatience that all found odious'. All these people had different feelings about justice and royalty on the evening of 10 July from those they had had in the morning. In their eyes the rest of Henri II's reign only developed what this duel had signified by analogy. Henri inaugurated his reign with a fatal duel: he closed it with a tournament in which he himself died. 'Many people observed that the tragic end of this reign answered the grievous portents under which it began; for the King who, against the laws of his duty, had permitted a serious and bloody combat, was killed in a pleasure fight.' More serious still: Henri, who had not dared to choose between two duellists, spent his reign simultaneously favouring both the Guises and the Châtillons, the two rival families who were then drawing the French around them in two separate camps, to lead them into civil war: 'and it seemed that the King had conspired with them to divide France between them, to the ruin of his children and his kingdom'.

There remains one point to be examined. Did Henri II forbid formal duels after La Châtaigneraye's death? Most narrative histories of duelling say he did, as if it were self-evident. But the documents in no way confirm this assertion.

Certainly the King did put into effect an edict 'against all murders and assassinations which are daily committed' on 15 July 1547, just five days after the fatal duel. But this measure mentioned neither duel, nor call, nor *démenti*, nor quarrel; it applied to all those, 'be they gentlemen or commoners', who committed 'murders and assassinations'. It was a measure prosecuting not the duel *per se*, but rather those responsible for violent deaths.

In 1550 Henri II issued a decree which did, this time, concern quarrels and challenges, and thus duels; but it applied only inside the army. Furthermore its aim was the regulation rather than suppression of disputes, which got in the way of discipline. Every quarrel had to be submitted to a superior officer and, if the colonel permitted it, a cartel could legitimately be sent.

In fact only one of the sources we have consulted spoke of a royal decision against duels. This was Jacques de Thou's *History*: 'the King ... swore never to permit any duel in the future'. It is a late source, but a serious one, and one which cannot lightly be dismissed. It seems that indeed Henri II did not grant a field again during his reign, but he never abolished the institution of the duel. Let us recall that two years after 'Jarnac's stroke', the King held a *lit de justice* during which the Chancellor proclaimed Parliament competent by custom in matters of duels. And soon afterwards we see the same Henri II sending letters patent to the Duc de Bouillon, sovereign of

Sedan and king's vassal, asking him to grant a field to two French noblemen who wanted to fight a duel.

So Henri II did not legally ban judicial duels. Rather he effectively devitalised them. Through the public spectacle of a duel in which he sided against one of his subjects and then did not dare use his sovereign right to interrupt the fight, he recognised in the duel a private procedure of superior authority to that of royalty and to which, in an extreme case, a king himself might be liable. In his over-sensitivity to aristocratic values, he precipitated France into a development already well advanced in Italy, and an eclipse of the role of royalty as dispensers of justice.

In itself, Jarnac's combat was no more a turning point, beginning or end than any other historical event. But, like other events which stay in the collective imagination or memory, it was a sign. As a result of the publicity surrounding it, the pomp of its staging and the echoes it made, it provided an opportunity for the crystallisation of certain ways of thinking and established a certain conception of the duel and its role in social and political life.

In the sumptuous and bloody spectacle by which Henri II wanted to represent his accession, in which he both staged and gambled it, the King, though physically present, was missing. 'Servile in mind and tongue, pitifully enchanted', as Michelet imagines him, Henri was not capable of being king and did not dare take sides. Just as in the representation of the court of Philippe IV of Spain that Velasquez gave when he painted *Las Meniñas* fifty years later, the King is 'represented, but absent', the *King's place*, felt to be indispensable, was excluded from the duel.*

What came out of this ordeal was an image of the duel which exalted the hidden God, honoured the man of courage (winner or loser) and effaced the sovereign. La Châtaigneraye's death certainly was a 'defeat for royalty'.

---

*The phrase is borrowed from Michel Foucault, *The Order of Things*, trans. from the French, London, Tavistock, 1970. Its value here is entirely rhetorical, and has no methodological implications.

PART II

The Turn of the Sixteenth Century: A Disputed Peak

Chapter 6

Transformations of the Duel

C'est un acte d'honneur d'escorter non-couard
L'ami qui vient tenter un donne-peur hasard.
                              (P. de Bousy, *Méléagre*)

They seek out-of-the way places, like witches do, and
sometimes in the moonlight ... not seing that God is
watching them.
                              (N. Caussin, *The Holy Court*, 1624)

During the thirty or so years separating the fight between Jarnac and
La Châtaigneraye from another famous duel, the one in which six of
Henri III's favourites killed each other, rapid changes altered both the
procedure of duels and attitudes towards them. During this period
they assumed the form that would remain theirs, at least until the end
of the seventeenth century.

Changes in Form

In most duels fought after 1550 the following elements either no
longer existed or were only memories: the request for and granting
of a field, the sending of heralds, checks and arbitration by godfathers and the master of the field, the suspension of the fight when
the royal baton was thrown down and the punishment of the loser
who was condemned by his defeat. Whether the political authorities
forbade, tolerated or encouraged duels, they no longer made of them
an official, public procedure.

And so the procedure became lighter, simpler and shorter. In
practice it was reduced to the exchange of cartels. Duellists took care
over the style of their cartels, balancing stinging irony with unshake-
able courtesy. Some opted for brevity, possibly just one laconic
sentence (a real epistolary death-blow), while others chose to write a
copious manifesto, a real defence speech crammed with sometimes
nitpicking arguments. Often they would refer to the murderous

nature of the meeting only by paraphrase. Thus Zamet challenges Balagny to 'show [him] that [he is] a man of honour in all [his] actions', La Valette, moved by 'a just desire to speak' to Ornano 'in the way that good people of [his] profession are accustomed to do', wished 'to have the good fortune to embrace [him] in [his] shirt-sleeves with a knight's weapons'.

In order to have more impact and to improve their personal publicity, the opponents sometimes had their cartels printed or posted up. In any case, enthusiasts and the curious would take on the task of passing manuscript copies of them 'from hand to hand'. Brantôme was greedy for such literature and the Chancellery officer L'Estoile collected it.

And when a private quarrel was between two important people, so that it became an affair of state, the cartels became tools in a campaign to win over public opinion. This can be seen, for example, in the dispute between Don Philippin of Savoy and Charles de Créquy 'over a scarf'. The former was the illegitimate brother of the Duke of Savoy, then at war with France, while the latter was Lesdiguières' son-in-law and assistant in the government of Dauphiné, commanding the royal army. They fought two duels in 1599; Don Philippin, who was hurt in the first, died in the second. The quarrel was widely documented on both sides of the Alps, their cartels were circulated and one or the other criticised for cowardice and lack of honour in relation to his word. Henri IV's final relief is easy to understand. 'The King, who had long been worried about the outcome of this quarrel, received the news with great joy.'

So cartels, which were the only written part of the procedure, were very much in vogue in the last decades of the sixteenth century. But this vogue did not, as it had in Italy, become a means to evasion, a talkative substitute for bloody confrontation. Although opponents accused each other of running away from the fight (a commonplace way of calling the other man's honour into question), it would seem that most quarrels were resolved by bloodshed. True, we have no statistics which allows us to state that there were few cartels without duels. On the other hand it is certain that there were many duels without cartels.

In this respect it is noteworthy that those enthusiasts who made collections around 1650 seldom copied out any cartels dated later than 1613–15. This is because many duellists abandoned this vestigial paperwork, and their *démenti*, assignation and choice of weapons became simply oral. This was partly due to the need for secrecy at a time when the King's agents were taking real action against duels, but more often it reflected a desire to forestall attempts at reconciliation and friendly arbitration and, above all, the protagonists' impatience with all intermediaries and delays which might prolong the insult and make others suspect that they were afraid to fight.

The more the ritual was whittled away, the briefer became the amount of time that elapsed between *démenti* and duel. In some cases they were separated by only a few minutes. Such duels were called 'encounters' (*rencontres*).

The word 'encounter' is at least as frequently used in sources as 'duel' after the beginning of the seventeenth century, and it completely supersedes the word 'combat'. Jurists and canonical lawyers discussed it at great length. Should this almost informal duel, which followed without delay on an argument or an insult, be regarded as premeditated single combat, or was it merely an unconsidered brawl? Behind them the whole society assimilated the encounter into the categories of duel or brawl, according to needs and preferences.

When St Jeanne de Chantal's son fought as a second and a nun wanted to console his pious mother, the latter replied at once, 'The accident that happened to my son? ... It was an unexpected encounter.' When two noblemen in the retinue of Louis XIV's brother Monsieur* had a quarrel which was given concrete expression in two letters of challenge and one missed assignation under the Paris city wall, they met 'by chance' in the Rue Richelieu, where it was not their fault that 'their valour was fatal to them'. On the other hand, for a member of the government who wanted to make legislation against duels more effective, 'those who claim to have received an insult ... and who meet or who fight alone, or in equal numbers and with equal weapons, will be subject to the same punishments as if it were a duel'. And a judge who wanted to condemn a homicidal defender asked him 'if he had sought an opportunity to encounter and fight the deceased in a spirit of hatred and vengeance'.

For the historian, however, encounters must be considered as a type of duel. First because they were always closely linked in contemporary minds (even for those who drew a distinction between them), and secondly because the popularity of encounters coincides with the period when the duel was evolving into an increasingly summary procedure.

Around 1660 one senses a kind of impatience among duellists. They were increasingly abandoning the form the more surely to reach the content: kill or be killed.

---

*The King's eldest brother was traditionally referred to as 'Monsieur'. – Ed.

Material Changes

The first change concerns the place of combat. Since the closed field was no longer either requested or granted, combatants no longer required a special, quadrangular place encircled by a wall. Any flat space that was sufficiently large, open and free of obstacles became an appropriate arena in which to fight a duel. Indeed the only real condition defining it was the agreement of the two opponents who decided to meet there. Those with an eye to publicity, or a strong taste for the spectacular, would choose a busy spot, easily accessible and with enough space to accommodate an invited audience, servants and casual onlookers. Those who wished to escape pressure or the religious and civil authorities would choose a place that was more out of the way, deserted or at least discreet.

Thus some duels took place in the centres of towns and cities, in streets, on public squares or in the suburbs of the larger conurbations. More frequently, however, duellists removed themselves from urban areas. These duels fought 'in the shade of woods and forests', in 'out-of-the-way places', were the exact equivalent of what the Italians called duels *alla macchia* or *alla mazza* ('in the maquis'). Curiously, however, this term was not translated into French, in spite of the fact that the thing itself became widespread in France. Brantôme kept the Italian word, writing, 'combat à la "mazza" ' and we found 'fighting *à la Machie*' in a 1559 translation of an Italian author. This was an exception. The word 'maquis', in current usage today, never appears in the literature on duels. And the idea of 'taking to the maquis' (*prendre le maquis*) (frequently done, because people often had to hide from the authorities in order to fight a duel) was rendered in French by 'taking to the countryside' (*prendre la campagne*). In France it is the term 'field' (*prè*), which designates the proper place for a duel, acquiring this sense in the early years of the seventeenth century, and not, no doubt, and whatever Littré says, 'by allusion to the area of the Pré aux Clercs' outside Paris, but because a mown field was perfect as the kind of empty, delimited but discreet place which those hoping to fight a duel were seeking at that time.

In this way the 'countryside' and the 'field' took the place in France of the transalpine *macchia*. The significance of this difference goes beyond mere philological curiosity; it indicates an important nuance. The duel had broken away from the highly socialised space of the closed field, but it had not been cast out into the completely foreign world of nature. It was located in a space which was not necessarily enclosed, but was always delimited by the divisions between plots of land; it was located on land humanised by agricultural work. The duel was removed from the town, but it was not expelled from society.

In choosing as the arena for his duel a place outside but close to his town, an ordinary place, but one that previous duels had in some sense fitted and possibly even consecrated to that function, the duellist went some way towards reconciling the contradictory requirements of discretion and publicity, while at the same time satisfying his nostalgia for the closed field. This was how the Pré aux Clercs gained its lasting notoriety: situated on the edge of the Paris conurbation, but within the jurisdiction of Saint-Germain-des-Prés, it was an open, uncultivated space, a place for walks and games on the banks of the Seine. It became well known so quickly that in 1608 Paul de Montbourcher proposed transforming it into an official closed field, where all the kingdom's duels could take place under the supervision of a captain who would live there and give out the weapons. Of course, no such designation was made. But the Pré aux Clercs was not the only place to be given a find of tacit preference. The French gentlemen who followed Marie de Médicis into exile in Brussels adopted the custom of fighting 'a good half-league' from the city, near Notre-Dame-du-Lac. In 1633 this place was termed the 'usual meeting place for the duels of this Court'.

Another change was that a duel would sometimes continue past dusk, and some took place entirely at night. These 'moonlight' duels impressed contemporaries, but seem to have been quite rare. However, even if they were exceptional, their existence bears witness to the fact that the duel, no longer restricted by the rising and setting of the sun, had ceased to be a public spectacle.

Like place and time, the appearance and equipment of duellists went through great and lasting changes. Duellists increasingly fought on foot. Duels were occasionally fought on horseback, but after the middle of the sixteenth century these very soon came to be regarded as exceptional curiosities. Pedestrian duellists increasingly abandoned all forms of defensive equipment, such as helmets, cuirasses and shields. By the end of the sixteenth century it was thought normal to remove the doublet and fight in one's shirtsleeves, sometimes even 'without a shirt', 'naked . . . in white canvas breeches'. Of course, there were cunning men who wore armour hidden under their shirts, but these would be caught out by the seconds, who checked 'to see if their lives were protected by any rampart other than a shirt'. Vulson de La Colombière tells how one duellist thought it clever to wear a 'very large, wide shirt, thinking to fool the judgement' of his opponent, who would then strike the air; but

Fortune, who 'favours rightness and openness', defeated the perpetrator of this stratagem.

The consequence, and indeed the desired goal, of this change in clothing was to make duels more lethal and more speedily decisive. Jean de La Taille was merely summing up the received ideas of his peers around 1600 when he declared, 'in shirtsleeves and on foot is the form that is considered the most generous'. This opinion was a long way from the 'habit of former duellists . . . who wanted their bodies covered, or else they would be fighting like beasts'.

The offensive weaponry also changed, or rather became simplified. The pike, which was a cumbersome and ineffective weapon for a fighter on foot, fell into disuse. Duellists disdained muskets and rifles, but pistols – which were to become the most frequently used weapon for duels in the nineteenth century – were introduced at the beginning of the sixteenth and became popular, being the only firearms compatible with the close, hand-to-hand combat which was the preponderant characteristic of the duel.

But duellists' preference continued to be for the naked blade. There were two reasons for this: first, duels were chiefly practised by gentlemen; and gentlemen were defined as men whose profession was to carry a sword. That 'gentleman's faith', which almost never left their sides, was always at hand in case of insult. Secondly, the sword, the blade and 'iron' (*le fer*, also used metonymically to mean 'the sword') were important elements in the imaginary sphere of society; an entire heraldic, allegorical and alchemical literature invested in these notions and designated them the supreme substance and instrument of justice. The sword was seen as the weapon of a man who did not count on any help 'beyond that of his heart, his sword and his valour'. More and more often the sword used was not the heavy Swiss or Germanic weapon, which sometimes had to be held in two hands and which dealt the opponent heavy blows, scarring and stigmatising him, but not always mortally wounding him. Instead, duellists chose the rapier or the *braquemart*, a pointed sword which killed more quickly and more surely, but did not mutilate or disfigure the loser. Sometimes duellists took care to fight with swords of the same length, but others did not bother about equality in weaponry, so great was their hurry to get it over with and their desire not to appear cowards.

Duellists' indifference to ensuring that each had an equal chance, like their preference for the most lethal weapons and their show of disdain for all forms of protection, bear witness to the fact that from now on duels had to be quick and fatal.

Seconds

One change on both the formal and material levels of duelling was the institution and generalisation of seconds.

In principle, seconds were two individuals who each accompanied one of the 'quarrellers' (*querrelants*) on the field. Sometimes there were more of them, but there was always an equal number on both sides. Sometimes the terms 'thirds' or 'fourths' were used, but more often the word 'second' was simply used in the plural. To some extent they were the descendants of the godfathers, comforting duellists before the fight and when necessary checking for type and length of weapons, absence of armour and amulets. But they were not passive witnesses: they fought each other. Moreover, once a second had killed his man, or put him out of action, he would go to the aid of the duellist he was seconding. When this happened the adversaries were no longer equally matched in terms of numbers, but nobody was bothered by this. 'Disparity and inequality is only judged and considered concerning the state of things at the beginning of the fray; for the rest, trust to Luck.'

This was an important innovation. Certainly in the Middle Ages battle pledges had been known in which two fought against two, three against three, and even fifteen against fifteen. But each of the combatants in these fights had a single opponent. These ancient duels had consisted of juxtaposed single combats. Later they became small collective battles.

The practice of seconds may be Italian in origin. At the beginning of the seventeenth century it was generally thought to have been inaugurated in France by the famous and scandalous duel in which six of Henri III's favourites killed each other. This is not certain, since contemporary chroniclers of the event did not present it as something unheard of. Let us simply say that it was around this date of 1578, and no doubt several years before, that the custom of seconds became widespread in France.

What requires more elucidation is the significance of this vogue for seconds, which lasted three-quarters of a century. Forms of social solidarity, such as family ties, client networks and friendships between companions at arms, undeniably played a large part here. There was also an element of prolongation of the 'private wars' of times gone by (or contemporary ones) in a ritualised, partially defused form.

But often the choice of seconds took no account of relationships between men, and sometimes even ran counter to them. A gentleman who had been rejected by one quarreller would sometimes offer his services to that man's opponent, while another might take the first man he met as a second in a cause which did not concern him. Yet another might draw straws to determine whom he was going to try to murder and another still have his 'soul impaled by the body of [his] best friend'. So the constitution of a team of duellists and seconds might transcend the most sacred of ties, for it was motivated by forces that ran deeper than simple social solidarity. Montaigne puts forward a motive of individual psychology: the 'cowardice' of many duellists who dared not face their danger alone, and were reassured by the presence of a companion (even if he were a stranger). This desire for a form of moral protection goes against the entire evolution described in this chapter, which is that of the search for an ever greater element of risk. But it is not absurd, for it might have been a useful form of compensation, permitting the duellist to attain full awareness of his vulnerability.

However, it is with the second rather than the quarreller that explanations should be sought. To help any man fight for his honour was considered an obligation, an imperative by all those who made a profession of honour and arms. To be a second sometimes meant renouncing ties of family or friendship, but it always signified an affirmation of a greater and more abstract solidarity, that of all gentlemen: 'It is unseemly to hold one's sword uselessly in one's hand while one's friends are fighting each other.'

For some it was also a game, and for most a fascination. The less the second was implicated in the quarrel, in which his opponent was neither his rival nor his enemy, the purer and more intoxicating the attraction of danger. La Noue clearly felt this: he makes a link between 'the rush to become one [of the seconds in a duel]' and the crowds that were drawn by the brotherhoods of flagellants which gained new strength during the troubles of the sixteenth century. In a period of worry and instability these phenomena held a morbid attraction. Signs of the times. In some circles, and doubtless for men of a particular age, to be a second in a duel was to assuage the harrowing, disturbing and reassuring desire to play with death, to play with one's own death.

And so the shape of the duel changed and became set in the space of a generation. Not, let us repeat, quickly, nor definitively for all places and all cases. But through a series of modifications all moving in the same direction.

The more honour became linked to appearances (*le parestre*), and indeed to appearance, the more duels lost their element of spectacle. They were witnessed only by those who took part and – invisible, but how present – God. In renouncing his emblazoned armour, his caparisoned horse and his liveried godfather, the near naked duellist chose to present himself unmasked. He slipped out of character, sometimes giving up his social rank in order to be simply a person. But this process of stripping down was rendered equivocal when the same duellist surrounded himself with seconds. This may perhaps not be as contradictory as it seems, for the facts of the quarrel and even individual honour itself faded in the desire for a hand-to-hand fight.

And the sword, which no longer disfigured, but killed, like the defeat which now exalted rather than condemned the loser, undermined the value of arbitration and stressed the sense of ordeal. Henri III gave proof of this when he erected monuments to the glory of his favourites who had died in a duel, and Henri III's detractors also proved it: they were scandalised by this gesture because of the life that these dubious heroes had led, but never because of the way they had chosen to die.

From the *démenti* to the fight, to death, 'is just an instant's time'. But this instant was unbearably long to any man who felt 'a longing for death, a scorn for life'. Italian fencing worked on speed, surprise and the suppleness of bodies that it rendered imponderable, bodies that slipped away in the moment they exposed themselves. It drew balletic figures, which were at once effaced and substituted by others. Once a 'ceremonial of slow, severe ritual [which] pushes aside or veils the face of death', the duel now drew 'death in movement'.

Duels were still symmetrical, but their symmetry was fragile. Their culmination was the *fente*, that figure in which the duellist's body, held in unstable balance, briefly outlined a diagonal from the heel of his left leg leaning on the ground to the tip of his sword, which had touched his slower opponent, an opponent who was still standing, still vertical.

An equally fragile and ephemeral symmetry is that of the number of combatants, whose balance was soon upset by death. The duel was certainly an ambiguous phenomenon after 1550.

As a spectacle without a spectator, played out in the twilight of a moment which was not daylight and in a place which was not closed, as a gratuitous yet valued act, ostentatious but furtive, 'a contradictory mix ... of tormented gravity and sensual exhilaration', as an unmasked appeal for illusory honour and an immediate search for an outcome without a future, in the thirst for a despicable, heroic death, the duel was a quintessential expression of baroque sensibility. During this period, in cosmogony as in architecture, harmony was primarily regarded as a state of permanent tension, a fluctuating struggle between opposites. It was quite natural for Scipion Dupleix to begin his *Military Laws Concerning the Duel* with a chapter entitled: 'That the whole universe is built on nothing but duels and combats'.

For him, the social phenomenon that he was studying fitted into an agonistic vision of the world, a vision taken from Heraclitus and to which even Christianity submitted. 'Furthermore I would make so bold as to say that even the Son of God, in making Himself a mortal man, fought a duel with two of our most cruel enemies, the devil and death.' The duel was one of the most perfect works of baroque style.

Chapter 7

In Support of the Duel:
A Sociology of Duellists

With a million other gentlemen, I am waiting for a general
pardon for all duels.
> (Malherbe, letter to Racan, 13 December 1624)

There is almost no family in the kingdom that has not felt
to its cost the lamentable effets of God's anger through that
scourge.
> (M. de Vulson de La Colombière, *Epistle, True Theatre of
> Honour and Chivalry*, 1648)

The qualitative changes in the duel phenomenon went hand in hand
with a quantitative increase of which its contemporaries were certainly aware, even if they did not rigorously measure it. Henri II's
reign, and above all the period of the religious wars, seems to mark
the dawn of its popularity, but the peak comes later. Boissat (whose
work was published in 1610) thought duelling had lessened 'over the
last twelve or fifteen years'. So there was a coincidence, if not an
actual link, between the end of the civil wars and the upsurge of
quarrels and duels, those 'internal wars'. There is no unanimous
agreement that duels were becoming less frequent, or had more or
less disappeared, until the second half of the seventeenth century.
Whether because of Louis XIV's efforts, or for some other reason,
duels declined after the Fronde.

Having thus situated the peak chronologically, we should like to
be able to give some further statistical information: the annual
number of duels in France, the numbers of fatal duels and of duellists
who died on the field, the proportion of commoners among duellists
as a whole, or the role of the duel as a cause of death among
gentlemen. We should like to be able to translate the statistics into
graphs, to describe and if possible explain the pace of change that the
phenomenon underwent. But the sources do not allow us to satisfy
these curiosities of quantitative history, these requirements of serial
history.

From 1602 every duel was considered a criminal offence. It should
therefore have given rise to criminal proceedings, traces of which

would be found in judicial archives (if they were well preserved). However, an elementary rule of criminology teaches us to make a distinction between the number of crimes that actually occurred and apparent criminality (that which leads to investigations being at least opened, of which only some end in the passing of a sentence). So even if a court's archives have come down to us intact, they could give us only a minimum figure of cases of duels where proceedings were started, and would tell us nothing of duels which escaped the attention of the law. And we cannot gather even this mediocre information for most of the seventeenth century, because of the state of preservation of the documents. For example, the criminal chamber of the Paris Parliament, which saw 110 trials for duels during the first quarter of the eighteenth century (a period when the phenomenon was in decline), has only left us fifteen trials for the first quarter of the seventeenth century (apparently the time when duels were at their most frequent). Even if many duels escaped prosecution at the beginning of the seventeenth century, we know from concrete cases that a number of duels tried by the Parliament (but how many?) do not figure among the fifteen which have come down to us.

Another method of approach would be to make an inventory of the letters of pardon or remission sent by the royal Chancellery to those guilty of fighting duels (or, if they were dead, to their heirs). In fact innumerable witnesses from the reign of Henri IV to that of Louis XIV testify to the fact that the sovereign more or less systematically granted a pardon to those guilty of duelling. But no archive has made such an inventory possible. We are therefore obliged to repeat the uncorroborated statistics of those who 'kept a record of pardons' granted to duellists during the reign of Henri IV. The average estimate of these contemporaries is that there were around 350 duellists brought to the attention of the authorities during the first years of the seventeenth century and almost as many killed in duels (which is logical enough, as it is harder to make corpses disappear than duellists!). So we only reproduce this figure with reservations, and it cannot tell us much about the actual number of duels, because of the almost universal practice of using teams of seconds.

Under Henri IV's successors no curious person consulted the register of pardons, apart perhaps from the Duc de Gramont, who, 'having counted', judges that duelling cost the lives of 940 gentlemen between 1643 and 1654. However, he does not tell us how he made his count. Then we find a first-hand document, which covers only the years 1656 to 1660: a list of names of those 'accused of the crime of duelling' who were as such excluded from the general amnesty granted on the occasion of Louis XIV's wedding. There are 218 of them judged guilty, of whom at least fourteen were killed in fifty-three duels. Twenty-four of these duels took place in the years 1658, 1659 and 1660, four were later, but twenty-five are undatable. And this list is certainly incomplete, because none of these duels took place in the south of the kingdom. This is an important source, bearing witness to the vitality of the duel and the seriousness with which it was regarded in the middle of the century. It is not a statistical document; it simply marks out a quantifiable development.

Another possible way of tracing the development of duels is to look at the family trees of noble houses. In the first half of the seventeenth century there were many expressions of alarm at the haemorrhage of blue blood that duels represented. Were they really a danger to the size of the aristocratic population, or at least an important factor in aristocratic mortality? Having drawn up a pat-ronymic catalogue of the 472 duellists we came across in the course of the present work, it was tempting to try and discover how many men from their families (mostly aristocratic) had died between 1500 and 1700 and among these how many had fallen on the field. We were soon disillusioned! La Chesnaye des Bois's *Dictionary of the Nobility* seldom states how people died (unless they were killed in battle). A few deaths in duels are mentioned; but not all those that we know of from other sources, far from it. Perhaps, by systematically going through the documentation on the great families it might be possible to gain more precise information. However, this would take the lifetime of an entire Benedictine community, and even then one could not be sure of a rigorous result.

Is this a statement of failure? Not quite. Reading this list of names one has the impression that most gentlemen who lived beyond adolescence had descendants. Even if many of them risked their lives in duels and some of them were killed (how many we cannot know), the duel was not the demographic catastrophe that some imagined or suggested it to be.

The only realistic figures concern a short period and the restricted area of the capital. The most trustworthy are those of the gazetteers and chroniclers. However, even here we do not have a valid record of the number of duels, but only a selection of anecdotes provided in greater or smaller numbers depending on the year, and which can almost always be counted on the fingers of one hand. The frequency of their appearance goes up over certain periods of years, but these rises do not correspond in the different sources. In short, duels are only mentioned when they are remarkable for the number of vic-tims, the strangeness of the circumstances surrounding them or the celebrity of the opponents. So instead of the intensity of the phe-nomenon, history can only record the degree of attention paid to it by authors. It must identify the different levels of interest in different periods rather than the periods of greater or smaller numbers of duels. If there are any statistics, they are, if we may be permitted the expression, impressionistic.

Overcoming all the Cartesian prejudice of French historiography (respect for homogeneous sources, in continuous chronological series, studied in their entirety or by properly justified periodic surveys) and following Stone's example in relation to the English aristocracy, we noted all dated duels which we came across in the course of our researches, without concern for the heteroclite nature of the documents (requiring only that they be contemporary to the reported event). This has given us perfect impressionistic statistics: the rise and fall in the strength of the echo left by duels among people writing in French society in the first half of the seventeenth century.

The results suggest four periods of increase in duelling: 1640–7, 1611–14, 1621–6 and 1631–3. Each period of increase is prolonged by a high plateau and followed by a drop, the sharpest of which corresponds to the years 1618–21. There is a slow decrease which begins around 1637 and only stops in 1649. Then there is a last upsurge until 1652–3, followed by a drop to the level of the 1640s.

After the place of the duel in time, let us consider its place in space. Was there a geography of duels? Some of the people of the time thought there was, but the links between individual writers and particular regions, and also stereotypes such as that of the Younger Sons of Gascony, who were regarded as a vindictive group, limit the value of such assertions. In the total number of anecdotes that we have assembled, an overwhelming proportion of duels took place in Paris. The density of the population, the presence of the Court and the influx of young gentlemen from the provinces are not enough to explain this effect. However, in the capital, men of letters, booksellers and readers ensure notoriety more easily than elsewhere and, conversely, the rarity of traces in the little-urbanised provinces does not necessarily reflect an infrequency of the phenomenon.

Study of judicial sources gives us no real geographical variation. No region shows a greater density than any other. However, our sources cover only the area within the jurisdiction of the Paris Parliament: they shed no light on the situation in Languedoc, Guyenne or Brittany.

We can therefore conclude only that duels were found over the whole of the territory of France, without being able to confirm that there were any regional variations.

In society – and this will come as a surprise to no one – the duel did not concern all individuals and all social categories, or was of very unequal concern to them. First, men did not fight women. And women did not fight each other. Apart from the odd anecdotal exception which proves the rule, the stronger sex monopolised trial by arms – even (and above all) if women were the cause of many fights. Among the male population, children and sick or old men were excluded or exempted from duelling. A man could be challenged only if he were of an age and in a physical state fit to carry weapons. But age limits were flexible and tended to disappear if an old greybeard or a young stripling were the challenger, or insisted on being a second. Voiture fought at the age of fifty, Zamet fought two duels at sixty and Malherbe is even said to have challenged a man at the age seventy-three. Young and even very young men must often have been seen on the field. Many contemporaries established an almost logical link between youth and ardour for duelling.

We would like (yet again) to be able to test this view against quantitative sources, but we are far from being able to draw up a pyramid of duellists' ages. In parliamentary interrogations for the first quarter of the seventeenth century there are only twelve duellists whose age is given or can be found for the date of the duel: they range from twenty-three to forty-six, the average being slightly over thirty. Clearly this tiny sample proves nothing, but it testifies to the fact that, although duelling might have gone hand in hand with strength and thus with youth, it was far from being the preserve of adolescents beginning their adult life.

So were duels the preserve of the gentry and nobility? This is the wrong question to ask. Less because there are examples of duels between commoners (valets, clerks, bourgeois) than because for contemporaries the criterion of aptitude to fight a duel did not depend on aristocratic birth, but on whether both opponents carried arms by profession and whether they were recognised as equals.

In consequence a common soldier could fight a duel with an equal. And even with a superior if the latter agreed momentarily to suspend respect for hierarchy and make himself the former's equal. In 1611 or 1612 an illiterate soldier, Monget, killed a Baron de Termes in a duel. This anecdote is worth telling because it illustrates a case of the socially acceptable limit at which duels could be fought. The Baron and the soldier quarrelled over a woman in Fontainbleau in the spring in 1611. Termes wanted to fight and was physically abusive to Monget. A Swiss guard separated them, saying 'that the King's service and the prohibitions against duels obliged him to do so'. Then in June or July, this time in Paris, Termes provoked his rival 'having told him to put his hand to his sword'. Monget 'did not want to fight'. This cost him dear: his opponent beat him with a stick and his captain discharged him 'for having born the said blows without having wanted to fight'. When he was beaten again in September in the church of St Honoré, Monget finally made up his mind to fight. He met his enemy in a street close to the Louvre. And he killed him. But he did it honourably; he did not take advantage of the moment when Termes stumbled, nor of the point when he broke his sword. Both accused and witnesses probably gave a biased account of the facts but, even so, it is interesting to note the degree to which the simple soldier's respect for social hierarchy went against the egalitarian treatment offered to him (with provocation and humiliation) by his aristocratic adversary. As we have said, it was an extreme case. The counter-proof is that Louis XIII thought it necessary to remind Pontis 'that an officer must never be permitted to fight a private soldier'.

As a consequence of the same principle, the most undisputed aristocrat who had renounced the wearing of a sword to put on the robe of a magistrate or a cleric was thus rendered unable to fight a duel. Jean-Pierre Camus, the Bishop of Belley, was well aware of this when he fulminated from the pulpit: 'No, no, my robe gives me enough shelter from your challenges and your all-out fights' to excommunicate duellists. On a more farcical note, Baron de Foeneste had misgivings about fighting a coachman, the argument in favour of doing so being that he was a sergeant (and therefore a career soldier), while the argument against was provided by the greatcoast which he wore as part of his job, and which made of him 'a man in a long robe'.

Within the world of gentlemen who carried weapons by profession (which thus extended beyond but did not comprise all the gentry and nobility), differences of rank made it possible for some to refuse to fight a duel, and put others more or less outside or above the sphere of the duellists. But these internal barriers were not always readily acceptable to public opinion. It was all right when the Duc de Beaufort, whose bravery was legendary and who was a 'bastard of France' – an illegitimate member of the royal family – refused to fight a simple gentleman in a futile quarrel: 'princes', comments Madame de Motteville, 'have often chosen to avoid fights with private individuals'. But when the Duc d'Elbeuf replied to the Comte de Brion's challenge that 'those of his quality did not act in such a manner' and left for his country estate, Gaston d'Orléans 'had verses written saying that M. d'Elbeuf had been called to fight and had not wanted to go'. Ultimately, the obstacle lay less in inequality of rank than in the adversary's relation to the majesty of royalty.

There were individual cases where a high-ranking dignitary (such as a member of the *noblesse de robe*) would voluntarily divest himself of his authority in order to be able to meet his opponent, but the royal family remained apart. The princes of the blood had very public quarrels, but never fought duels as a result. The brothers of successive kings, who were often friendly with famous duellists, never fought. As for the kings themselves, after the exchange of cartels between François I and the Emperor, they did not even challenge other sovereigns. It is true that Henri IV challenged the Duc de Guise in 1585, but, as he was then King of Navarre, in France he was merely the leader of one faction who wanted to confront the leader of the opposing faction.

At the end of this chapter, which has accumulated more questions than certainties, we can form a few impressions. In the first half of the seventeenth century neither French society nor its 'flower', 'these poor gentlemen who are killing each other', were threatened with disappearance by the duel. Nevertheless, duelling weighed heavily in the consciousness of that society. It certainly concerned only fit men who carried arms by profession. The King escaped it, as did his relatives, the high officials of the Crown, women, magistrates, priests and clerics, those wearers of robes, and the labouring masses. But all men of war were potential duellists, as was any civilian commoner, bourgeois, adventurer or servant who carried a rapier. At that time the carrying of weapons was unregulated, apart from a few vain decrees. Age did not prevent a man fighting a duel as long as he still had the strength. No region escaped and no year was exempt. We now come to the essential problem: what were the reasons for this intensity of duelling?

Chapter 8

In Support of the Duel:
The Motives for Duels

Today frenzied courtiers think it more valiant and brave to
fight over a Whore than in the service of the King.
(A. Favyn, *The Theatre of Honour*, 1620, p. 1689)

Why did a man fight a duel? Because he had received a *démenti*. This
was the simple and universal reply, but it gave only the immediate
cause. The *démenti* itself was a response to certain words, gestures or
attitudes considered insulting or offensive. These words, gestures
and attitudes could in themselves be gratuitous, unpremeditated, and
might not have been aimed in a personal way at the individual who
found himself their victim, but often they insulted someone with
whom a man already had a quarrel. Although at the time the duellists
might have fought without hatred or desire for revenge 'over a small
matter', 'over a very minor matter' or 'over a glass of lemonade', in
fact the duel was often a reactivation of long-standing and serious
rivalries, which could go beyond the individuals concerned to impli-
cate families, cliques, social groups and even nations. For example,
when the Comte de Coligny challenged the Duc de Guise in 1643, it
was because the latter had made public Coligny's secret love for
Madame de Longueville; it was also because they each represented
opposing factions at court; it was also to 'resolve the old quarrels
[between their two houses] with which the whole history of the last
century is filled'.

It was rare for a duel to spring from a single cause, as it is for
several sources to give the same reason for a particular duel. Nevertheless, the real or claimed reasons given by our sources for each
event can be reduced to certain types, and we have made such a list
for the century spanning 1560–1659. Apart from duels 'for fun',
which often had their origins at a ball or at a game of tennis or cards,
most were the outcome of five categories of quarrels. In descending
order of frequency, these were: duels fought over women (twenty
cases), by men belonging to rival factions or clans (ten cases), over
public office (seven cases), following differences or legal cases concerning family or seigniorial inheritances (seven cases), and lastly

because of rivalry over precedence, or some other honorific distinction (six cases). This list does not differ greatly from that drawn up by the Sieur de Chevalier in 1609: 'Duels are fought by those seeking to marry, to gain homages, because of legal trials, to win precedence in church and public assemblies, in fact for all sorts of quarrels.'

Let us look a little closer at these categories.

Over women. This category is larger, but also more precise, than 'by those seeking to marry'. Indeed we did not discover any suitor engaged in 'a combat which has Chimène as the prize'. The sociological reality was different from the mythological and literary models, such as Atalanta and Hippomenes' race, Aeneas' fight against Turnus for the hand of Lavinia, or the exploits of Roland and Renaud for the love of Angélique, although these were familiar in the culture of the time. No one fought to win a lady's heart, although a duel might be fought for revenge against the man who had won it. Duels were mostly fought to defend, avenge or exalt the honour of a man's wife, daughter, ward or mistress, or even that of a lady to whom he dedicated his respectful admiration or entirely platonic passion. In this respect the words with which La Béraudière ends his book on *Single Combat in a Closed Field* are highly significant: 'One must love one's mistress and not dishonour her: but it is the duty of the valiant gentleman to preserve her honour with the point of his sword.'

By men belonging to rival camps. This is a category which Chevalier does not mention. Moreover, this reason was seldom presented as the only or even the most important one underlying a fight; it was seen more as something that encouraged it. The cases we have found are concentrated into two periods of deep division in society: the Wars of Religion and, to a lesser degree, the Fronde. There is of course a link which deserves further consideration between political troubles and single combat; but it is not a simple causal link.

Over public office. This is a cause which contemporary authors often mention. But, as with duels fought over women, it was never a question of two ambitious individuals meeting with swords in their hands to decide who would get this seneschalsy or that galley command. The duel would be fought to test the merit of the man who had already got the job. It would be fought – without putting it so brutally and insolently – to prove that the sovereign's choice was not the best. It was an indirect but serious way of challenging the authority of the Prince.

It also happened, particularly with young gentlemen and those newly arrived at Court, in the army or in the entourage of one of the high aristocracy, the *Grands*, that by proving his worth in a personal quarrel – or by offering himself as a second – a man could give an indication of the qualities he would bring to bear in public office.

How many times did cold calculations concerning ways to distinguish oneself and advance one's career lie behind the unthinking intoxication of a public display of courage? It is hard to say. Especially since venality and heredity were more usual routes to honours than duels. However, the Capuchin monk Zacharie de Lisieux complains of such an attitude among contemporaries of the Fronde, as did Montaigne's brother-in-law Pressac at the time of the Ligue. After stating that valour is refused to spies and 'merchants who risk their persons', Pressac observes that those who are punctilious about honour act no differently from such bold defenders of their own interests, 'those who parade their desire for such fights and who, voluntarily, seek them out, assuming that they will thus acquire the reputation of being men of worth and of good service: in which they are in practice doing nothing other than seeking personal profit and advantage.'

Because of legal cases. Half a century after Chevalier, René de Menou judged 'most quarrels to be based on legal disputes'. In our survey, legal disputes concerning family property or seigniorial rights led as often to a duel as did rivalry over public office. But here again it was not a question of appealing against the judgement of the courts with the judgement of arms. Of course, trials were often interminably lengthy; of course, the magistrates' dialectic was hard to understand and seemed dishonest to men of honour who were (or considered themselves) 'open men'. However, they did not dispute sentences or arbitration. They were exasperated rather than disconcerted by labyrinthine legal procedures and resented only the opposing side who, according to them, were carrying out the sentence in an insulting manner. Trials or disputes over inheritance crystallised hatred between families, whose numbers were swelled by their allies and faithful supporters. An individual who was particularly sensitive to the behaviour of an opponent would extract a quarrel over a point of honour from it, challenge him and meet him in the field. But if there were a death, or simply a large number of seconds, then the duel would become just the prelude to a private battle or even a local war. In such cases the duel, which was formally speaking fought with no idea of revenge, would effectively become the principal link in the chain of a vendetta.

Because of quarrels over precedence. This cause should not be confused with the futile motives of the more fastidious men of honour, the *raffinés d'honneur*, who were quick to fight 'for fun'. In a civilisation of ostentation, a baroque society ruled by appearance, power expressed itself essentially through prestige, and prestige through material symbols such as dress, seating or rank in ceremonies. No one was indifferent to these things, from workers to dukes and peers of the realm. So it is understandable that in such a society those who would draw their swords to defend their women and their property and to advance their political or military ambitions would also draw them in disputes over 'pre-eminence in church' or 'pre-eminence in council'.

Beyond the reasons for actual duels, we should also look for factors which motivated the frequent recourse to duels in the peak periods described in the previous chapter. For contemporaries, these were essentially twofold: the influence of wars and the weakness of monarchs.

The links between duels and wars are numerous and complex. It was primarily 'men of war' who had a vocation for fighting duels. Armies in the field were breeding grounds for quarrels and fights, whether in Flanders under Louis XIV or in Italy under François I. Civil and foreign wars offered brave men the chance to challenge each other as champions of the opposing causes. Many observers thought that the Wars of Religion 'engendered these particular disorders', or at least that 'it is from the heart of our civil wars that our duels have taken their vigour, so well do these two evils go together'. But others judged it to be the end of the civil, and indeed international, hostilities under Henri IV that produced so large a number of quarrels, these being the only 'way by which young men believe that they can gain greater praise in times of peace'. This was also the opinion of the King himself. In a letter to the Pope in 1609 he described the failure of his policy against duels, attributing it to 'the heat and courage which is common among those of this nation who during this happy time of peace ... find themselves without employment'.

These words of Henri IV lead us to the second reason underlying duels: the weakness of monarchs. This can be seen in three different, successive or simultaneous manifestations.

There was a proliferation of duelling because it was no longer an institution authorised (or refused) by kings. After the duel between Jarnac and La Châtaigneraye, Henri II and his successors renounced their role of supreme judge and controller of affairs of honour by ceasing to 'grant the field'. Of course, sovereigns were keen to settle quarrels that sprang up between the *Grands*; but they did not always succeed before blood was shed, and they could do nothing (and their officers little) to settle quarrels between opponents who were less noticeable than men in their immediate entourage.

The King lacked authority, either because he was too young to rule effectively (the minorities of Louis XIII and Louis XIV), or because his right to rule was disputed by a proportion of his subjects

(Henri III, Henri IV until 1598), or because his administration was paralysed by civil troubles (Wars of Religion, the commotions of Louis XIII's reign, the Fronde). This lack of authority gave free rein to an extra-legal, if not illegal, procedure. Sovereignty had been 'silently abandoned' by the King, and those 'individuals' who took to duelling were 'manifestly usurping it'.

The repressive legislation of the Bourbon kings reinforced the very phenomenon it was aimed to crush. First, because disobedience to the law brought risks that added to the attraction of that act of audacious bravery, the duel; secondly, because it was generally well known that legal sanctions were rarely applied, and that if prosecution was brought against a 'criminal', he would almost always obtain a letter of remission. Lastly, and this is the most serious aspect, because the sovereign, like his courtiers, regarded duellists not just with indulgence, but with esteem and admiration.

These political interpretations of the strength of the duel are supported by our impressionistic statistics. A certain number of chronological coincidences can be seen between periods of great increases or decreases in duelling and the political climate of the time.

- The peak of 1604–7 corresponds to a period of peace at home and abroad.
- That of 1611–14 occurs during the minority of Louis XIII and in the run-up to the meeting of the Estates General.
- The decrease over the years 1618–21 accompanies the resurgence of politico-religious conflict in Europe.
- The peak of the years 1621–6 corresponds to the years in which Richelieu became a minister and established his authority; these were also years of military operations against the Protestant faction.
- The peak of 1631–3 accompanies the policy of 'covert war' when, by dint of much subtle manoeuvring, France managed to delay its entry into the Thirty Years War.
- The long period which followed, when duelling was less frequent, coincides with France's open participation in the general European conflict.
- The last burst of 1649–53: following the partial re-establishment of peace abroad with the Treaties of Westphalia, France was prey to civil troubles in the Fronde of the Princes.

If we take these points of coincidence as indications of a particular conjuncture of attitudes in society, they do make clearer the links suggested by contemporaries between duel, war and political crisis.

Foreign wars, if they were generally regarded as acceptable by public opinion, reduced the number of duels. Individual aggression was in some sense channelled towards a common discharge. And although it is undeniable that quarrels flourished among those living the military life, these quarrels were isolated in the vast social closed field of the army.

Civil war stimulated duelling. During these wars institutional prohibitions no longer, or scarcely, had a role; in these conflicts combatants and civilians were no longer separated, the politico-religious cause intersected with private rivalries and the enemy was also a brother.

Even more conducive to duelling were periods preceding or immediately following conflict. Post-war periods were times of bitter idleness and impossible reconversion for men who only knew and loved fighting. Thus some authors proposed getting rid of these brave but burdensome men by sending them off to fight the Infidel. The utopian Crusade was also a form of policing.

Pre-war periods were at least as conducive to duelling. The years and months preceding the outbreak of hostilities or troubles were periods during which aggression built up without yet finding a collective outlet. For those who enjoyed a fight, notably the young, these were times of tension aggravated by humiliation. Of course, there is no formal proof of such states of mind, but accounts of the years preceding the Wars of Religion or France's actual entry into the Thirty Years War help us to understand that these periods were ripe for quarrels and duels.

We cannot discuss statistics on duels (even if they are only impressionistic) as if they were statistics on prices or burials. Nor can we give a strictly determinist explanation to a phenomenon of collective attitudes. This is why we do not claim here to explain why the France of the last Valois and the first Bourbons was also the golden age of duels. But we can achieve a better understanding of what duels represented for those who lived through this important time in their history. The duel has its place in a politico-military ambience formed of an aspiration towards unity and authority combined with the experience of division and a refusal to submit oneself to a disputed authority. The duel was a way of distancing oneself from the sovereign, and often of teaching the sovereign a lesson.

But, while it resolved or at least expressed contradictions, the duel was in itself a contradiction. Many felt it to be a gratuitous, irrational act, performed by individuals who were deliberately placing themselves beyond the pale. But many others felt duelling to be a constraining social obligation and submitted to it without the least sense of 'fun'. 'They often do it to keep up appearances rather than because they want to,' says P. Caussin in 1624. 'Their blood runs cold at the thought of the danger to which they are exposing themselves.' Some fought out of conformism, others to affirm their difference.

Fighting a duel meant placing oneself on the fringes of society; but avoiding a duel had the same effect.

Chapter 9

Opposition to the Duel: The Church

It is the action of an atheist, since all sorts of religions condemn it. It is the action of a man in despair, possessed by the devil, hurling himself into perdition in cold blood, like the man who hangs himself and brings about his own death.

(J. Chenel de La Chapperonaye, *Revelations of the Solitary Hermit*, 1617)

'Show me,' I said, 'with all your direction of intention that it is lawful to fight a duel.'

'Our great Hurtado de Mendoza,' said the Father, 'will give you immediate satisfaction, in this passage ...'

... These passages made me wonder at seeing piety inspire the King to use his power to forbid and abolish duelling in the State, while it makes the Jesuits devote their subtlety to permitting and authorising it in the Church.

Pascal, *7th Provincial Letter.*

The forces which gave strength to the duel came from the depths of French society. The drive against it, on the other hand, came from the highest levels of that society. Pitted against the almost visceral and often unspoken drives that led to duelling were the reasoned speeches of authorities such as the Catholic ecclesiastical hierarchy and its Protestant equivalent.

The Gallican Church had a fundamental horror of bloodshed and risk to life (even in martyrdom), unless on the express orders of a superior authority representing God's will on earth. Medieval canon law had been hostile to trial by ordeal, judicial combat and tournaments.

It was from this point of view and within this tradition that the Council of Trent passed the 19th canon in the last meeting of its 25th and final session. In order to rid the Christian world of this diabolical practice, dangerous to both life and soul, the Church forbade princes to grant a closed field, on pain of excommunication and dispossession of the place soiled by combat. Duellists, godfathers, accomplices and ordinary spectators were condemned to excommunication and it was not permitted to bury in consecrated ground those killed in a duel.

This was a very severe decision, worded in such as way as to cover all private and public duels, judicial combats and encounters for points of honour. It was a massive condemnation valid throughout the universal Church, but for France, the Church's Eldest Daughter, it had little validity, and that only gradually acquired.

In fact the Council's decrees were never 'received' as laws of the Most Christian Kingdom of France. And one of the stumbling blocks was precisely the 19th canon. After consulting the lawyer Du Moulin, Charles IX protested that it was an abuse of spiritual power to appropriate the temporal right to take the place of combat out of the jurisdiction of a legitimate prince and give it to his sovereign or, if there were no feudal lord, to the Church, 'Neither the King of France nor his kingdom can be subject to the Pope.' This was to remain the doctrine of the Gallican monarchy on the subject. Although the King and Gallican Church struggled against duelling, unlike the Italians they did not use the Council of Trent's decision, beyond drawing inspiration from it regarding excommunication and the prohibition of Christian burial.

As a body the Gallican Church met, took decisions and formulated its wishes when the Estates General met, as they did four times between 1560 and 1614, and at General Assemblies of the Clergy, which were ten times more frequent. At each session of the Estates General, the clergy devoted one or two articles of its General Register of Complaints to duels, quarrels and *démentis*. This must be seen as an act of its religious ministry: the clergy stated that this type of combat is 'unsuitable to the Christian state' (1560) and proposed (but not until 1588) that duellists' corpses should be 'deprived of an ecclesiastical burial'. But we should perhaps view it still more as a reflection of a political concern that the clergy shared with the lay orders: the Registers of the Third Estate and even those of the nobility also always had one or two items devoted to the fight against duels.

The clerical assemblies had no items concerning duels on their agenda until 1616. As late as 1615 only individual men of the cloth were attacking duelling as a sin. Taking publications as an index, they must have been very few and isolated individuals, for we found only three books for the whole second half of the sixteenth century. This does not point to a great effort to combat duelling. However, these books do voice three themes or arguments which later became classics of the religious anti–duel panoply. First, the idea that to fight a duel was to 'give oneself to the devil' through voluntary sacrifice.

Secondly, the idea that a duel was the worst possible preparation for a good death, that most important moment of Christian life. Lastly, the idea that noblemen should keep their ardour for the only really honourable form of combat, 'the fight of good against evil', for 'there is nothing more honourable for a Christian than to suppress his passions with reason'.

In the years 1614–15 there was a sudden change from isolated preaching and *ad hoc* arguments to the establishment of an ecclesiastical anti-duel strategy. As we have already stated, 1614–15 was a peak period for duels and also for publications on duels. The duel was perceived as a major phenomenon of the period, a sign of those times of uncertainty, of royal minority and the meeting of the Estates General. Every individual and authoritative body in the headless kingdom was obliged to adopt a position on the phenomenon. So the Church moved from moral and political complaint to a pastoral offensive.

The clergy, first order of the kingdom, devoted one article of its Register of Complaints to duels among noblemen, but this article was different from those it had presented to previous meetings of the Estates, in that punitive laws were now in place and the clergy was asking for their enforcement. But for this to be carried out – and here the text becomes urgent – a change of attitude and ethics was required on the part of the rulers. It was necessary not only that the laws be strict, but also that the King should look with disdain upon the guilty and that magistrates should resolve to take no account of those letters of pardon which were 'extorted from the King by importunity'. The clergy wanted the second order of the nobility to adopt this text and include it in its own Register. The nobility refused and even put pressure on the clergy to abandon publication, at least as the text stood. The clergy became more entrenched in its position. Fenouillet, the Bishop of Montpellier, pronounced a homily before the lords which was immediately published. He set out what was essentially a religious argument in the accepted form of the time, a mixture of erudite allegories in a pathetic tone. In the twenty-two pages of the printed pamphlet, the word 'blood' occurs twenty-seven times, like a pulse beating on the King's door and obliging him to assume his responsibilities.

And there was more. Every Sunday deputies from all three orders gathered in the Augustinians' church to hear a sermon preached by a deputy from the clergy. Three of the first six of these sermons fulminated against quarrels on a point of honour, a major temptation for the nobility, and against their chief sin of duelling. Two of the three sermons which have survived in their entirety do the same. These are homilies by Camus and a short quotation will give us the general tone: 'this kingdom is afflicted with the three scourges spoken of by the prophet . . . these being the *plague* of heresy in the Church, *war* within the nobility, through duelling, and *famine* among the Third Estate as a result of extreme oppression.'

The clergy were also campaigning outside the Court and the Estates General, among the general public. There is an echo of this campaign in the conclusion given by *Le Mercure françois* to the account of a duel in January 1615: 'To go to mass full of devotion, and then, on leaving, to go and cut each other's throats over another man's quarrel is something that was never seen in centuries gone by.' Other writings display more obvious propaganda of an edifying nature. An anonymous pamphlet tells the disturbing story of a duel which took place the day after Fenouillet's homily in which one second, a stranger to his partners, mysteriously disappeared after dispatching his man. He could only have been a demon. 'So from now on,' concludes the pamphlet, 'remember that you will no longer be fighting against men, but against devils.'

Between the dissolution of the Estates General and the Fronde, the Church consistently followed the line it had set itself in 1614–15, although not always with the same ardour. Clerical assemblies ceaselessly called for duellists to be more mercilessly prosecuted. One by one the synodal laws of each diocese made explicit the fact that duelling led *ipso facto* to excommunication and that only the Bishop had the power of absolution in this 'special case'.

Exhortation and censure went hand in hand. There were oratorical campaigns during which, according to Richelieu, 'one heard nothing in church but preachers' complaints on the subject'. The entire active element of the seventeenth-century Catholic Reformation applied itself to the task, including the new regular orders, secular congregations and pious laymen, each in their chosen style.

The Capuchins, those robust and popular last-borns of the Franciscan family, many of whom had noble origins hidden beneath their cowls, were particularly active. One of them, Philippe d'Angoumois, founded the Company of the Holy Sacrament with the Jesuit Suffren. One mission this devout society gave its members was to renounce duelling and keep their fellows from it too.

Officials of the 'so-called reformed religion' could also be seen dealing out bans and admonishments, on the example of the Catholic hierarchy. The consistory symposia were constantly drawing up and reaffirming articles 'to be read on a Sunday by every pastor in his church so that considerations of conscience and religion restrain those who cannot be restrained by respect for human laws and the edicts of kings'. Synods invited pastors to censure those guilty of duelling. Ministers delivered exhortations to the faithful from the pulpit, and sometimes in print.

Churchmen saw duelling as a manifestation of literally infernal libertinism or neo-paganism, although not always at the level of visible behaviour. Underneath the surface of duellists' practices, they saw and denounced a serious subversion of values. To the transcendent values of revealed religion duellists preferred worldly values, such as honour, values for which they were prepared to sacrifice themselves. In the attraction of duelling the Church perceived not so much real atheism (in spite of certain expressions of holy eloquence) as a diversion of religious feeling away from orthodox Christianity, for, whether clearly or more confusedly, the nobility and all those who followed their ethics saw the judgement of arms as a judgement of God. It was a sacred act in reverse, a sacrifice in which the combatants, simultaneously priests and victims, made themselves 'martyrs to the devil'. The duel was not just simple disobedience, even of a serious nature, to this or that commandment from God or the Church. It had the mark of Mortal Sin.

Having been alerted to the moral and religious problems posed by duelling at the end of the sixteenth century, the French clergy increased its severity in the first decade of the seventeenth century, then increased it further around the middle of the century, ending up in the 1680s with a ban which, although it was beginning to lack any concrete object, was none the less total for all that. But beneath the increasing severity and clear consciences of the ecclesiastics, their silences and softening translations betray the lasting subconscious presence of an almost complicit indulgence on the part of these men of the Church, who were also men of this world and of their time. We have no intention of minimising the first impression of restriction, which is the most clearly expressed and can be read in black and white in so many works, on the grounds of these few indications. However, we do wonder how such theoretical opposition responded in practice to the test of the everyday, to individual motivations for duels, all of which were seen as unique, exceptional, incommensurable and irrefragable – when the priest, having closed his books, was sitting in the dark of the confessional, faced with the particular, trembling case of a penitent duellist, a man like himself, his brother.

For the attitudes of the clergy as individuals were far from homogeneous. Doubtless clerics like the Cardinal de Retz, who reconciled wearing a robe with carrying a sword, were extremely rare. However, more numerous were the priests and monks who paid very little attention to canonical bans. There were those who confined excommunication only to the most extreme cases, those who took no account of the special case and confessed and administered the sacraments to dying duellists and those who, without batting an eyelid, buried the victims in consecrated ground, or beneath the stone flags of their church, sometimes with great ceremony. Worse still, perhaps, some convents offered asylum to guilty duellists pursued by the law.

Casuists and Confessors

It is the famous passage from Pascal's *7th Provincial Letter* standing as an epigraph to this chapter which leads us to examine the vision of the duel in the confession manuals and summaries of casuistry.

The Jesuits acted chiefly through spiritual directors. One of these, Father Caussin, Louis XIII's confessor, wrote a book called *The Holy Court*, a manual for Christian courtiers which was enormously successful, in which there is a chapter on honour, courage and duels. Its conclusion distances it greatly from the too-indulgent priests caricatured by Pascal: 'So, by rejecting duelling, one cannot avoid dishonour in the eyes of the world? Of whom does this world consist? A lot of scatterbrains. . . . So you must leave this world. Leave it!'

However, this unequivocal attitude was not shared by all. As the lack of discussion of duelling by sixteenth-century authors of confession manuals and casuistry shows, understanding of the duel as a practice hazardous to eternal salvation came late in the century and even then did not worry the majority of spiritual directors. The seventeenth century offers us a quite different picture: thirty-four of the forty-five such authors we found discuss duelling. With one exception, those who do not mention duels were first published in the last third of the century, and their silence clearly does not have the same significance as that of the sixteenth-century casuists. On the theoretical level, it signifies an unqualified condemnation so obvious that it leaves no room for discussion (of the sort we find in the work of those of their contemporaries who persisted in writing about duels); on the practical level it signifies that the problem was no longer urgent and acute.

We can trace the pace of change over the period in which religious souls were vigilant with regard to the sin of duelling by following the same text through its subsequent editions and, where appropriate, its translations. The most deliberate, and thus spectacular, transformations of a text, are those of the *Aphorismi confessariorum* by the Jesuit Emmanuel Sa, sixteen editions of which appeared in France between 1600 and 1702. In 1603 the work was placed on the Index, but reappeared 'expurgated and reworked'. The Index commission cut three clauses from the passage on duelling. One clause affirmed that a sovereign could authorise a fight by special dispensation with regard to the canon law of the Council of Trent. The other two cited cases which the author judged legitimate grounds for a private duel. So the evolution was towards restriction, with duelling tolerated only in exceptional circumstances (for the champion of an army following David's example, or in self-defence), and even then with reservations.

Other changes we have found reflect a similar evolution towards ever greater strictness. However, we also found two cases of more discreet modifications in the opposite direction. The first is in a French translation of a Latin work by a Jesuit Regnault Valère, which contains a chapter on duelling. In the 1623 translation published in Lyons, the chapter is faithful to the original and is called 'Of him who fights a duel'. But in an equally complete and exact translation published in Paris in the same year the title is given as 'Of him who challenges to a duel'. So a hasty reader who stops at the table of contents might conclude that the *appelé* could go and fight with a clear conscience. The second instance comes later in the century, in a free translation published in 1674 of a work listing sins related to military life, in which the word *duel* is erased in passing. Whether or not this omission was deliberate, it proves that not all casuists had the same opinion of the seriousness of the sin of duelling.

Further proof of this is provided by an examination of the principal cases of conscience which led duellists into bloody fights, as identified by the theologians. The casuists accepted that in such cases different moral arguments as to the correct way to proceed were in conflict. They attempted to distinguish right from wrong according to the precepts of the Church and the intentions of the person involved, where necessary trying to lead those intentions in a direction they considered compatible with Christian morality.

The first and most ancient of the cases relating to duels was that of a duel fought 'to establish the truth of something'. This case was linked to the tradition of judicial duels and discussion of it was developed mostly by authors of the end of the Middle Ages and the beginning of the sixteenth century; but it always remained at the heart of the notion of the duel in the analysis of religious minds, even when buried under other forms of duel. Seventeenth-century casuists consulted the work of their predecessors and often linked duels to the *probatio vulgaris* (trial by water, by red-hot iron . . .), or recalled Jesus's words: 'Thou shalt not tempt the Lord thy God.'

The duel, which was supposed to settle intractable quarrels, to let the truth shine through and justice triumph, was indeed a form of temptation of God. The Church of the humanists, Cartesians and the Council of Trent was not only generally prudent where miracles were concerned, it was also utterly opposed to God's created setting himself up as a miracle-worker with the willing participation of his opponent.

The confession manuals seldom discuss (and it is moreover not in their brief) the fact that in duels, as in all forms of ordeal, it is not always the best man who wins. But they condemn in principle the procedure which consists in 'wanting to extort a miracle from God'. The scandal is not that God does not reply, it is that the duellist calls on Him, charges Him to make a decision, to choose. To tempt God is, in the literal sense of the word, to test His providence. It is to provoke God at the same time as the adversary. It is to force Him to prove Himself at the same time as one proves one's own courage. Such arrogant insolence, presumptuous 'trust' in God and waste of His providence were opposed by those of austere and parsimonious faith, who worshipped the silence of the hidden God and whose religious attitude – which extended far beyond the Jansenist circles – was defined by a tragic rejection of the miraculous.

Two cases linked to the above, but which were looked at with more indulgence, concerned judicial procedure. Many casuists considered that an innocent man condemned to death or to bodily mutilation could agree to exchange single combat for death at the hands of the executioner. Most casuists expressed reservations about this, made conditions and insisted that the condemned man must hope not to show his innocence by fighting the duel, but only to save his life (his opponent must be undeniably guilty to deserve death). To our knowledge, this procedure was completely obsolete in France, and the reflections on it purely theoretical.

Why then should theologians spend time analysing situations that did not arise in the society of their time? Were they simply using them as exercises, passed down from one generation to the next regardless of historical changes? Did they think that situations that had once been real could become so again and therefore deserved constantly to be studied? Or was it rather that they were expressing their private conviction that human justice is not the whole of justice, that the sword of justice cannot be entirely subject to reason and its norms and that this is so precisely because of its supernatural privilege of ending human life? The taboo nature of both the executioner's work and the situation of the prisoner condemned to death led the most rational of theologians to take care – even if the problem were entirely theoretical – to give these functions inherent to but on the margins of society to someone who stood in an exceptional relation to that society: a duellist. Giving a chance of life to a condemned man, forcing him to fight a duel, was a way for a human court to hand over its role to divine justice, it was an implicit (and possibly unconscious) recognition of the notion of a judgement from God. It was a way of leaving things to the mercy of the source of all mercy. At the same time, and at an even deeper and more obscure level of consciousness, it was a way of breaking the never-ending chain of revenge for spilt blood. Since the Church 'abhorred blood' and handed over those it condemned to the secular authorities for execution, the magistrates might prefer that the responsibility for bloodshed should fall on the dead man's honest opponent, rather than on those professionally responsible for his death.

So these two cases of procedural duels, although they were residual if not fossilised in the actual judicial practice of the sixteenth and seventeenth centuries, were not anachronistic. They were expressions of a conception of justice which was certainly traditional, but also very much alive in contemporary hearts and minds until the last decades of the seventeenth century.

One frequently mentioned case was that of two soldiers from opposing armies facing each other in single combat as champions of their causes. The *exemplum* of David and Goliath had a crucial place in the gentleman's mental universe and the fact that Holy Writ supported an intellectual process familiar to the social elite could only encourage churchmen to be indulgent towards it, or indeed to approve it. Two types of reasons supported the adoption of such a position. Some casuists thought this type of combat was licit because it strengthened troops' confidence in themselves in times of trial. From this point of view the 'duel' was simply an element in a wider conflict. But for most such a fight was the ultimate form of combat, substituted for the general conflagration in order to end it; its aim was to spare human life, bring immediate peace and ensure the victory of the just cause, the one being defended by the weaker army, state or faction.

So here again we can see the miraculous judgement of God appearing. The strength of this idea can be measured by the consensus among casuists published before the end of the seventeenth century. Any who may have disagreed preferred to keep silent on this point rather than take the risk of rebutting it. For this case of conscience had a concrete existence in contemporary reality, for example in the fight between Marolle and L'Isle-Marivaut during the League, Bayart's duels during the Italian wars, or Henri of Navarre's challenge to the Duc de Guise in 1585. In the following century, examples became rarer, but the practice did not become completely obsolete: in 1602 the Chancellor of Poland and the King of Sweden exchanged cartels, and, when Christian IV of Denmark seized Calmar, Christian IX of Sweden provoked him 'so that less blood might be spilled and so that your renown might not be completely obliterated'. Certainly, these events took place in foreign and predominantly non-Catholic countries, but many French manuscript collections tell their stories: a proof that potentially this case still retained its power.

Another cause of duels was also frequently mentioned but gave rise to many more reservations. This was concern to avoid a reputation for cowardice which might be prejudicial to the career of a man professing honour. If he were considered a coward, he could 'no longer show himself at Court, nor hope for any promotion in the army, following the custom of a number of princely Courts'. Whether the theologian allows or forbids such a case, it is never without reservations and a degree of confusion. Such confusions and subtleties show that we are touching on concrete and contemporary problems here and therefore on problems which are also complex and ambiguous. The spiritual director was obliged to take account of antithetical but respectable criteria: the inanity of the glories of this world and an evangelical concern 'not to retire from the world but to protect from evil', respect for human life but also respect for social conventions outside of which all life becomes impossible. For moral problems of this density, there is no easy solution. Circumstances must be examined in their specificity, and the choices open to the penitent must be considered with a view to charging the latter to choose the lesser of two evils.

Besides these causes which might justify recourse to duelling, the authors mention two formal causes, depending on whether or not the penitent was the challenger. Two casuists allowed that it was possible for the appellant not to be criminal. His intentions should still be led away from murder of his opponent and towards the defence of his own honour, or else he should not fix the place and form of the fight, thereby ensuring that the combat kept the appearance of a chance brawl. The *appelé* was generally given greater indulgence. Villalobos sums up the opinion of more than one of his casuist colleagues by recommending him not positively to accept the duel, but to announce that he will not change his habits or timetable in any way, that he will therefore be easy to find, and that if he is attacked he will draw his sword.

So there were basically two licit or possibly licit cases: the defence of truth by the champion of an army and self-defence. The first was a theoretical case, with no real concrete applications; the second was far more real and even everyday, and its application is infinitely extendable. Direction of intention made it possible to apply it both to the *appelé* 'out for a walk' on the field where he knows he will meet his opponent and to the gentleman to whom life is not worth living if he cannot repair honour which he knows deep inside himself to be nothing but social convention.

Pierre Milhard, the Benedictine monk whose *Guide for Priests* was one of the main instruments in the popularisation of moral theology in France, gives us a kind of average vision for casuists as a whole. His work very explicitly articulates all the condemnations and other 'very strange punishments' which strike the main actors and extras in a duel and in no way softens the seriousness of an excommunication 'so reserved that nobody, whatever their social position, can absolve it'. But he recognises that honour is an essential component of morality, even for non-gentlemen, and for him this honour is indissociable from reputation. The intention to defend this honour then allows a man to have recourse to arms without going against 'the prohibition on duels'. After having proclaimed his opposition in principle to duelling 'because of the law of God, the Church and his Prince', Milhard goes on to suggest to the gentleman that he may defend himself, indeed even give a preventative *démenti*, indeed even 'forestall' his opponent who wants 'to have his life ... anticipating him by doing that for which the opponent is probably prepared'.

Like a great number of casuists (at least until the middle of the seventeenth century), Milhard shows us with a kind of naivety that he recognises the morality of honour, a morality belonging to aristocratic circles and quite separate from ordinary Christian morality. The casuists' vision of the duel was a vision of a reality torn between two equally demanding and austere moralities, between eternal precepts and the legitimate imperatives of the time, and between religious and social values both of which had aspects that changed and aspects that remained the same, but at a different pace.

Over the course of time we find a change in the notion of the duel in moral theology. For the earliest authors, the sin of duelling consisted in the illicit search for truth, the action which forced providence to give up its secrets. But for the more modern writers (and in fact for the greatest number), it was the pact between two individuals determined to ignore the legal frameworks of society. This shows a radical transformation of moral conceptions. At the end of the Middle Ages single combat was essentially a sin of a metaphysical order, a sin which disturbed normal, logical and honest relations between man and God, between the finite, sinful creature and a God whose 'name is Truth'. After the end of the sixteenth century the dominant view in France was one which saw the duel above all as a rebellion against social order, a crime which disturbed normal, logical and legal relations between the individual and the magistrates, between two men on the one hand and, on the other, the whole social corpus as it was constituted hierarchically under the authority of those in political control. Without ever completely ceasing to be of interest to the City of God, the duel mainly preoccupied the City of Men.

Chapter 10
Opposition to the Duel: The State

This crime is one of those which have most held the attention of our sovereigns and which have given rise to the greatest number of edicts.

(P. F. Muyart de Vouglans, *Institutes*, 1757, p. 543)

The classification of duelling as a crime and the establishment of repressive legislation happened slowly. This slowness is easily explained by the genealogical link between the formal, official duel (outmoded, but not abolished, after the middle of the sixteenth century) and the spontaneous duel for a point of honour (never legal, but for a long time regarded as extra-legal rather than illegal).

In a general way, all those who had a sense of state and Church as hierarchical, disciplined and coherent bodies were opposed to duelling. Most important among them was the King, whose vocation was to exert temporal and spiritual authority. The King was Emperor in his kingdom, Bishop beyond it in the Gallican Church, and Protector of the reformed Churches.

François I, in 1532, considered that, as quarrels of honour could not be settled by ordinary justice, they should be submitted to him, with a view, as he put it, to 'obtaining from us such permission as it shall please us to accord them'. This is the archaic conception of the duel in its purest form: as a legal procedure but one which it is the privilege of the King – the supreme arbiter – to authorise or to forbid. It was only when the parties in a particular case disregarded a royal refusal that the combat could be considered a crime. In one of these cases we see François I charging the Governor of Guyenne to prevent 'on pain of hanging and confiscation of property' a duel for which he had refused to grant a field; and for the first time – to our knowledge – this disobedience to a particular royal wish was described by the Chancellery as a 'crime of *lèse-majesté*'.

As we have seen, Henri II legislated largely by keeping silent, although he tried with his 1550 decree to regulate the practice of *démentis* and quarrels within his armies, under the control of the colonels. His son Charles IX promulgated a decree at Moulins in

1566. He stated formally that there had been a rapid increase of duels and observed that 'the source and foundation of these quarrels usually proceeds from *démentis* that are given'. But he could only reply to these new (in their number) events with a traditional idea: the banning of 'assemblies of people and the carrying of weapons' (totally futile in 1566) and an order to those who received a *démenti* to refer the affair to the Constable, to the Marshals of France or, failing that, to the Governor of the province 'to settle it as they see fit'. There was nothing here about granting a field, but nor was there anything about refusing it or recognising that the practice had become obsolete. It was simply that the highest officers of the Crown, nobles who had covered themselves in glory by their martial exploits and who had been invested with a portion of royal sovereignty, were – in the name and place of the King – declared competent to decide cases of honour simple enough to be resolvable without recourse to arms. They were respectable and indisputable arbiters who could decide in a given quarrel who had ridiculed the honour of his rival, who should make reparation to whom, and what that reparation should be.

The rise of tension and confrontations in his entourage led Henri III to make a 'Decree on quarrels which might arise in his house or in the Court'. This decree established an obligatory and minutely defined arbitration procedure. The text of the decree was published on 12 January 1578. On 27 April the King's favourites killed each other in a duel. Clearly these preventative measures were 'very badly observed', even in the milieu where the authority and power of the monarch were most immediately felt.

The following year, the great Paris Decree of May 1579, 'relative to the general policing of the kingdom', devoted two sections to duels (but without naming them). Henceforward all subjects were required to 'separate those whom they see fighting each other with swords, daggers, or other offensive staves . . . and deliver them into the hands of the law'. All local officers of the administration were required to inform royal authority of 'any quarrels which flare up in their province', while trying at the same time to settle them. Lastly, the expression 'crime of *lèse-majesté*' is no longer applied to the actions of a particular individual who has rebelled against a particular and precise injunction issued by the King, but applies generally to 'all gentlemen and others [who] bring people together on the pretext of individual or other quarrels'.

It is a short text, vague in style and anyway impossible to apply during a period of unrest. But it testifies to a maturation of the hostile governmental attitude to duelling.

The decisive step was taken only after the turmoil of the civil wars.

It started with a decision by the Paris Parliament reached on 26 June 1599, when, at the time of the trial of two homicidal duellists, the sovereign court made a ruling destined to set a precedent. It mentioned duels by name, described them as crimes of *lèse-majesté*, and clarified the reasons why they were incompatible with monarchial order: 'neither by divine nor human law is it permissible to seek or pursue vengeance other than through the usual channels of the law'.

The lawyers were expressing themselves here with an audacity that the kings were a long way from showing. They simply ignored the fiction of the Crown's high officials delegated by the King to arbitrate in quarrels and grant the field. Only 'ordinary judges' are mentioned as capable of assessing the 'reparation for insults and injuries' received.

Three years later, Henri IV signed the first anti-duel edict. This was the beginning of a long series of royal decrees. In an attempt to reveal the spirit that informs them, we propose to analyse the preambles of the six edicts on duels issued by the Bourbon kings during the first half of the seventeenth century. In principal these official rulings were irrevocable. Each of them makes specific reference to the ones that preceded it and all repeat the same ideas, often word for word. We can thus consider them as a single text in which the monarchy expounded the motives for its opposition to duelling, as long as we qualify our synthesis by taking note of the dates of each edict, those themes that are not repeated and also possibly the preambles of the eight declarations made by the Bourbon kings in the same period (rulings in a much drier style, often much more limited in scope).

The most frequent term used to describe duels in these documents – and most at home in a legal text – is the word 'crime'. They are described as crimes of *lèse-majesté*, which should be 'punished as such' (1609).

The first two texts, signed by Henri IV, while using the word 'crime', denounce the duel above all as a regrettable practice. But even in 1609, and constantly after that, duelling was essentially seen as licentious, a positive abuse, and the epithets used to describe it stress its seriousness, for example 'pernicious disorders' (1651). These legal texts, like the moral literature of the time, readily adopt a passionate tone to speak of duelling as the manifestation of a *passion*, a sickness touching minds and bodies: 'frenzy ... brutal passion, prodigious mania, rage' (1643), 'a disastrous wrong' (1651).

The duel was a social disorder and individual 'disturbance', an 'obstinate wrong' (1643) from which people and the state must be preserved; 'disastrous generally and to the principal families of our realm' (1651). So it threatened and concerned noble duellists, the nobility and gentry as a whole, society in general and the person in charge of it, the King. Twice the duel–nobility link appears as a privileged relation within wider society: 'many within our Nobility and others of our Subjects whose profession is to carry weapons' (1602); 'our subjects and especially our nobility' (1651), but more usually the link between the practice of duelling and noble birth is shown be an exclusive relation.

The French nobility appears as an elite corps 'whose famous valour is redoubtable throughout the world' (1643). It is the 'principal nerve of our State' (1602), 'one of its principal columns' (1626), which 'has always held honour to be dearer than life' (1609) and has a vocation for heroism. Gentlemen were guilty of duelling because they interpreted this vocation wrongly. It was 'a false and erroneous opinion' (1609) which led them to confuse the highest pinnacle of noble honour with the behaviour of 'the lowest slaves', those among whom circus gladiators were once recruited (1643).

In the eyes of the monarchs, the 'generous sages' among gentlemen knew 'that it is by maintaining the work and perils of war with invincible constancy that one proves the greatness and steadfastness of one's courage' (1643). But there were also, and perhaps in greater numbers, 'frenzied' gentlemen who thought that they 'could find satisfaction for an insult by no other means than arms without ruining [their] reputations and making themselves noted for cowardice and lack of courage' (1609) among their peers and by the King himself. The first 'participate in the only real glory which is acquired in the service of one's Prince and one's Country in a legitimate war' (1643). The others, 'very badly informed' (1609) of the real attitude of their sovereign, condemn themselves to becoming 'unhappy victims' (1643). By killing each other they lose their lives and/or that of their peers. They lose the honour they think to preserve, 'which nevertheless obliges them above all other things to show respect to their sovereign Prince and obedience to the laws of their Country' (1602). By placing themselves outside the law, they also lose their military responsibilities, and so still fail 'their honour by failing to be in our armies' (1643). By preferring honour to life, they arrive at the absurdity of constantly losing their honour and sometimes their lives, not to mention eternal life.

The preambles portray the gentry and nobility as caught, in their hunger for the enhancement of their reputations, between 'true glory' and 'false honour', between reality and illusion, good and evil, the King and the Duel. The edicts make the King the symmetrical counterpart of the duel, although he occupies a disproportionate place in these texts of which he is also the utterer. The King appears in a triple role, triply concerned by the existence of duels, and triply determined to put a stop to them: as father of the nobility and gentry, head of state and image of God (1602, 1609, 1643). He is a Bourbon, a monarch and the Most Christian King.

The King first proclaims the sympathetic link which joins him to the nobility and gentry whose most eminent member he is and whose chivalric ethics he cannot fail to share. He can only be 'touched by an extreme pain' faced with the mourning of the country's 'principal families' (1651) and he cannot 'think without horror' of the cause of so many deaths (1643). But nor can he remain indifferent to the solicitations of those close to him who plead for leniency towards this or that guilty duellist (1609, 1651). He inclines to a 'readiness to pardon' when he considers 'the service that most of the nobility and gentry rendered him in his armies' (1643). He cannot refuse a general remission solicited by his mother, his sister or his wife at a moment of joy for the whole family of France: the marriage of Henriette to Charles I of England (1626), or the birth of the Dauphin Louis Dieudonné (1643).

However, in the name of a better understanding of the interests of the nobility, he owes it to himself not to give in to a simplistic type of clemency. He owes it to himself to 'serve the health, honour and preservation' of his nobility and gentry (1602), if necessary against their wishes, and in order to do this he must maintain an implacable severity (1609–43). So he swears 'by the living God to grant no pardons' (1609, 1643).* This severity arises not from a sense of the state, but from the feelings of a 'very good-natured father' (1609). The phraseology of these edicts places them within the tradition of chivalric romance rather than absolutist chancelleries. If the King is doing the nobility good against its will, it is only at the request of the healthier parts of the body of that nobility. Every one of the edicts enumerates by name the people whose 'opinion' the King has asked and who approve of his action: members of his family, the princes of the blood, the peers of the realm, the 'officers of our Crown and other persons of note close to us' (1609).

The last edict, drawn up in 1651, is moreover presented as having been prepared in consultation with 'our cousins', the Marshals of

---

* This role of the oath in a legal document reveals much about the concrete, personal and extra-rational character of the law at the beginning of the seventeenth century. A few months after making 'the most solemn and inviolable of all' vows, 'by the living God', Henri IV broke it by granting pardons to duellists. Some good souls saw Ravaillac's murderous knife as the instrument of God punishing the royal perjurer.

France: those valiant captains who, as a college, held the long-vacant post of Constable and were to preside over duels if it were the King's pleasure to grant a field. The earliest edict, that of 1602, goes even further in its affirmation of a consensus between King and nobility and gentry: in it Henri IV declares himself moved to legislate by the 'just complaints of several fathers and others who fear the reckless-ness of youth [in] their children'.

As the father of his peers, the King's intervention follows the purest of chivalric traditions: he is the champion of all insulted gentlemen, and at the same time the arbiter of doubtful cases. He 'has taken upon [himself] all that might be imputed in this respect' to those gentlemen who respect his prohibition and he has the responsibility for ensuring that their honour is respected (1609).

The King is also the living law. It follows from this that every duel is a direct affront to his 'sovereign authority' (1609, 1643). He intervenes against them less because they are acts 'prejudicial to France' (1643), leading to the loss of its finest children, and more because such procedures 'violate the respect due to a sovereign on the part of his subjects' (1643). Here the King is no longer the equal of his gentlemen, for they have been brought down to the level of all the French and drily treated as simple subjects of the King. Every duellist, every man who gives a *démenti*, is a private individual, 'who has presumed without our permission to grant a field for combat in our kingdom and to pass judgement himself' (1602). The King is condemning not the principle of judgement by arms, but the pri-vatisation of a royal prerogative. The duellist is ignoring, and worse substituting himself for, the King. He is trying to establish a 'custom against our laws' (1651).

The seriousness of the crime is accentuated gradually as the kings pass more and more acts banning duels and organise a procedure for settling affairs of honour. The inobservance of the edicts and declara-tions shows 'the insolent disdain' of duellists for the King's will (1609, 1623, 1643). The King – and everything maintaining monarc-hial order – cannot therefore suffer these 'combats [which have] greatly wronged and insulted [his] sovereign authority' (1609). In the most literal sense of the word, the duel is a crime of *lèse-majesté*.

However, the King is also the Lord's Anointed, 'the living image of God whose pleasure it has been to grant some participation in his power' (1643). In this respect the fight against duels is to the King an affair of 'conscience' (1602, 1609, 1623), as is his firmness in applying his own legislation: 'the position of being the Most Christian King obliges us to be infinitely more sensitive to God's interests than to our own' (1643). Above and beyond the King's personal feelings and the interests of the state, Christianity requires that he fight against duels. The duel is in fact a case of both human and divine *lèse-majesté*. Through the monarch, and independently of him, duellists are insulting God as 'their Creator and their Judge' (1643).

Two religious arguments militate against duels. Two among the best-known sentences from Holy Writ condemn them: 'Thou shalt not kill' and 'Vengeance is mine'. The duel is murder and God 'detests the spilling of human blood' (1602, 1623). The duel is an encroachment upon the divine prerogative of vengeance, which God has expressly 'reserved' for himself (1602, 1643). The King himself can avenge insults only through God's delegation and as a 'participant in his power' (1643). So if a simple creature decides to avenge himself (even without killing his opponent), he is acting 'in contempt of God's commandments' (1602, 1609, 1623); he is violating religious law (1626, 1643). This sin against God's authority is more serious than that committed against his neighbour's life (and against the sinner's own life) and it repeats and expands the manifest affront to the Prince's authority. This is why the edicts proclaim duelling to be a crime of divine *lèse-majesté*.

To set oneself up as judge in place of the law-giving King and the God of Justice was a profoundly impious act. Those who were guilty of it did not perhaps always realise this, but the King was well aware of it, as is shown by the way in which, in the same declaration (of October 1614), he punishes duels and encounters on the one hand, and oaths and blasphemy on the other. His edicts implacably develop the implicit logic of those members of the nobility and gentry who are fastidious about honour, to show the incompatibility of their conception of a gentleman with the description of a Christian. Duellists, in their contempt for God, were rejecting salvation. They preferred to be gentlemen rather than Christians and that was something the Most Christian King, who was also the first gentleman of the kingdom, could not tolerate. By placing themselves outside divine and human law, they were banishing themselves from Christianity, and it was just a small step from the renunciation of God to acceptance of the devil, particularly for those preachers who were keen to show that duellists were worshippers of Satan. Only the 1643 edict goes that far, but it would be no misrepresentation to state that it merely puts the finishing touch to the attitude expressed by the others. It denounces 'the Demon under a false veil of honour' and describes the illusion, 'opinion' (1602), 'error' (1609) and 'imaginary shame' (1643) of those adherents of false honour as a result of 'the artifice of that immortal and capital enemy of men'. According to this edict, the cult of honour is paganism, and duels human sacrifice. To participate in duelling is to practise a false religion, or rather a religion of falsehood, the counter-religion of those who have devoted themselves to the Prince of Falsehood, the Evil One. To go on to the field is to 'sacrifice their body and soul to this Idol of Vanity whom they adore'.

The monarchy's struggle to eradicate duelling from the nobility and gentry took both punitive and preventative forms. It involved three types of judicial procedures corresponding to three different stages of the crime: to prevent disputes becoming quarrels over affairs of honour, the King urged that they should be referred to ordinary judges; to prevent quarrels from leading to duels, the King made it an obligation that they must be referred to the point-of-honour judges; to prevent duels from becoming precedents in an aristocratic counter-jurisprudence, the King urged his public prosecutors to refer them to the parliaments.

To dissuade gentlmen from 'making a quarrel' out of their disagreements, the legislation provided for the 'aggressor' to suffer 'the total loss of the thing in dispute, which from now onwards we shall judge on his behalf'.

Knowledge in matters of challenges and quarrels (up to the point of armed confrontation) was the direct preserve – if the King did not take the business in hand himself – of members of the high *noblesse d'épée:* the Constable, the Marshals of France and governors of the provinces, or their subordinates. But their role became refined and modifed over the successive royal decrees.

The 1609 edict expressly recognised them as competent to judge in a legal judicial combat. Section 5 invited gentlemen to 'ask us, or them, for combat; which will be granted by Us according to whether We judge it necessary for their honour'. Later decrees no longer mentioned this power to grant a field which had, in practice, long been an anachronistic fiction. Neither Henri IV nor Louis XIII nor Lesdiguières ever showed signs of applying Section 5 of the 1609 edict. In fact this edict (like those which followed it, and like the earlier 1602 edict) describes, in minute detail, only cases where arbitration was possible and the sanctions to be taken if one of the parties failed or refused to submit to it. One might wonder, therefore, if there were still cases in which it was unclear who was the aggressor, and in which, at the same time, the two adversaries decided to submit themselves to the decision of the Constable or marshals, which would be the only case in which a legal duel was possible.

Furthermore, the fiction of the sovereign who granted the field, which was never explicitly renounced, was in fact invalidated after 1626 by a provision which literally contradicted it and which was reaffirmed in the edicts of 1643 and 1651. It concerned gentlemen 'who, having begun a quarrel in our Kingdom', made a 'rendez-vous to fight outside the frontier of the latter [in order to] elude the authority of our edicts'. These gentlemen were liable to the same punishment as those who fought on French territory; they had even less right to indulgence 'because the time they take gives them the opportunity to recognise their error, surprise and the first actions that one takes in the heat of a newly received insult cannot excuse them'. Richelieu considered it normal to prosecute in cases of duels fought on foreign soil; how different is his position from that of Du Moulin, who refused to accept the decisions of the Council of Trent because, by forbidding the King to grant a field, the Pontiff was disposing, in an abusive manner, of land in a state which did not belong to him. In these texts of the second quarter of the seventeenth century, the King's sovereignty weighs less on his territory and more on his individual subjects. The crime of duelling is no longer so much one of removing a portion of the kingdom from his jurisdiction as of coldly and deliberately excluding some of his subjects from obedience to him.

The Constable, marshals and governors were therefore essentially arbiters who decided questions of honour by naming the offending party and condemning him to make the reparation fixed by their sentence. For half a century the edicts repeated almost word for word that it was up to these people to 'command satisfaction' (1626, 1643) by a 'sovereign judgement' (1602, 1651) of 'disputes concerning a point of honour and the reparation for offences' (1643).

So that they could achieve this, the texts gradually gave them an administrative organisation. In the provinces, it was the Governor or his lieutenant-general who passed judgement in the first instance, hearing complaints 'in the presence of lords and gentlemen who shall meet in the place and others who shall be called by them', until the 1651 edict charged them to 'appoint from each bailiwick and seneschalsy one or several gentlemen [according to the size of the area] of the required quality, age and capacity to be informed of disputes'. These magistrates with fixed jurisdictions were then called 'point-of-honour judges'.

Their powers were gradually reinforced, and the means at their disposal refined. The level of reparation was entirely left to their discretion. They were empowered to give prison sentences, fine recalcitrants or confiscate their property, to have their gentlemen's status degraded and to have them inscribed on the roll of tailles or taxes paid by commoners. The 1651 edict even granted them the power to banish the guilty and to 'use the marshals' provosts, their lieutenants, exempts and archers in the execution of their orders'.

This evolution gradually transformed fairly toothless proceedings into real and concrete powers. But at the same time it also profoundly altered their spirit so that they lost the major part of their social prestige. In the early years of the century the arbiters of honour were gentlemen whose known prowess and recognised wisdom qualified them to decide satisfaction between equals. The point-of-honour judges of the middle of the century were – at least in the exercise of that function – highly positioned clerks, whom the King had empowered to put impudent men of quality in their place.

There are a few comments to be made on the development of this repressive legislation.

The death penalty was not always openly required against all the guilty. However, it was always suggested as possible, and even desirable, according to the judges' discretion. The earliest and least precise text, the edict of 1602, describes all those breaking the law on duels as 'criminals of *lèse-majesté*', including the onlookers who chose to watch them, and says that they should be 'punished as such ... without the death penalty and confiscation of property being moderated'.

Seconds were always prosecuted, and after 1609 were always explicitly punishable by death. However, in later texts (1643, 1651) the *seconded* were pursued more severely than lone duellists. The use of seconds became an aggravating circumstance. A rebel against the King was all the more guilty if he had accomplices and so formed a kind of embryonic faction.

The edict of February 1626 breaks with previous and later decrees with its less severe punishments and a massive batch of pardons. This leniency displeased Parliament, which did not pass it without re-monstrance. But it was tactical leniency, and in no way a recantation. It was simply aimed to produce a repression more fitting to the crime, and therefore more correct. In its basic thrust, this edict goes further than its predecessors. It made it a duty to report quarrels and duels and encouraged 'informing' with the promise of favours. It assimilated all encounters fought by equal numbers on both sides into the category of duels. It was the first to provide for the prosecution of those fighting duels beyond the French borders. It was the first to punish those using seconds (and their descendants, who were declared ignoble and unfit for public office). Lastly, it was the first to make challenging a superior into a separate crime. So 1626 did not mark a hesitation in the attitude of the state; it marks a turning point for the ever more determined opposition.

In the texts of 1626 and 1643, the superiors whom one was most surely forbidden to challenge to a duel were 'guardians, lords of fiefs and leaders' in general. In 1651 these were designated slightly differently: 'benefactors, superiors or lords, persons in command, persons of quality [and in particular] generals of our armies'. The challenge was particularly bad if it contested a decision made by this moral, social or military superior: 'considering that there is nothing more necessary to the maintenance of discipline than respect towards those in command'. The edict of 1651, which was especially vigilant where challenges between army officers of unequal rank were concerned, identified even more abominable criminals: 'people of ignoble birth ... insolent enough to challenge gentlemen'. As their rank forbade them to use weapons personally, they used champions of noble extraction. These indirectly duelling commoners were to be hanged and strangled, and their property was to go to the family of their dead opponent. Such civil compensation represented a break with all known jurisprudence. For the first time a gentleman who was killed in a duel was to be treated as a victim rather than a guilty man. This was because the non-noble who defied both him and the royal edicts was recreating the solidarity between nobility and monarchy by this double affront. He was putting the final touches to the definition of the duel's significance to royalty: a challenge to established authority.

Marshals and Arbiters

The kings and regent queens were the first to strive to reconcile *Grands*, courtiers and even members of their family; indeed no one who dreamed of wearing the crown (such as the Duc de Mayenne, or Gaston d'Orléans) could fail to perform this regal action. The example from on high was zealously followed, not only by the marshals and governors and those persons they chose as arbiters, but also by all those who spontaneously appointed themselves to this type of good office. The list of all those who worked to prevent duels is long and includes prelates, the entire nobility and gentry of a province and an isolated gentleman with no commission other than his influence over the local squires or his family. But how long is the list of quarrels that were really and definitively appeased by their efforts, and was as much ardour put into being reconciled as it was into reconciling?

Certainly one comes across people like Bassompierre and Termes who challenged each other to a duel, were brought together and, by their own admission, were 'ever since extremely friendly'. Certainly, the judicial archives often present the arbitration procedure as requested, sought by one of the parties, if not both. But examples abound of people who were reconciled against their will, often for a very short time, and we are a long way here from the Italian situation, where a challenge to a duel was only a ritual performance which unleashed the expected interventions of conciliators. In

France, up until a third of the way or halfway through the seventeenth century, while it was unseemly and sometimes impossible to dismiss arbitration, it was often possible and always desirable to avoid or elude it. The reconciliation itself was only perceived as authentic if there had been an armed confrontation and blood had been spilt (even a tiny amount); then the insulted party regained his honour without the insulter losing his.

A quotation from Crucé's *Nouveau Cynée* perfectly sums up the position of the would-be duellist faced with established procedures of dissuasion:

> Should he complain to the courts? He will be laughed at, for the little reparation they will grant him. Should he ask permission to fight a duel? This will be attributed to his cowardice. And all the more if he accepts a satisfaction given before five or six people. Being so reduced to these miseries, he must hide himself away forever, not daring to appear in company, or else he must avenge himself by murder at any price.

In short, while it was honourable to reconcile other people, it was equally dishonourable to allow oneself to be reconciled. Although the arbitration procedure was frequently used, it was often ineffectual.

Judges and Public Prosecutors

Did repressive laws work better than preventative laws? The reiteration of legislative measures in itself suggests not. Even if the judges were vigilant and strict, we know that their efforts were disrupted by the incurable propensity of sovereigns to grant pardons to those condemned for duelling. But were the judges as strict as all that? Were they vigilant?

A random sample gives us the records of fifteen trials, of which nine carry a final sentence. Only one of these sentences is severe, and it is to punish an affront which was not followed by a duel: the accused slapped and provoked the Lieutenant-Governor of the town of Ardres and failed to respect his duty to be obedient to the King. In this affair Parliament confirmed the sentence passed in the first instance by the bailiwick court: a public admission of guilt, yoke and six years' banishment. The eight other judgements confirm letters of remission granted by the sovereign. Thus the court, strict in the case of a challenge to a duel which did not lead to an actual fight (but which, it is true, concerned a representative of the state), was, like the monarch, lenient regarding actual and fatal duels. This leniency does not, in our small sample, seem to discriminate on grounds of social status: authentic gentlemen benefited from it, but so did a bailiwick lawyer who had murdered a colleague, and an illiterate soldier who had murdered a baron.

In the prison registers of the Conciergerie du Palais for the years 1610, 1620, 1630 and 1640 we have looked at a total of 4,363 prisoners. None of them was explicitly incarcerated for duelling. The word 'duel' was written on only a single occasion, and that in the margin of the register: when a 'dead body' was transferred from the prison of Fort-l'Evêque to the Conciergerie, the margin note added four days later specified that it would be 'dragged on a rack to the closest place to where the duel was fought'. We may suppose that out of the eight absent gentlemen executed in effigy and among the thirty or so gentlemen who gave themselves up as prisoners to have their letters of pardon, abolition or remission of sentence recorded by Parliament, a certain number were guilty of duelling. However none of the twenty-three duellists we have identified elsewhere for these four years figures among them. Anyway the absence of the word 'duel' is noteworthy in these registers, which do not scruple to indicate that knights, grooms and even counts and marquises have been imprisoned for debt, theft, rape or murder.

By collecting all the sentences we have come across in our unsystematic examination of the documents, we can glean a few figures: twenty-nine sentences were passed on six living, present prisoners, twenty-one corpses and twenty-five absent suspects.

Our first impression is that the sentences passed on corpses were perhaps the most frequent (as those against absentees were often only warrants for arrest). Certainly a dead body would be more of an encumbrance and less easily made to disappear than a guilty man who was still alive. Nevertheless, the total we have is derisory compared to the number of those we have recorded as killed in duels over the same years. Of the condemned and executed dead, seven are soldiers. These belong to a group apart in the society as a whole, among whom the requirements of obedience and discipline weighed more heavily. They were also on the lowest step of the social ladder of those who 'carry arms by profession'. The unidentified bodies, such as a 'dead body dressed in a white doublet', were also obscure people and the law was able to take it out on their corpses only because there was no one to pay them their last respects. However, other bodies were systematically ignored by the judges, such as the sole victim in a 1623 duel between four men, when the Aix Parliament settled for issuing warrants against the three survivors – who were, of course, absent.

Execution in effigy was used against some absent duellists, who had gone into more or less distant exile, or had simply taken refuge in a friendly place, even in their own houses. This practice marks a failure on the part of the law. If those condemned were apprehended later, or if they voluntarily presented themselves to the court, the death sentence (already carried out on the effigy) could no longer be applied. They would be retried and, except for the atypical and possibly unique case of Bouteville, the court was always more lenient the second time. Indeed this second trial, when it took place, was often carried out simply to confirm a letter of remission which restored to the guilty duellist all the rights and privileges he had enjoyed before committing the crime.

In spite of these mitigations in practice, it is notable that sovereign courts seldom sentenced duellists to execution in effigy. For this punishment, although notional at the level of actual experience, was serious on the symbolic level. And when they did decide to do so, the public did not always support their verdict. People took the effigy of Moussy down from the gibbet in 1618, that of Bouteville in 1627.

It was very rare indeed, exceptional even, for an effective death sentence to be passed. Three were passed in fifty years, with ten years between them. We shall look more closely at the most famous of these, the execution of Bouteville and Des Chapelles, in a later chapter. The large number of offences committed by these two and their links with opposing aristocratic groups turned this trial into a political affair whose importance went beyond the crime of duelling. The two members of the King's guard put to death in 1610 no doubt had the misfortune to come before the courts just after the promulgation of an edict and at a time of ideological stringency, when examples were needed. As for the Chevalier d'Andrieu, who was executed in 1638, he was just an accumulator of duels who had killed seventy-two men before he was thirty. He was an arsonist, necrophile, rapist and blasphemer, a kind of monster that society rejected with horror.

These few actual executions of duellists caused such a stir that it seems reasonable to think that there may have been no others (or at least almost no others) during the whole first half of the seventeenth century. So on the rare occasions when the letter of the law was applied it was to individuals against whom there were other charges besides the crime of *lèse-majesté* under examination here.

The rest of the time, that is to say for most of the time, the accused were forewarned and legal pursuits never reached them until they had obtained letters of pardon. Even more often, they were not pursued at all – particularly when the duel had not caused any man's death. Let us hear what Retz has to say in his *Memoirs* about the combats of his youth, fights which he had hoped would lead to the scandalous publicity of prosecution. First duel: 'The public prosecutor began proceedings, but discontinued them at the request of our families; and so I was left with my cassock and one duel.' Second duel: 'There were no proceedings, and I was left still with my cassock and two duels.' Third duel: 'I neglected nothing to give the duel publicity, to the point of bringing in witnesses; but one cannot force destiny, and no one thought to inform on it.'

So in the jurisprudence of duels, the death penalty was a freak event, legal pursuit an exception, and absence of prosecution the rule. But present-day research into the judicial history of the Ancien Régime has accustomed us to seeing laws not being applied and punishments as exceptional. Perhaps this is just another case of that 'necessary illegalism' in the society of the time which Michel Foucault has described.* By being either too visible or too obscure, most duellists had the same *de facto* exemption in relation to the punishments set down against the crime of which they were recognised as guilty. Rather than dwell on this non-specific impunity of duellists, we should note the very real afflictions which often befell those who committed this serious crime.

Sentences were passed and applied concerning the property of dead or otherwise unpunished criminals. Louis de Chabans complained of this in 1615: 'As soon as a duel has been fought, the law does not fail to seize the combatants' property and confiscate it'; and about fifty years later Tallemant des Réaux echoes his words. We cannot rigorously establish the frequency of fines and confiscations, nor the degree to which they reduced the patrimonies of duellists' families, but anecdotes we have come across at random during our reading confirm our impression of their frequency.

Another unpleasant consequence for duellists was the exile to which they were almost always constrained. Although sentences of banishment were rare, the guilty man usually took the initiative and left the Court, the town or the kingdom. This departure meant in practice that he renounced his functions, prerogatives and dignities. Obviously this was a prudent act and a manifestation of modesty while he awaited some measure of pardon. But it was also an act of self-punishment which interrupted the guilty man's career, broke up his network of acquaintances and distanced him from his milieu for what could be a long period of time. The duration of this purgatory varied enormously. If it went on for several years – which was often

---

*Michel Foucault, *Surveiller et punir: naissance de la prison*, Paris, Gallimard, 1975, 'The non-application of the rule and the inobservation of the innumerable edicts or ordinances provided the conditions for the political and economic functioning of the society.'

the case – it was a serious sanction against a young, ambitious man keen for glory. It is one of the paradoxes of the phenomenon that a man who fought to make himself known was obliged at the same time to go and get himself forgotten in retreat while waiting for his pardon.

And lastly the pardon was neither free nor total. Although in theory it was a sovereign act of royal power, it had no effect unless it was ratified by Parliament, which meant that the pardoned man had to give himself up and be tried. The court could dismiss the duellist's suit and refuse to ratify letters of pardon that it judged to have been wrested from the King's mercy against his real will. And when it did sanction the King's indulgence (which was apparently more frequent), it was only after interrogations in which the accused had to prove that he was guilty of homicide but not of duelling. The same scenario reappears in each of the trial transcripts we have been able to read: the fight was an unexpected encounter, with neither challenge nor premeditation, the numbers of combatants on each side were unequal and the enemy had drawn his sword before the accused had got his out of its scabbard. So the duel was disguised as an encounter, or better still as a brawl, even as a murder in self-defence. Only then could the Parliament reconcile with any logic its duty to uphold the strictness of the edicts (if necessary against the King's wishes) with its desire (analagous to that of the King) to be lenient towards a brave gentleman. In denying that he had committed a duel as a result of a *démenti*, in lying himself, the man of honour and of his word denied his duel: it was at this price that he could take his place in society once more, absolved, but not totally innocent. In fact, the ratification of a duellist's letter of pardon or remission was always accompanied by a sentence on him to make a religious offering for the victim's soul, to give alms 'for the prisoners; bread', sometimes to make civil reparations, and always to pay costs.

Even if one did not risk prison, death or loss of rank for having killed a man in a duel, one did not commit such an act with impunity at the time of the first Bourbons.

This severity in theory and leniency in practice with regard to those guilty of duels do not reflect inconsistent thinking on the part of churchmen and lawyers, but form a logical whole. The horror that duels aroused went in tandem with the respect inspired by the duellist, this man who had dared to look death in the face. The ambiguities and contradictions we have noted all through our research find resolution here. The desire of the authorities was not to suppress, but to punish. They were trying not to wipe out a crime, but to purge a sin.

To commit a duel was to step outside the ranks of social conformism and respect for everyday norms. It was to inspire an almost sacred fear which required an expiatory ritual in order that one might be reintegrated into society – but at a higher rank than that which one had occupied before all the publicity. A bloody duel and its indispensable accompaniment of punitive and self-punishing sanctions constituted a rite of passage: exit from childhood, the rank of commoner or illegitimacy, and entry into a function, an alliance or simply fame.

An anecdote told in Louis de Pontis's *Memoirs* illustrates this logic of united transgression and expiation as a means to aristocratic promotion. A certain Du Buisson, a young officer in Pontis's regiment, challenged his superior. They fought and injured each other. Pontis requested and received Louis XIII's pardon, but only for himself. For his subordinate and adversary (henceforward his protégé), he obtained only a promise that his life would be safe and that he would remain free. 'But I want him to be tried as an example,' added the King, 'and during this time he should retire to Holland, and not return until the affair has been hushed up and I have pardoned him.' The Council of War sentenced him to be executed. A year later, when a lieutenant's post was vacant, Pontis asked that it should be given to Du Buisson. Louis XIII, touched by such generosity, agreed. And Pontis concludes: 'I got him his letters of remission and his commission.'

What a *felix culpa* the duel could be!

Chapter 11

The Attitude of the Gentry and Nobility

David the King and prophet fought and killed Goliath in a duel. Then he also fought and killed Sobach in a duel. Abner killed Asrael in the same way. The fight is described in the same book and lastly also described there is the fight of the twelve from David's army who fought another twelve from the army of Isboseth, son of Saul. . . .

All that I have said about permission for duels has been said with the intention of permitting them to put an end to them, something I consider impossible otherwise.

(L. de Chabans, *Advice and Means to prevent the Disorder of Duels 1615*, pp. 72 and 80)

After 1585 the classical treatises of the Italians and the *Dialogues* of the Spaniard Urrea were no longer published in France. Henceforward it was the French who wrote on affairs of honour for their compatriots. From 1585 to 1650 they devoted no less than thirty books to these problems. But in all this output not a single book was designed as a code of the point of honour, or an apology for duelling, or a defence and illustration of the practice of individual quarrels. Among the authors, members of the *noblesse d'épée* seem to have been very few and far between and the titles, prefaces and sometimes also the conclusions of those few treatises or texts which uphold the aristocratic view in favour of duels present those texts as indictments of the excesses and abuse of duelling and of the degeneracy of a practice which had become a scandal. It would seem that gentlemen who supported duelling wrote nothing on the subject that was so important to them – apart from cartels and manifestos. Was this because of a feeling that their cause was indefensible, does it reveal a mute despondency in the face of the arguments of the opposing side, a tacit recognition that the defeat of their point of view was obvious and unavoidable? The facts easily refute such a hasty conclusion. First, duelling flourished in days, indeed over decades, when no apology for it was written, right until the middle of the seventeenth century. Also, the gentry and nobility, who were otherwise most sensitive to religious precepts and the arguments of reason, thought duelling a normal practice. Let us quote a few names. La Noue, known as 'Iron Arm', who was a valiant captain and an austere Protestant, wrote one of the clearest and strictest treatises against the duel; nevertheless he recognises that in particular, well-defined cases the sovereign must authorise combat, which alone can put an end to certain disputes.

Agrippa d'Aubigné was another zealous Huguenot who wrote a text called *Hell*, condemning the excesses of young duellists. However, in the *Adventures of the Baron de Foeneste* he enumerates 'cases when it is legitimate to fight', and he accepted challenges and accompanied his friends in duels until an advanced age. Under Louis XIII the Baron de Renti, a sort of soldier–monk, the model of a 'Christian gentleman', was challenged one day to a duel; his biographer Saint-Jure (his hagiographer, one should say) shows how he was able to reconcile this with his conscience by means of direction of intention: he met his enemy in an encounter, wounded him, beat him and very charitably bandaged the wound he had given him. Around the age of thirty, when he was writing his *Regulae*, René Descartes fought a duel for the love of Madame de Rozay. At the end of the century, when (in a quite different atmosphere) Baillet was writing *The Life of Descartes*, he thought it necessary to state that this event was a sort of accident which should not make us question whether 'his predilections were for other things than philosophy'. We do question it, however, if only because much later Descartes did not think it beneath him to write an *Art of Fencing* 'in which it appears that most of the lessons he gives are based on his own experience'. For Descartes, that 'French knight', philosophy and the practice of arms were neither incompatible nor contradictory. For Descartes, as for Renti, d'Aubigné, La Noue and the hundreds of gentlemen who neither wrote nor read an apology for duelling, but who often heard or read condemnations of it, there were more pressing imperatives than those of their Church's teaching. There were reasons for duelling of which reason knew nothing.

In order to uncover these reasons, we shall begin by examing the only piece of writing which is not reticent on the subject and totally supports the phenomenon, Brantôme's *Discourse on Duels*. Pierre de Bourdeille, Sieur de Brantôme, was a prime example of that nobility whose profile we have sketched out here. After a mediocre education (he knew no Greek and little Latin) he had an adventurous life of fighting and intrigue, which took him from Morocco to Scotland and from the service of the Valois to that of the Habsburgs and the Holy League against Henri III. A serious riding accident then forced him into a long retreat which he devoted to writing. This last characteristic is important: the *Discourse on Duels*, like all Brantôme's

work, was not published until long after his death. It would seem
that this man of the sword, who had come to the pen because of his
infirmities, was not interested in being published, indeed that he
prided himself on not appearing to be an author – at least during his
own lifetime.

Brantôme's stated reason for writing the book is to give his
opinion on matters of form and practice in duelling, based on his
long experience. This links it to the Italian tradition of *pareri*, in
which a gentleman gave his opinion on the validity of certain
practices commonly used in affairs of honour. However, it is in fact a
very different sort of work, as is obvious from the second page. Of
course here and there Brantôme does discuss a particular problem
(such as which of the opponents should choose the weapons, can a
young man challenge a mature one, can a captain fight a private
soldier?), or examine positions hostile to duelling (those of the
Council of Trent). But this is not what takes up the most space in his
Discourse, it is not the essential thing. The book is primarily a
collection of anecdotes, a series of 144 tales, some of which occupy a
few lines while others cover several pages and still others are referred
to again and again. These tales are often connected by pure
association, with no chronological link, nor often one of subject
matter. Some of them do not even relate directly to duelling.
Reading this book is like walking through a gallery of historical
paintings in which frescos, canvases and miniatures are all piled up
together and where the fight of the Horatii is next to that of Jarnac.
So we have tried to introduce a bit of order, to find a way of
classifying this collection of images, in order to define Brantôme's
overall vision of the phenomenon of the duel.

The first of our classifications is that of the chronology of the
events recounted. This chronology is not easy to establish. Some
tales are taken from legend, others involve people who are too
obscure or too vaguely situated for us to assign a time to them, yet
others are dated only in terms of the reign of a particular sovereign
(who, like François I, may have been on the throne for a long time),
while the more recent ones are referred to by phrases which are
meaningful only if one knows the date at which the passage was
written: 'one of the last few years', 'just recently' or 'during the
recent wars' However, we have been able to establish that most of
the events took place between 1550 and 1580, that is to say that they
were exactly contemporary with Brantôme's active life. In general
they are events that he witnessed, which happened to people close to
him (brothers, nephews, friends) or to himself, or which were told
to him by one of the heroes of the tale. The accounts are introduced
by 'I saw it', 'I knew', 'I remember', 'I heard it said to Monsieur . . .',

'I heard a tale of an Italian knight of Malta', 'I was present . . .' But it often happens that his sources are printed texts: annals, biographies, 'true stories', manifestos and other leaflets, many of them Italian, but more often Spanish or French. He does not scruple to quote these sources, even to copy them out. However, he is less happy with this type of information that with oral testimonies. Recounting a fight which took place outside Florence in 1530 – and which he obviously could not have seen – he indicates his printed sources while at the same time making clear that he prefers others: 'Paulo Jovio tells the story, but not so nicely as I read it in a Spanish book and heard it told in days gone by in Florence.' Elsewhere he recounts a dispute which arose in Gaeta in 1558, 'which I was told about in the place at the time, as I was passing through there'; in fact, Ludovic Lalanne, Brantôme's nineteenth-century editor, was able to establish that Brantôme learned of this fight from a Spanish account which he simply copied word for word. That Brantôme should be caught in the act of disguising a book as an oral source in this way reveals an important characteristic of the gentleman lover of duels: a duel was all the more interesting to him if he had seen it or had known the protagonists or at least the witnesses. An event he had witnessed or at least heard of had more value to him than one he had read about. Brantôme was a man of the spoken rather than the written word.

For the most part the duels and quarrels that he lists were between Frenchmen and took place in France (at Court and in the provinces), to a lesser degree in Italy and, for those at the end of the century, in Flanders, where a number of French soldiers were fighting. Among the foreigners there are only Italians and a few Spaniards. For Brantôme those who had authority on the matter of duels were the men of arms of the Latin countries, and above all his compatriots. He seems to have had a predilection for exploits which happened during the French expeditions in the Italian peninsula which, from Louis XIII's reign onwards, followed each other in quick succession. Lautrec, Bayart and Gaston de Foix were recent enough for him almost to have known them and far enough in the past to be mythical figures.

The number of duels recounted decrease the further we get from Brantôme's own century, but the arena in which they take place remains remarkably stable. Of course Brantôme based himself on written texts for all his medieval and ancient tales, but symptomatically whenever he can he reinforces the descriptions he has read with an image that sidesteps the screen of words and letters with the kind of deferred ocular vision given by a work of art. Here are two examples:

Telling the story of the fight between the Horatii and the Curiatii, he refers to 'what some have written', does not mention Livy until the fourteenth line, and instantly follows that with a visual memory: 'I saw this fight better represented than I had ever seen anything, at the town hall in Lucca....' There follow nine lines describing what we have taken to be a fresco. No matter that, chronologically speaking, the author of the figurative representation was further from what he shows than the narrator of the written text. The visual image, because of its lesser degree of abstraction, has a perceptible authority which gives weight to the historical or mythological anecdote.

The other case is similar. Following the 'Annales of France', Brantôme recounts the fight between Carrouges and Le Gris, and concludes: 'I saw this fight represented in an old tapestry hung in the King's bedchamber at Blois, with the old furniture, and the first time that I saw it King Charles IX, who was very curious about everything, looked at it and had the story explained to him' (there follows a description of the tapestry).

Brantôme's duels are a 'string' (his word is *enfilade*) of events that he saw with his own eyes, either directly or indirectly, and this is, in the first instance, the significance for us of Brantôme's anecdotes. But for *himself*, when he was dictating them to his secretary, Brantôme seems to have had two intentions: to entertain and to instruct.

First, to entertain. The aim to delight is undeniable. Brantôme enjoys telling stories and he hopes that the reader – or at least the listener to whom his manuscript is read – will enjoy the stories he tells. Phrases abound to show us how concerned this reader of Amyot's translation of Plutarch was to make his tales fine and complete, even if it meant digressions, repetitions and incoherences of composition – phrases such as 'I have perhaps been too long over this story, but because it is a fine one, I did not want to leave anything out....' The beauty of the tale excuses everything, justifies everything and explains everything. Analysis of a page by Brantôme will shed light on what we shall have to call, for lack of another word, his method. This page is an attempt to cut short a series of anecdotes which are taking him too far from his subject. 'So let us finish, although I have a very wide field to sow with many fine disputes, arguments, questions, examples, tales, stories; but that is for those who know more about these things than I do.' So the only thing that makes him fall silent is an incompetence which is in some sense aesthetic. If 'Admiral, Dandelot or the great Guise' had spoken in his place, 'it would have been the finest thing ever seen'. Anyway, this turns out to be a false end because he cannot stop himself from telling stories: 'However, I shall not yet depart from my discourses to string on another concerning a dispute which I have often seen carried out among the great captains and men of war ... on which dispute I shall cite this example, which is very fine ...' This very fine example is the tale of one of Vandenesse's duels, a tale which is expanded to include the whole life of the duellist, and takes him to his death, long after the duel itself, which is in a way just a pretext. The prime motivation behind Brantôme's *Discourse on Duels* is thus this pleasure which we all feel if someone tells us a good story.

The second aim pursued by Brantôme the narrator of fine fights is that of instruction. This aim takes him back to the intention he initially stated of giving *pareri*. In fact his stories do express a morality. Like the short stories of his contemporary Cervantes, they are exemplary tales. A word here and there reminds us of this. Brantôme's anecdotes are presented like arguments, as we saw from the way that he introduced Vandenesse's duel. They do not illustrate a demonstration, they support a discussion, or, more precisely, they take the place of both discussion and demonstrations. In Brantôme's exemplary tales, morality is of a piece with the narrative.

So in his accumulation of 'exempla, tales, stories', Brantôme reveals his desire to set out a doctrine using concrete cases, a doctrine which is limited (but also clarified) by the related desire to tell fine stories. On a given theme (for example, may a simple gentleman challenge a Prince, and should the Prince agree to fight?) he does in fact give arguments for and against, without coming down on one side or the other. Are we seeing here the scruples of a specialist who is content to gather information, leaving to his reader the task of constructing an objective point of view? Certainly not: that would be the procedure of a scholar or a politician, the people most foreign to Brantôme. Brantôme's 'method' arises more out of a deeply felt, platonic conviction that the finest story is also the truest and best; that the reader (a potential duellist) will recognise himself in it when he reads it and will remember it when a quarrel places him in a similar situation to that of Renaud de Montauban, the Prince of Melfi or the Lord of La Châtaigneraye. Thus Brantôme concludes one of his narratives: 'This fight was fine and gallant, and whoever chooses to consider any of its particularities would have more than a little to gain from it.'

A fine tale is a model to imitate: such is the implicit maxim that underlies the *Discourse on Duels*: such is the great argument with which Brantôme defends the practice of duelling. Brantôme's way of thinking is traditional; the rhetorical procedure and logic of the *exemplum* that he uses held great sway during the Middle Ages. It is therefore an inherited method, opposed by more modern methods such as abstract, Aristotelian reasoning, which scholasticism had

spread among theologians and jurists, or the reflection and medita-
tion on a verse of the Scriptures or a classical quotation made familiar
by the humanists, and then by the Protestant preachers. The first of
these methods is the same as that used by the Italian 'doctors of
duelling'; for them, examples were simply more or less pedagogic
illustrations of a demonistration by deduction and dichotomy. Brantôme knew their work, appreciated it and refers to it, but he does not
imitate them. His aim is different from theirs. This first method, and
also the second, were those employed by French enemies of duelling,
preachers and members of the *noblesse de robe*. Brantôme hears but
does not listen to them. Their speeches do not undermine him; he
and they do not speak the same language. So he challenges them, but
does not attempt to refute them.

Does this mean that Brantôme's attitude was anachronistic, that he
was alone in adhering to a logic which was no longer current outside
the rooms of his château, a Don Quixote of the *exemplum*? No, since
the procedure of the *exemplum* was the normal procedure for the
gentlemen moralists of his time, authors who were very successful
during their own lifetimes and became practically unreadable after
Descartes' generation. Such was the method used by Montaigne in
the 1580 edition of his first *Essays*: a series of anecdotes that do not
seem to follow any law other than that of free association. Their
aim, underneath the contradictions of exemplary tales, is not simply
to entertain. They demonstrate the logic of men of the sword as
opposed to that of men who wear robes, the clerics, theologians,
jurists and pedants. When Brantôme apologises for quoting a pro-
verb 'which is, however, pedantic', when he opposes real 'knightly
cartels' to those whose gibberish smacks of lessons learned in Geneva, he comes close to Montaigne, who praises writing that is 'not
pedantic, not monkish, not lawyerly, but rather soldierly'. In this
second half of the sixteenth century, the *exemplum* was the corner-
stone of aristocratic thinking.

The approach of other gentlemen who have left writings concerning
duelling is similar to that of Brantôme. These authors were either
ignorant of culture or could not have cared less about it. The lack of
learning among the gentry and nobility, noted and deplored by the
lawyer Savaron and the churchman Camus at the Estates General of
1614, was something to be proud of for those in question. Well-bred
men saw booklearning as something foreign, as laborious as a
mechanical technique and therefore an almost demeaning activity.
Among young gentlemen, the group who were keenest on duelling,
many 'of twelve or fifteen years old can neither read nor write'.
Among gentlemen who did write about duels (of whom many were

Greek scholars or poets) it was the done thing to pretend lack of skill at the writing desk, and to publish over one's dead body. Vital d'Audiguier, author of *The True and Ancient Practice of Duels*, said 'that he trimmed his pen only with his sword'. In the same vein a 'gentleman of very high rank' maintained his anonymity when he wrote a *Discourse on Quarrels and Honour*. It was, he said, 'my first attempt at writing, in which I had more trouble making myself intelligible than in putting down fine words'. A similar attitude made the editor of La Noue's *Political and Military Discourses* sign a letter in which it is claimed that the work was published without the author's knowledge.

So contempt for and suspicion of the written word were common traits among supporters of the duel, and this explains why the publication of theoretical treatises, in vogue up until the middle of the sixteenth century, ceased, without other publications taking their place. French gentlemen certainly did observe a code of honour, but it was purely oral. It had a limited audience, but its every clause was guaranteed by the word of honour of the gentleman who proffered it: the word of honour of a man of honour. The whole of Brantôme's *Discourse* illustrates the existence of this code, which was unwritten and thus ephemeral and changeable, as the anonymous author of the *Discourse on Quarrels and Honour* clearly showed. 'There have never been', he wrote,

> any rules by which one could definitely establish what was an offence to honour, at least for most things, and also no one would ever have accepted a law and furthermore each man changed something on his own authority and reformed something every day. The most sure and esteemed rule was founded on the practice at the time, which did not last more than five or six years, and which was furthermore formed on the example of a few men of whom one had a good opinion or who subtly, or with some semblance of rightness, knew how to introduce it: I can say of myself that I produced one in favour of the maimed.

'Rules formed on the example of a few men': these words well encapsulate the aristocratic code of honour at the end of the sixteenth century and beginning of the seventeenth, a code as strict as it was arbitrary. Like Brantôme, those gentlemen who wrote on duelling were fundamentally sensitive to *exempla*. But, while Brantôme happily reeled off a series of anecdotes with a clear conscience, these other authors claimed to denounce the abuse or excess of duelling and to base their ideas on both arguments and examples. At least this is the line they follow while they are setting out the arguments; once they start on the stream of anecdotes their reservations and criticisms gradually melt away in the face of the enthusiasm generated by their evocation of fine fights. Although he set out to condemn duelling and 'the misfortune it gives rise to every day', to stem the haemorrhage of aristocratic blood and eradicate a practice which nearly caused the death of his son, old Jean de La Taille soon begins to reel off anecdotes and, at the end of the book, admits that he does not believe in the efficacy of a rigorous enforcement of the edicts because the demands of honour are absolute and go before everything else 'as I would say myself if I was the age I used to be'. The role of the *exemplum* in the codification, justification and persistence of duelling is clear. La Noue was right when, giving four reasons for the duelling vogue, he gave second place to 'the example of a few lords and distinguished courtiers who have been seen to fight at Court and in the middle of cities'. More than a century later, Vulson de La Colombière knew that the prestige of examples was still the most important thing in gentlemen's eyes: 'I include several of these two sorts of combat because the Nobility will greatly enjoy reading them; and they will make them appreciate with more patience and satisfaction the arguments I give in favour of the Duel of the Ancients.'

The examples contain the entire doctrine of gentlemen concerning duelling and points of honour. So if we are to obtain a clearer definition, it will be at the price of a mistranslation: we must leave behind the language of examples to adopt that of arguments, making gentlemen stammer in the categories of scholars (categories which are largely the ones we use today).

First, it would seem that not any single combat was legitimate in the eyes of gentlemen, even if it could properly be defined as a duel. Among motives for fighting and forms of combat, the authors set down a certain number of conditions which alone can authorise a duel. These conditions first concern the nature of the quarrel. Even those gentlemen who have the most reservations about the use of arms recognise that there are cases where other proof is lacking and such a procedure is the only way, if not of telling right from wrong then at least of clearing suspicion from a man's honour. Others go further and list three or four cases in which they regard the practice of duelling as legitimate: *lèse-majesté*; treason; single combat by army champions, to avoid spilling the troops' blood, or to raise their morale; as a last resort to avoid undergoing 'an execrable punishment'. This is a classic list inherited from the Middle Ages; but among French gentlemen of the period in question it was extended to include two cases which open the door to precisely those 'excesses' against which our authors claim to be struggling: to defend one's mistress's honour, or generally that of any woman who is maligned;

to avenge a murder or 'to have satisfaction for an offence which cannot be repaired any other way than by the blood of him who caused it'.

The formal aspects were more constraining in practice than this elastic list of causes: the only valid duel was one which was fought openly, formally and publicly, and with offensive and defensive weapons. In other words, almost all the aristocratic authors denounce duels *alla macchia* and call on the King to start authorising judicial duels again. Some even go so far as to reject the practices of fencing and using seconds.

The virtual unanimity of those against combat *alla macchia* may seem surprising. Certainly formal combat had the prestige of the past, but as we have seen with Brantôme this prestige carried less weight than recent examples, and examples of contemporary duels *alla macchia* were mushrooming. More important was the face that this literature was intended to influence the King to revoke his previous punitive measures; its aim was to show him that repression resulted only in the proliferation of an evil which would on the contrary be reduced if it were authorised in principle. Such an authorisation, given in particular cases and publicly, would, according to these authors, be the best way of returning to the moderate number of duelling deaths of the good old days when previous kings granted the closed field.

But at a deeper level, even though gentlmen practised duels *alla macchia* (constrained to do so by the antithetic requirements of honour and prohibition), they did not like them, and indeed disapproved of them. For the practice ran contrary to the very reason underlying the phenomenon of the duel, the importance of appearances. How indeed could one prove one's worth without the presence of witnesses, and how could one found a reputation on a furtive, dissimulated act?

We might want to add that this 'shirtsleeve' confrontation without helmet or shield, this risk to which the duellist exposed himself almost naked, placed him at the mercy of blind, capricious fortune, reducing the thinking being to the level of the wild beasts, who were the usual inhabitants of the 'wilderness' where the fight took place. It tore the gentleman from the civilised universe to hurl him into primitive chaos. However, only one noble author, the very humanistic La Taille, dwells at all on this argument. This old man was something of an anachronism in a world which was no longer that of the Renaissance, and indeed he notes – in spite of his personal reservations – that a fight 'in one's shirtsleeves and on foot is the type of fight considered the most generous'. In fact for most nobles who – as their attitude to their studies and writings suggests – placed themselves on the side of nature as opposed to the upholders of culture, the primitive aspect of clandestine duels in the field was an added attraction. And while Brantôme, whose contradictions once again crystallise the mentality of his milieu, deplores the lack of glamour of duels *alla macchia*, he admires the complementary brilliance they can add to the discretion of a *Grand*.

Above and beyond the conscious contradictions which the practice of duelling, and of duelling *alla macchia*, made gentlemen suffer, on an imaginary level it resolved the conflict created by their situation in a society which still placed them at its highest level, but in which at the same time they felt like outsiders. For them duelling offered a return to a conflictual state of nature, which was at the same time a garden of Eden, a state to which Brantôme's formula for duels *alla macchia* also applies: 'There, everything is war.'

This attitude, this ideal of the gentlemen duellists, was most clearly expressed by one of their enemies, the anonymous author of a leaflet against duellists called the *Prodigious History of the Ghostly Supplicant Knight*. The first pages of this work deserve to be quoted in full, but we can give only a résumé of them here, thereby also summarising universal history as the writer saw it. In the beginning there were men 'scattered here and there in the countryside and wildernesses . . . without laws'. Duels were numerous at this time. Then a society 'of towns and laws' was created and 'they began to cultivate their land and their customs'. In order to acquire extra perfection, gentlemen (a bit like hermits) then 'preferred to stay in the fields', a retreat favourable to physical and intellectual exercise and 'to contemplation'. But some of them contemplated only an 'imaginary honour' and (with the help of rustic solitude) fell back into the primitive ways of the first humans, for 'as demons communicate themselves more easily in the middle of the countryside', they inspired the country squires with a frenzied desire to kill each other in a flood of duels. This may be a worthless account from the historical point of view, but the psychological analysis is accurate. And this little anti-duellist leaflet merely reproduces – though with an added tone of disapproval – the model of the men 'carrying arms by profession' themselves.

To summarise the attitude of the noblemen – using a procedure which is, as we said before, foreign to them – we can say that all of them acknowledged that there was something excessive in the contemporary practice of duelling and that there might even be a danger on the biological level if no brake were applied to the number of fights between sovereigns, *Grands* and indeed all gentlemen indiscriminately. But all of them said that the best remedy for these excesses was to authorise duelling, as the lesser of two evils. All of them thought that duelling could never be stopped completely because it met an irreducible need: no consideration, however honourable, could be so categorical an imperative as the requirement of honour. Brantôme gives the following verdict on two gentlemen whom he had himself once reconciled, and who had then had another quarrel: 'they were seen to go off without having fought each other, almost like friends. Many murmured about this, for challenges should never be left without men coming to blows, and one had, as I have said, to win or die.'

So how did the gentlemen reconcile the Catholic or Protestant faith that they all professed – and which was constraining and categorical on the matter – with the practice of duelling? In religious matters almost all gentlemen were utterly conventional, their adherence to their Church being all the more solid for its general lack of subtlety; duelling, on the other hand, was a deliberately and definitely marginalised practice, a rejection of conformism that was all the more powerful for being beyond the reach of classical arguments.

Gentlemen seldom posed themselves the awkward problem of God's judgement and the possible judicial errors of Providence, for it was more important to them to demonstrate their bravery than to leave the field victorious. They gave greater consideration to the prohibitions of their Church, but without suffering unbearable anxiety in that direction. The Council of Trent had fulminated against duels, but France had not 'received' its decrees, and besides the Council condemned only judicial duels for which the sovereign was asked to grant a field, a form of combat which had anyway become obsolete.

In any case, all these discussions and minute arguments were of no consequence next to an example which had the authority of Holy Writ, involved a king and, because it had given rise to an abundant iconography, was extremely well known: the duel of David and Goliath. Every nobleman whose writing we have studied here refers to it with a greater or lesser degree of smugness, while none of the enemies of duelling dares leave it unmentioned, even though it means coping more or less unconvincingly with a burdensome *exemplum*.

The constant reference to this example shows it to have been the most solid argument of the supporters of duelling. It was also one of the most traditional. Once again, it is Brantôme who sums up the debate most bravely, in a tone of definitive conclusion: 'But, say the good Christians, all these combats are neither holy nor Christian and are forbidden by God. In this regard I shall say nothing, not being a good theologian, but all the same David and Goliath fought each other, and God approved of the fight.'

This striking certainty is surprising. In fact the story of David and Goliath as told in the Bible does not greatly resemble an authentic duel: one of the combatants is an adolescent, the other a mature man; one is an obscure shepherd, the other a valiant warrior, and, above all, David fights with a catapult and Goliath with a sword. So there is no respect for equality of age, rank or weapons. Furthermore, David's weakness is strengthened by divine grace, which does not re-establish equality but simply reverses the inequality: to fight when inspired by the Holy Spirit is certainly not to give oneself up to the 'luck of arms'. But these details are only a problem to us who read the sacred text verse by verse. As we have said, men like Brantôme were much more impressed by what they saw than by what they read and for gentlemen of the century which extolled the primacy of the Word, divine revelation expressed itself less in the Book that they consulted than through the preachers that they heard and the images that they contemplated. So we must look in our turn, and since we no longer have the canvases and tapestries that decorated churches and châteaux, we must look at the engravings in illustrated Bibles and picture Bibles that were circulated frm the beginning of the sixteenth century to the middle of the seventeenth. There we have to admit that the differences between the Old Testament fight and a judicial duel in the Western tradition are greatly reduced.

First, the artists seem to have preferred to show the moment when David has seized Goliath's sword and is plunging it into him as he lies on the ground, rather than the point when he is catapulting the stone. This means that the difference in height between the opponents remains visible but is less striking than if both were standing up and facing each other. The inequality of weapons is also blurred in this final use of the sword, that most favoured instrument of Frenchmen 'whose profession is honour'. Above all the setting and onlookers surrounding the fighters very closely recall the layout of a closed field and the spectators of a judicial duel. In the famous *Icons* of 1538, the Hebrew and Philistine armies are symmetrically placed at each side of the composition, frozen in contemplation of the fight. They are holding their lances upright, forming a kind of barrier around the flat, empty space where David is facing his enemy, who looks like a large Swiss Guard. Behind Goliath are two tents surmounted by standards, which recall the 'thrones covered in cloth' in which sat the champions of a public duel. In the background the outline of a hill also places a boundary round the space reserved for the fighters, and the sun's rays lend all their brilliance to the event. A later engraving, which was apparently very popular, delimits the closed field with a stream, a line where the ground is uneven and a boulder, making a natural boundary. Here too the two armies stand immobile, their lances in their hands. Very few changes would be necessary for such representations to be used to illustrate the story of a duel, as it was practised until around 1550, and as its idealised image remained preserved, long after, in the minds of the French aristocracy.

So the iconography of the fight between David and Goliath allowed the latter to acquire an exemplary analogy with the duel. But the images are such because for the artist this analogy was already present, and indeed had been established from the earliest centuries of the Middle Ages. This poses the question of why this episode remained in the collective imagination, and why it became so intesely important, preferred to so many others that were equally venerable. We should like to advance a hypothesis here, which takes us to the heart of the problems raised by the duel. This image was fundamentally chosen because French gentlemen were interested in the complex relations between King Saul and the young David which fill the first Book of Samuel. David is the King's favourite, he protects him in battle and entertains him with music. He is his most brilliant military supporter, saving his life and state, and precisely because of his success and his generosity, he becomes the object of his King's jealous hatred. As the protégé who becomes a protector, an exile who does not kill the King whom he twice has at his mercy, but shows him the greatest respect in the most unselfconscious way, David is a prototype for the French gentleman of the years 1550–1650 in his relations with royalty. The story offers the symbolic image of a nobility and gentry allegorically represented in Corneille's *Nicomède*.

And although the kings of France unsuccessfully renewed prohibitions against duelling that the nobility (referring to the example of David) treated with contempt, it should be noted that in two great crises which brought the tension between aristocracy and monarchy to its peak the duel gained in strength and took on a deeper meaning, while the figure of David acquired the exceptional quality of a political symbol.

Let us consider the link between them in relation to two events.

1589: Paris, held by the League, was under siege. The great excitement that such a situation generates in a human community was exacerbated by the fact that in the camp of the besieging heretics, and more or less at its head, was the man who, in spite of his scandals and sterility, was still the Lord's Anointed, the Most Christian King Henri III. On 2 August a Dominican monk killed the King: was this sacrilege or divinely inspired vengeance? The next day a young Leaguer and a young royalist challenged each other to a fight with lances 'for the love of women'. This personal significance of their duel (likening it to a tournament) was marginal in the eyes of the mass of people in both camps, who were seeking a divine judgement. The more prudent wanted to dissuade the champions from fighting, while the League beauties paraded on the scene of the combat dressed in green, signifying that they were wearing the colour of madmen in mourning for Henri III. Both armies suspended all action for a day and the duel took place 'after all the formalities of chivalry had been observed', following the ceremonial which had not been seen in France since Jarnac's duel (except – for obvious reasons – the request to the King for a field). Marolle, champion of the Catholic Parisians, killed his opponent and returned to the besieged capital 'amid trumpet fanfares and public exclamations'. Priests and monks preached to the galvanised inhabitants that 'the young David has killed the Philistine Goliath' and 'augured from this the destruction of the party of Béarn'. For a community rebelling against its monarch, victory in a duel between equals justified murder committed against an impious king.

1649–51: Paris, under the doubtful banner of the *Grands*, was once again in revolt against the power of the monarchy, incarnated at the time by the minister Mazarin. The revolt was called the Fronde – the Catapult – the weapon that David used against Goliath and there was nothing coincidental about this link, as an engraving by Abraham Bosse indcates. Although some pamphlets of the time portrayed the young Louis XIV as the Israelite shepherd, at least two of them pitted David–Beaufort against Goliath–Mazarin. The Duc de Beaufort was in fact the leader of the Fronde, if not in terms of his responsibilities then at least on the symbolic level of popularity. He was a constant opponent of absolute power who, from the Cinq-Mars* conspiracy onwards, was involved in every cabal; but he was also the son of one of Henri IV's illegitimate sons, a kind of negative image of the legitimate King, the 'market King', 'King of the Frondeurs'. And he owed a great deal of his popularity to the fact that his life was studded with quarrels of honour, and also that he was one of those who turned the period of the Fronde into an Indian summer of duelling. During one of Beaufort's quarrels Gaston d'Orléans – another negative image of the King, who at one time proclaimed himself Lieutenant-General of the realm – thought of 'authorising combat according to the ancient custom'. And when this same Gaston simultaneously named Beaufort and Nemours (who were brothers-in-law) to his Council, such similarity of treatment led them on to the field. In killing Nemours in the duel,

---

*A conspiracy to overthrow Cardinal Richelieu in 1632 involving Louis XIII's favourite, Cinq-Mars. (Ed.)

Beaufort had the sorrow of losing both an esteemed rival and a beloved relative.

There seems to have been a complex of ideas and representations which meant that noblemen could rebel against the power of the monarch only if they also tested themselves against each other in fights between equals, as though obscurely searching among themselves for another monarch; and this double procedure seems to have gained consistency and unity by reference to the figure of David.

The preceding considerations have led us some way from our immediate concerns of the reconciliation of duelling with Christian religion in the minds of the nobility. But they have brought us to the central bastion, the castle keep of aristocratic attitudes, which is where we must stand to understand the religious attitude of duellists. With the formidable example of David, in whom they saw themselves as in a mirror, they did not feel they were returning to the naturist paganism they were accused of, but that they were fulfilling their Christian vocation by defending their honour.

Indeed the simple fact of being gentlemen placed them within the chivalric code, conferring upon them a modest equivalent of an order of knighthood. An analogous argument demonstrated that honorary orders (the Golden Fleece, the Holy Spirit), actual military orders (like that of Malta) and monastic orders were all the same. To be a gentleman was thus to be a member of a sort of congregation and to obey the rules of that congregation. 'This religion of chivalry', wrote Brantôme, 'has also been called the religion of honour, and those who profess it are called knights of honour, for as the virtues are the rules that must be observed in this religion of chivalry, they necessarily follow honour.' To observe the rules of honour, the point of honour, was to belong to a Christian elite who imposed upon themselves a stricter ethical code than that of the common Christian morality of ordinary lay people of all ages and conditions. And where there was a conflict between ordinary Christian morality and chivalric morality, it was no sin to renounce the former to satisfy the latter; it was no violation of the more lax morality to submit to the more demanding. Just as chastity within holy orders was not a sin against the laws of marriage, to cause, meet with or at least risk death in a duel that one's honour demanded was not to sin against the commandment 'Thou shalt not kill'.

The attitude of those noblemen who accepted, practised and exalted the duel was archaic. They supported the idea of a traditional human community (no matter if it had only ever existed as such in their imagination), employed the rhetoric of the *exemplum* and were unaffected by or hostile to new forms of civil, political and Christian society. Faced with weighty texts, strict edicts and blistering anathemas, they went forward with the calm assurance of little David going to meet Goliath. In a civilisation of the written word, in a Church founded on Holy Scripture, in a 'religion of the Book', the duel was the ritual of a people without writing.

It was also a kind of religious act. This is why those who believed in it did not feel the need to justify themselves with human discourse. This is why, through this act about which they had nothing to say, they told us so much. The theme of David, which was always present but blossomed with dramatic intensity during the great events of the 'crisis of the French aristocracy', points to a link between the religious and the political in the unconscious of an entire social group. The polemics on duelling are inseparable from those on tyrannicide. Considering themselves as primitives, the nobility touched those fundamental points of collective psychology whose outlines we have only begun to perceive in the last century. The regenerating murder of the old King could be carried out only if it were announced, presaged, justified and also continued and annulled indefinitely by the mortal combat of his two finest warriors. It would seem that, for French gentlemen of the sixteenth and seventeenth centuries, a collective Oedipus complex was overlaid with a collective complex of Eteocles and Polynices.

Chapter 12
The Attitudes of the Bourgeoisie

> *M. Jourdain*: So like this, without having to be brave, a
> man is sure to kill his man and not to get killed himself.
> *Fencing Master*: Without doubt. Did you not see the
> demonstration?
> *M. Jourdain*: Yes.
> *Fencing Master*: And that shows what consideration we
> should be given in a state, and how much better is
> knowledge of the use of arms than all the other useless
> knowledges, like dancing, music....
> (Molière, *Le Bourgeois Gentilhomme*, II, 3)

However one defines the bourgeoisie, it consisted of people who did
not 'carry arms professionally'. In principle therefore they did not
practise duelling. They did, however, have opinions on it. In this
chapter we shall consider as bourgeois those commoners who lived
in the city for all or most of the year, did not work with their hands,
had some education (at least knowing how to read and write) and
remained above the breadline (except in times of exceptional crisis).
This certainly gives us a complex amalgam, taking us from the shop
to the private mansion, from the self-made man to the schoolboy,
from the Parisian financier to the lawyer from Aix. We cannot expect
such a varied group to have a unanimous and unchanging attitude.

Having seen them pass through the courts, we know that at least
some of the bourgeoisie were neither indifferent nor hostile to
duelling. We shall start by looking at two substantial documents
from the time. The first is the *Journal* written between 1574 and 1611
by Pierre de L'Estoile, an officer in the Chancellery, contemporary
of Henri III and Henri IV, austere Gallican and inveterate collector.
The second is the *Historiettes* by Tallemant des Réaux, a wit of Louis
XIV's time, a lukewarm Protestant from the world of finance, who
frequented the *Grands*. True, their writings, originally circulated in
manuscript form, are subjective accounts and tell us most about their
authors; but they also tell us about a particular milieu, the small
group of friends for whom they were destined. We can use them as
touchstones in a wider analysis.

Throughout his life, L'Estoile was undeniably interested in everything to do with quarrels, cartels, fights and reconciliations. Such things are frequently mentioned between 1578 and 1583, then from 1599 to 1611, with particular frequency in the years 1606–9. In general he either refers to or recounts combats that took place locally in Paris and the surrounding area, sometimes (and more often as he gets older) adding moral considerations to the anecdotes. He also records quarrels which did not end in bloodshed, legislative measures and pardons granted by sovereigns, and lastly he collects the satirical or laudatory poems that circulated about famous duellists.

L'Estoile's writing gives the immediate impression that for him a duel was a tragic affair, where things went quickly from words to swords and from life to death. This is expressed by the following figures taken from the whole of the *Journal*: nine quarrels did not end in a duel; thirty-four encounters took place; fifty-seven duellists died on the field or immediately after the duel; twenty-two were injured, some so seriously that they cannot have survived for long; nineteen duellists survived, but we do not know whether they were injured or not.

So L'Estoile saw the duel as a basically lethal phenomenon. He notes this without sentimentality or emotionality. Words of the family of 'cruelty' and 'blood' do not appear at all, while the adjective 'bloody' is used only once and applies not to flesh but to the sword: 'the naked sword all bloody'. Wounds are mentioned, but never detailed and even less described, apart from a single exception (which confirms the rule) concerning a grotesque duel between two clerks in which one cut off two of the other man's fingers. So the fights L'Estoile records do not produce in him the reactions of someone visualising the scene, nor does he use concrete adjectives. For him the duel is something serious, not a drama full of pathos.

However, there is a noun which he places twice in apposition to the word 'duel', and that is 'monster'. This almost allegorical apposition occurs in the work of more than one of L'Estoile's contemporaries, expressing an idea of the duel as a kind of infernal beast, a gigantic and frightening creature which escapes the bounds of reason and feeds on human life. There are also associative lists in which the words 'duel' and 'quarrel' occur and which form the mental context in which L'Estoile almost spontaneously classifies – and thereby qualifies and judges – them, for example: 'Continual ballets, duels, blasphemies and all sorts of debauchery and foolishness'. These lists indicate a strongly felt link between the practice of quarrels of honour and life at Court. The most frequent link is that between duelling and debauchery, followed by insolent luxuriousness and murderous cruelty, with insult to God, 'blasphemy', coming last. One word sums up the whole (a little like 'monster', but including all the vices bordering on duelling), 'madness'. For this austere and economical member of the bourgeoisie who, because of his rank, never set foot inside the grounds of the Louvre, duelling was a social scourge linked to the sumptuous, dissolute life of the courtiers, and its practice indicated mental aberration.

The explicit judgements and moralising with which L'Estoile accompanies some of his tales are always on the level of civic and Christian morality, and his judgements are always severe. Certainly when he was young his curiosity dominated his indignation, and he was more interested in collecting songs about the duel of Henri III's favourites, the Mignons, than sighing over the impiousness of their behaviour, even if he disapproved of it. A quarter of a century later, on the other hand, he clearly distanced himself from those who admired the death in a duel of a gentleman of 'valour and good nature . . . who was said to have made a good end. And I, as a good Christian, would call it a bad and poor end, unless it pleased Him who alone can make a good end out of a bad one, by his great mercy, to have touched his heart to make himself known.' During the last five years of L'Estoile's life, passages in this vein abound. This was an unexceptional development in the attitudes of a sick, morose old man, for whom everything modern was scandalous; but it also reflects the overall evolution of the whole religious section of society which, be it Catholic or Puritan, was becoming increasingly moralistic.

For L'Estoile the duel was fundamentally a phenomenon of the gentry and nobility and almost all the potential or actual duellists he presents us with are noblemen or, to use his more precise term, 'gentlemen'. All the same, three times in the *Journal* there appear bourgeois men – or men who had recently been raised to the ranks of the gentry and nobility – who fought a duel. In 1581 a former merchant from Lyons 'and, since the troubles, captain of a château of Port Ancise', showed mercy to his adversary, over whom he had the advantage, and L'Estoile bestowed on him the ephithet 'generous'. In 1607, it was the famous and extremely rich banker Zamet who dispatched a nobleman who had mocked his way of dancing. The following year, a clerk from Montauban wounded a colleague on the Pré aux Clercs defending the reputation of a marquise. In the latter two cases, L'Estoile records that the nobility was 'scandalised' that challenges and fights should be tolerated on the part of people of such low social standing; but how did the average bourgeois man regard bourgeois duellists? L'Estoile did not feel the need to say and appears

neither shocked nor flattered by such occurrences. He tars all duellists with the same brush, whatever the colour of their blood, 'all as
wise as each other on this point'.

Although L'Estoile regards the duel as a gentleman's practice from
the outset, he does not judge it in terms of social criteria, any more
than he responds to it emotionally with horror or excitement. In
exceptional cases he admires a duellist for having spared his adversary's life, but consistently disapproves of duelling from his point of
view as a magistrate, because he sees in it an element of disobedience
to royal authority, and even a symptom of the failure of that
authority. As a Chancellery officer he felt very strongly that the
practice of single combat was an affront to royal power and later he
reproached Henri IV for the guilty leniency that made him grant
pardons to murderers. He also condemns it from the increasingly
strict point of view of Catholicism after the Council of Trent, as
disobedience to the commandments of God and the Church, and
discreetly (and more and more openly as he gets older) he laughs at
its absurdity. Pierre de L'Estoile's reactions are not those of any old
average bourgeois. They are the reactions of a devout Catholic with
a strong sense of the state, a sense of order which, on earth as in
heaven, among the *Grands* as among the obscure, did not permit the
ridiculing of authority. Nothing sums up his overall attitude better
than these words which he wrote in 1607: 'That is how this monster
went on devouring the French nobility and gentry, through *God's
good judgement and the connivance of the Prince.*'

The image of duels given by Tallemant des Réaux is still that of a
homicidal phenomenon. Among his anecdotes he cites or recounts
four duels in which two adversaries kill each other and twenty-four
in which one of the combatants dies, as opposed to only sixteen
which end in wounds alone. So duels were deadly in the middle of
the seventeenth century, even in the very particular atmosphere of
the *Historiettes*.

But this picture requires qualification. Tallemant does not often
describe duels as 'bloody' and when he mentions the Chevalier
d'Andrieu, who 'at thirty had killed seventy-two men in duels', it is
as a monstrous case; this character, who was convicted of various
abominable crimes, had been condemned by public opinion and
executed by royal justice. More representative of an average attitude
(although Tallemant rails against him) was Boisrobert, who 'in one
year had eight quarrels and made eight reconciliations'. Out of the
total number of challenges and duels that Tallemant mentions in
sufficient detail, we find: thirty-two duels which did not take place
(through reconciliation before swords were crossed); thirty-four
duels which were not fatal; twenty-eight fatal duels. These figures

clearly reflect the degree of seriousness of the phenomenon in the eyes of the teller.

Although Tallemant's writings are full of bourgeois men whose concern for their honour lasts only until the death-blow, one also finds, alongside the rabid 'gladiators', noblemen from the finest stock and not suspected of cowardice, who are economical when it comes to spilling blood. The Duc de Rohan-Chabot, for example, fought two or three times, but always 'in fairly bloodless fights'. Having 'a great need to enhance his reputation a little' because the legitimacy of his ducal title was in dispute, he accepted a fight in which 'he slightly wounded [his adversary] on the hand; but the two seconds, who were brave men, killed each other'. So, unlike the seconds, two squires from Saintonge, the great aristocrat, who wanted public esteem, declared himself satisfied at first blood. The dividing line between simulation and fatal duel ran not between commoners and gentlemen, nor between robe and sword, but between the provinces on the one hand, and the Court and Paris on the other.

Tallemant gives duelling a positive aristocratic value. The word 'crime' never appears in the context of duels, but 'brave' and its derivations and 'reputation' do. Among the gentlemen duellists he presents, we find only one empty blusterer and three men described as cowards, compared to seven models of courage and generosity.

But bourgeois and recently ennobled office-holders also have an important place in the duels of the *Historiettes* (even if such and such a duke refuses to obtain satisfaction for 'the presumtuousness of this bourgeois' President of Parliament otherwise than by murdering him). These portraits of bourgeois can be divided into three types:

– those ridiculous enough to fight, such as the King's secretary who furiously challenged his son-in-law, thus causing the unhappy man's death – from a seizure; or the paymaster who was very jealous about his wife and learned fencing to take on a councillor from Touraine; or the two business associates who wanted to balance their muddled accounts on the Pré aux Clercs and who, when they got there, abandoned 'this madness' and went 'to dine together'. The desire to duel quickly passed for these bourgeois who, more or less clearly, thought the same thing as L'Estoile: 'He will beat me, and will laugh at me twice as much';
– those cowardly enough to evade duels, such as Chapelain, a notary's son and young tutor, who thought it elegant to wear a sword until the day someone tried to take him for a second, when he 'hung his sword on a hook'; or a master of accounts who rode through the countryside dressed as a squire until, fooled by his

appearance, some duellists called him to second them. At this he abandoned his horse, fled to the law courts and did not come out until he had obtained a ruling 'that no master of accounts should disguise himself as a gentleman';
– those clearsighted enough to refuse duels. Such was the case of the councillor from Touraine mentioned above; he 'laughed [at the appellant] and did not want to fight'. Such was also the case of a 'rich parvenu', the President de Chevry, who, in a moment of 'madness', promised a courtier that he would give him satisfaction according to the ways of honour. When the other reminded him of his promise a little later on he replied with a laugh: 'You should have taken me at my word. I'm no longer in that mood.'

So Tallemant's bourgeois do not resemble Molière's M. Jourdain faced with duelling. Although some of them regard the pretension to fight duels as a failing, they are also critical of those who avoid making reparations for a fought duel. A clear-sightedness resembling courage leads more than one of them to refuse this dangerous game. The key to the complex attitudes of Tallemant's bourgeois is offered to us in the form of an anecdote which is worth repeating. A younger son of the de Coustenau family insulted one of his bourgeois neighbours. 'The bourgeois wanted to give in; no quarter.' They fought. The bourgeois had the advantage. Coustenau cried out: 'Don't kill me!' 'Go on, I'll let you live,' said the bourgeois. 'But since I shall have to go away, give me money for my journey.' The author concludes: 'He took all his money and left.' This conduct – which Tallemant clearly enjoys describing – is significant. The brave bourgeois did not fight lightly, for peccadilloes; he did it after considering all the facts of the case and as a last resort. But he fought well; the intoxication of the fight and concern for his reputation did not lead him to neglect his interests.

In the duelling world of the *Historiettes* the dividing line does not, as we have seen, run between commoners and gentlemen: there are shopkeeping Don Quixotes and retiring types with a full complement of noble ancestors. Nor does it fall between prudent cowardice and intrepid generosity: one of the most valiant gentlemen duellists comes under the heading of 'Eccentrics, visionaries, the whimsical, bizarre, ect.'. The line is drawn between those who do not count the cost and those who do, those for whom life has no price and those for whom it does. That price is calculated on the double yardstick of honour and wealth, those two submultiples of social position.

It is in this sense and this sense alone that one can speak of a bourgeois vision of the duel in Tallemant's writing. The price of blood is not fixed according to whether it is blue or red.

For Tallemant des Réaux, as for Pierre de L'Estoile two generations earliler, duels were things that happened to other people. They could be petty or laughable, but they were never insignificant or derisory. Even for those members of the bourgeoisie who were the furthest from practising the accepting them, duels retained great prestige for a long time. This was because in their attitudes hostile reasoning and favourable arguments cohabited.

One of the favourable arguments was the fascination of *exempla*. The logic of examples was as powerful for commoners as it was for gentlemen and the former had to make an effort to throw it off. This is apparent if one reads dissertations written 'against the damnable custom of duels' by magistrates and officers of justice during Henri IV's reign and Marie de Médicis' regency. They deploy verses from Scripture and aphorisms from the Ancients, they skilfully decipher a symbolic system borrowed from mythology and the Kabbala and sometimes force themselves to comply with the rigours of formal logic. They sense and say that examples are harmful to their theses. But they cannot help using them, thereby undermining the points they are trying to make.

In 1612 Joly, a lieutenant of the Constabulary, was the first to criticise those authors who 'certainly condemn [duels] in general, but tolerate them in particular'. He himself resisted the charm of heroic examples to the end of his work. His *Antiduel* is a single narrative (entirely invented) purporting to be the last words of the famous duellist Balagny, in which this hitherto impenitent fighter recants. Joly explains that this 'well-reasoned story might have more effect than the great collections amassed by other writers before me of all the exploits that they considered relevant to the similarity of duels in all ages and countries. I have avoided this as a pitfall, seeing that it could only make things worse.'

So resistance to the fascination of *exempla* was difficult, even in the minds of magistrates who wrote books against duelling. We can guess from this how hard it was for more modest members of the bourgeoisie, or for those less associated with new currents of thought and the exercise of public office. In his reading notes taken in 1656, an officer from Arles, an isolated but no doubt representative character, appreciates Muzio's *On the Duel* primarily for the 'quantity of examples' that he gives. So here is a commoner and *honnête homme* (the seventeenth-century ideal of the 'decent man') in the middle of the seventeenth century reading a work by a humanist mannerist Christian in a fashion worthy of a knight of the autumn of the Middle Ages. We can be sure he was not alone.

The second factor, which prolonged and expanded on the preceding one, was that the French bourgeoisie had long been bathed in a culture which exalted noble values and confrontations between two equal and armed individuals. Their reading and education bear witness to this. For a long time even modest bourgeois loved to read chivalric romances, or their cheap and vulgarised derivatives, the 'blue books'. Those cultivated commoners who abandoned chivalric romances to a popular or childish audience soon found other reading matter which exalted single combat, such as the stories included in Scarron's *Comic Novel* or (to cite titles dear to the milieu in which Tallemant des Réaux lived) *Le Grand Cyrus, La Princesse de Clèves*, or *Le Journal amoureux d'Espagne*. These were all heroic models of aristocratic individualism, offered for the admiration of a peaceful and refined bourgeoisie.

Even more than the reading of novels, which was a pleasure for only a part of the adult bourgeoisie, the education dispensed in colleges to the elite of the commoners and to young gentlemen perpetuated the aristocratic values of confrontation. Classrooms were decorated like lists, school exercises, *disputationes*, compositions and the awarding of prizes were all run as symmetrical competitions: pupil against pupil, ten pupils against ten, class (headed by the teacher) against class. Schooling was a perpetual joust. True, these intellectual combats and mimed confrontations may have fulfilled a function of sublimation and diverted the aggression of young gentlemen away from bloody fights. The Jesuit Father Dainville noted: 'Instead of containing and aggravating energies which want only to be spent, [the masters] "like skilful grooms" put them to use in the advancement of studies. They disarmed their pupils of their swords to arm them with the pen.'

But for the children of the bourgeoisie, this 'heroic ambience', combined with the daily presence of gentlemen of the same age as themselves, was an effective school for diffuse propaganda in favour of duelling. In 1615 a secular master gave his pupils the legitimacy of single combat as a subject for *disputatio*, which he published as a *Controversy on Duels*, in the form of an oratorical joust performed by his pupils. It matters little that he rewrote it, that he begins by describing the duel as a 'monstrous foolishness', that the arguments on both sides are hackneyed and that at the end of the debate he condemns all duels carried out without the authorisation of the King and magistrates. The essential point is that this scholastic exercise gives a strictly equal place to those for the those against the duel, and that the figure of David is frequently mentioned. In the colleges, where glory was 'the last word', many sons of prosecutors, doctors and money-changers must have learned – at the same time as the art of fencing – the prestige of, and indeed the taste for, duelling.

The main arguments militating against duels were those of Christian morality and obedience to the King. But these arguments were not specifically bourgeois, and as long as they were the only ones they were ineffective in practice. However, two themes which first appeared in certain bourgeois circles after the beginning of the seventeenth century were to have greater effect. These were the notions of archaism without glory and biological waste.

Any idea of duelling as an anachronism is absent from L'Estoile's writing. It is vague in that of Tallemant. It was first developed by the small and inward-looking but audacious group of erudite free-thinkers, some of whom collected documents concerning duels. One of these men, Peiresc, a magistrate from Aix, intended to make a book of them, but eventually confined himself to gathering the material which now constitutes a large manuscript archive in the Bibliothèque Inguimbertine in Carpentras, about which we can make the following observations.

There is a total absence of stories of single combat from biblical and classical Antiquity, although for his contemporaries these provided exemplary and indeed providential justification for duelling. Peiresc's attitude is 'modern': he is not looking for the authorisation of *exempla*; he wants documents to help him understand.

A quarter of the documents date from the fourteenth century. Peiresc saw the time of the first Valois as one of flamboyant chivalry in which, when monarchial values were partially eclipsed, a ritual of aristocratic honour was established in France and the Low Countries. Implicitly, and perhaps consciously, he suggests that for men of his time to hark back to that ritual was to risk the return of the troubles and conflict which had prevailed at the time of the Hundred Years War. Peiresc is a peace-loving man, a lover of order and authority. His apparent lack of interest in duels which took place closer to his own time and his almost complete silence concerning those contemporary to himself have a conspiratorial significance. To turn duelling – a question of burning topicality for general opinion – into an object of study was to exorcise it.

Lastly his interest is orientated towards all that is French, legal and ceremonial. He is interested in procedure rather than fine swordplay and lingers over the wording of cartels and their answers rather than the theories of the Italians. He rejects any form of ethical judgement, aiming merely to describe the form of the phenomenon. This almost scientific approach denies all sense of affinity or repulsion and distances the writer from his subject. The duel is no longer a monster, it is a thing.

In a sonnet in praise of a duellist from Aix which Peiresc copied out, the former spared his floored and pleading opponent: 'One speaking of life and the other of glory'. This poetic choice of

Peiresc's accords with the single element of admiration for duellists that we found in L'Estoile's writing and with Tallemant's attitude, which, as we have seen, distinguished not between those who fought and those who refused, but between those who knew what blood was worth and those who did not. These attitudes fit into a whole bourgeois vision which was expressed and grew stronger in the course of the seventeenth century, a vision which made a distinction between courage and temerity, between life foolishly risked and life usefully spent. The countless appeals to save the precious lives of the French elite for war and the service of the King arose from this current of opinion.

The most lucid and systematic formulation of this attitude appears in the work of Pascal, who polished off the duel in his *7th Provincial Letter*, and gave it a few other scattered mentions. Pascal is profoundly hostile to all forms of duelling. What scandalises him the most about this kind of homicide is that it is supposedly done in defence of honour and with no desire for revenge, that men are killed without hatred, and that the Jesuits 'do not even want a man to desire the death [of his enemy] in a movement of hatred'. This he interprets as a sinful dissociation of ideas, seeing in it a clear illustration of the ruses and hypocrisy of the moral doctrine of spiritual direction.

As a polemical demonstration, his arguments are impeccable, but at the level of psychological and social analysis of the duel he shows a complete incomprehension of the phenomenon. Pascal understands nothing of reparation which is not vengeance, of a fight desired and agreed upon by both parties, a confrontation which is the outcome of a pact, a murder which is proof of esteem for the victim, indeed which gives him back this esteem, and which can be a proclamation of profound solidarity between the two combatants. What he disapproves of most in duelling, what makes the practice seem to him worse than brawling or murder, is that it is the result neither of cold calculation nor of boiling anger. It is a gratuitous act. Therefore, it is absurd. It is outside the framework of reason. Here we should not forget that the Latin *ratio* at the root of 'rationalism' had the sense of both 'reason' and 'calculation', or that the enemy of 'probable opinions' was a specialist in the calculation of probability; and we should not forget that even in his thirst for poverty and Christian charity, as well as in the dialectic of the wager, Pascal knew what things were worth, what money was worth and what life was worth. He does not justify avarice; but he understands it better than prodigality. He takes a bourgeois stand for saving against all waste.

In short, Pascal sincerely believed the morality of the Jesuits to be a sordid calculation devised to suit their world and time. But – at least as far as duelling is concerned – it is he who is the real accountant and man of his time (indeed the precursor of time to come), while the Jesuits, who were lenient where murder was concerned, as long as it was done without hatred, were echoing a morality of generosity which was soon to be outdated.

Pascal understood nothing about duelling; but this is a sign of his greatness. By this he shows that he had entirely completed the intellectual and moral mutation which the whole of French society was not fully to achieve for another generation or two. He analyses duelling from the point of view of reason and passions and measures it against the length of human life (biological and eternal). Instead of an absolute, he sees it as an abnormal phenomenon, an action which is inexcusable because it is irrational, something which cannot be accounted for. Worse than an evil, duelling is a vanity. It is not a mode of matter, it is a modish whim.

While the Chevalier de Méré was still stumbling around trying to extract a model for the *honnête homme* from the ideal gentleman or courtier, Pascal, with certainty and ease, resolutely accomplished and proclaimed a bourgeois ethical revolution of the symbolic problem of duelling.

Pascal was, to our knowledge, the first to use the word 'fashion' in relation to duels. After the end of the seventeenth century, and during the whole of the eighteenth the link between these two terms would be frequently made and would seem as obvious as that between 'duel' and 'monster' had seemed in the years 1610–20. The term 'fashion' in fact encompasses the two complaints of anachronism and waste that we have seen gradually forming in the thinking of certain bourgeois circles opposed to duelling. An outdated and therefore temporary phenomenon is a fashion, as is a gratuitous and therefore futile fad.

One generation after Pascal, La Bruyère gave the definitive expression of the thinking of laymen and commoners (whether of free-thinking or Jansenist tendencies) on these problems. The author of the *Caractères* devotes a paragraph to duelling, and puts it in the chapter 'On Fashion': 'The duel is fashion's triumph, and the place where it has exerted its tyranny with the greatest brilliance. . . .' The past tense here proves that La Bruyère chooses to consider duelling as dead. His main condemnation of it is on the grounds that its judgement is irrational, that it grades an individual's chances of survival according to his bravery and that it paradoxically sets the esteem in which a man is held according to his readiness to get himself killed. He gives thanks to the Great King for having put an end to this murderous frivolity with a kind of sumptuary law. For him the duel was a harmful craze. For him the duel – like Racine or coffee in the eyes of others – was on the way out.

There is another way besides using the spoken or written word to express one's thoughts on a social phenomenon, and that is to practise it. Although duelling was commonly considered to be a preserve of the *noblesses d'épée*, we have seen in the writings of L'Estoile and Tallemant that commoners fought duels, against either men of equal rank or authentic members of the *noblesse d'épée*. Before concluding this chapter, we should therefore examine the group of bourgeois duellists and their motivations.

What strikes us from the outset is that we encounter bourgeois duellists throughout the two centuries under study here. Some of them are properly speaking recently ennobled men who want to break with their common origins through a duel and, to the horror of authentic gentlemen, have themselves recognised as members of the gentry or nobility. Zamet, whose quarrel with Bidossan we read of in L'Estoile's writings, was one of these. But this Italian parvenu financier had at least one other duel: he sent a cartel in the purest chivalric style to the most famous swordsman of his generation, Balagny. Another such duellist was the grandson of the great Castilian merchant André Ruiz, himself a lawyer from Nantes who died in a duel. Another, at the end of Louis XIV's reign, was the heir to a dynasty of Rouen merchants, the Legendres. In its origins, alliances and relations, this family belonged to a cosmopolitan and mainly Protestant milieu. The father, ennobled by Louis XIV and also by Charles I of England, was a presiding judge. The son killed a man in a duel. It was possibly to this bloody episode that the men of his generation owed their accession to privileged functions open only to the *noblesse d'épée*. The duellist himself became a diplomat (because a duel necessitated exile), while his brothers were respectively brigadier-general and lietenant-general in the King's armies.

These cases illustrate a certain mentality. The man enriched by commerce, who was also of foreign origin, did not really feel integrated into the aristocracy, even though its members heaped flattery upon him. Like those who were 'assimilated' by colonisation in the twentieth century, he had to comply with the most extreme requirements of this culture in which he was undergoing a laborious, and indeed painful, apprenticeship. He needed to be all the more of a purist in comparison with those to whom this culture came naturally. In order to feel himself to be a gentleman and be recognised as such by the others, he had to be more careful than other people about defending his point of honour. Businessmen who had gained riches and titles and sought to fight duels were not simply illustrating what has been called 'the betrayal of the bourgeoisie'. They display the profound anxiety of individuals at the crossroads between two value systems and whose ontological status is thus undermined. For these men whose status as gentlemen – lacking ancestors and military exploits – was doubtful, such as the Duc de Rohan-Chabot, whose birth was not indisputably legitimate, the duel had kept its role of ordeal intact.

So it is not in the heart of the nobility and gentry but on their fringes that we find the fiercest partisans of the ethic of the point of honour. In a society where money was powerful but condemned and despised by morality, even when honestly acquired, a fortune built on trade and banking was a stain. To bring about the transmutation of the man of money into the man of honour, a kind of alchemical operation was necessary, in which steel dipped in blood purified gold: the duel.

A second category of bourgeois duellists, while making this aristocratic act their own, were not trying to escape their common condition. By the beginning of the eighteenth century, these duels fought by modest members of the bourgeoisie were simply archaic relics which were kept up only in primitive, isolated regions, and involved only older men. Their practice died out with their generation.

The place of the aristocratic values of duelling in provincial bourgeois life is shown in the record of the interrogation of a lawyer called Gousset, charged with killing his colleague Magnan in a duel in 1611. One afternoon they were playing skittles with other bourgeois of their town. The loser had to buy everyone a meal. Magnan lost and requested that payment should be put off to a later date. Gousset agreed to this, but made jokes about those who did not honour their gaming debts (traditional jokes, which had even given rise to a local expression: 'to give alibis'). Magnan became annoyed: By God's death, he was no giver of alibis. The said respondent *had lied*.'* Still, they apologised to each other and all went to the inn. Then, going into the kitchen, Magnan said to his opponent, 'By God's death, if you were a *man of honour*,* you would come and meet me tomorrow at the place called Chaumont-le-Bois.' The dialogue continued with an exchange of harsh words. They parted. Gousset finished the evening conversing with local ladies at the house of a friend, an older man who was thinking of remarrying. Magnan came and made a row under the windows and as a result the evening was spoiled and curtailed. Before returning to his own home, Gousset escorted two ladies to theirs. On the way they met Magnan, who had sword in his hand and said: 'By God's death, you know very well what we have said to each other. I must kill you.' Gousset let go

*Italics FB.

of the ladies' arms, drew his sword, parried and saw his opponent 'impale himself' on his sword. In a most detailed way, this anecdote ties together bourgeois, even folkloric themes (society life in a small bailiwick capital, jokes from the gaming repertory, disturbances perpetrated on widowers who want to remarry), and the patterns and expressions of chivalric honour (quarrels over gambling and women, the utterance of the *démenti* and the oath, the idea of the man of honour, the lofty brevity of the challenge, a meeting fixed without it being either necessary or seemly to state clearly that it was to fight).

In the cultural milieu shown in this tiny news item, two value systems are superimposed, or rather enmeshed. Let there be no doubt: what gave duelling its strength and ensured its longevity was the prestige that it had, not just among those members of the bourgeoisie who wanted to be gentlemen, but even more among those bourgeois who wanted to be bourgeois in a society dominated by aristocratic ideals.

Whether or not they actually practised duelling or remained outside observers, the bourgeoisie had very particular and varied ideas on the subject. However, we can make out certain convergent themes in this plurality; from the heir to the Ruiz family of merchants who did not hesitate to get himself killed to be *recognised* to Molière's M. Jourdain who wants to be 'sure of killing his man and not being killed himself', from the unqualified admiration and support of sixteenth-century commoners to the fascinated horror of the bloody monster which characterises the beginning of the seventeenth century and the ever more determined and open contempt for an outdated fashion of the beginning of the eighteenth, we can trace the overall evolution of bourgeois attitudes.

At first these attitudes are scattered, isolated and partial, then they grow together, becoming coherent in the thinking of Pascal and finally taking hold throughout the bourgeoisie and spreading beyond it.

We shall cite three examples from this last stage where the bourgeoisie exported its attitudes.

In 1648 Vulson de La Colombière published his *True Theatre of Honour and Chivalry*, a book which had a lasting success in aristocratic circles. Tales of duels abound in this book, but they no longer have the value of heroic examples; they are classified chronologically and above all reproduce ancient documents, introducing the archaeological attitude of the erudite free-thinkers to an aristocratic readership. Such an attitude at the height of the Fronde says much about the power relations then operating between families of thought.

In 1662 came a tiny but highly symptomatic event. As an educative example of a syllogism the *Logic of Port-Royal* offered its pupils (and chiefly the young Duc de Chevreuse) a sentence which ended with this proposition: 'Therefore a Christian's duty is not to praise those who fight duels.' This is a long way from the teaching methods of the Jesuit colleges and their indulgence towards single combat.

In 1671 the Académie Française proposed a choice of two subjects for a new poetry competition: 'Either the glory that the King acquired by putting an end to duelling or that which he acquires every day by building up Navigation and Commerce'. The destruction of duelling and the restoration of commerce, the linking of these two speaks volumes.

And so the cultivated bourgeoisie gradually substituted the ideal of the *honnête homme* for the figure of the gentleman. They turned away from duelling, although not without difficulty, and even succeeded in discrediting it among the nobility and gentry.

Chapter 13

A Crucial Collective Trial: The Bouteville Affair, 1627

In the first half of the seventeenth century in France both the practice of duelling and the opposition to it were at their peak. In the middle of this period, halfway between 1602 (first royal edict against duels) and 1651 (formation of the first brotherhood of gentlemen who vowed to renounce duelling), came an event, or rather a collection of events, which crystallises the situation for us: the duels, trial and execution of Comte François de Montmorency-Bouteville.

Between the ages of fifteen and twenty-eight, Comte de Bouteville was involved in no fewer than twenty-two duels. Extraordinarily, he was present rather than absent when tried; more extraordinary still, he was executed by the executioner in the public square. His cousin, Comte des Chapelles. who had seconded him in his last duels, accompanied him to his death. This was an unprecedented event, and nothing afterwards really resembles it.

Bouteville's death offers a unique chance to grasp the deepest significance of seventeenth-century men's attitudes towards behaviour that both frightened and fascinated them.

The first social group interested in the Bouteville affair was that of the gentry and nobility, to which Bouteville and Des Chapelles belonged, and from which almost all duellists were recruited. Among gentlemen – particularly young Parisian gentlemen – the feeling of solidarity with the two condemned men was very strong and far from passive. As early as 24 April 1624, after a duel against Pontgibault, Bouteville and his partners were able to flee the forces of the law thanks to numerous accomplices. Parliament initially investigated two hundred people who had helped them in their flight 'in a coach pulled by six horses', before condemning the duellists in their absence and hanging them in effigy on the Place de Grève. Then, on the night of the 28th, the gallows were cut down by persons unknown and the effigies removed from degrading display. On the 29th Parliament had the gallows re-erected by decree and, indicating where its suspicions lay, forbade 'all lords and gentlemen, their lackeys and all others to go in a group' across Paris. Similar incidents were feared during the 1627 trial and execution, when the consequences would have been more serious. For instead of effigies, it would have been the accused themselves who would have been taken from the grasp of the authorities. Hence the deployment of exceptional forces for an affair which Richelieu simply described as 'singular'. A detachment of more than five hundred soldiers accompanied the coach carrying the prisoners from Lagny to Paris. Three hundred and sixty men surrounded them during their transfer from the Bastille to the Conciergerie, which took place at night for greater security. On the day of the execution, Paris was like a city under siege: chains had been stretched across the streets, six companies of soldiers occupied the Place de Grève and the surrounding area and an order was given not to 'allow any man on a horse to pass'. These precautions were enough. There was no open act of rebellion against the royal decision on the part of the young gentlemen. Their solidarity with Bouteville led them to push as hard as they could against authority, but not to break with it.

The upper echelons of the nobility, including the princes of the blood, were equally resolved to defend the accused, but without going so far as to disobey royal orders. Bouteville was a Montmorency, related by blood and marriage to the most illustrious families in the realm, and the 'relatives and friends' who, in the words of *Le Mercure François*, 'were intriguing and praying here and there', were influential people whose attitudes did not go unnoticed by the public. The Princesse de Condé, the Duchesses de Montmorency and d'Angoulême and Cardinal de La Valette all tried to put pressure on the Minister of Justice and the magistrates. The Marquis de Molac, Des Chapelles' brother, spoke to Richelieu's councillors and to the Cardinal himself. The Comte de Montmorency and the Prince de Condé sent requests for pardon to Louis XIII. Their pleas were addressed as much to the public as to the King: they were circulated in pamphlets and *Le Mercure* reproduced them, along with a 'Reproof from Lady de Bouteville to the King'.

Although neither the *Grands* nor the young gentlemen were able to save the condemned men, they did at least manifest their unswerving and unequivocal loyalty to the two accused, without explicitly opposing the royal will. Within the walls of the Palais de Justice, while the trial was going on, Madame de Condé 'went to the Holy Chapel of the Palais, had six masses sung and took holy communion there'. When Madame de Bouteville and other ladies repeated their request for an audience with the King to make him change his mind, the latter charged Bassompierre 'to go and tell them that they could not see him'. Bassompierre, who had agreed to send three companies of Swiss guards after Bouteville three weeks earlier, refused, saying

'Sire, they are my relatives.' After the execution, the bodies were returned to their families, who laid them out in the Hôtel d'Angoulême, then had them buried 'both in the same vault in the sepulchre of those of that House of Montmorency'.

So the highest nobles demonstrated that they did not repudiate those who received the death penalty for duelling. They also revealed something more. Des Chapelles belonged to the middle stratum of the Brittany nobility; he was related to the Montmorencys only through his mother. It was certainly because he had fought duels in contempt of the royal edicts, because he was the victim of a paritcular royal order, that he received the posthumous honour of lying in the sepulchre of the 'First Barons of France'.

Although duelling was a mark of courage and an inevitable phenomenon in society as conceived of by the nobility and gentry, it was still a crime, even in their eyes. But their requests for mercy show that to them it was a minor crime, 'a simple contravention of civil law, without cowardice against His Majesty, the State or the persons of the dead'. 'The two men have done nothing against the King's person, against the State.... They have violated the King's Edicts.' Here is the distinction which holds the key to the arguments of the nobility and gentry: the King's person, which was sacred and undisputed, was contrasted to the King's edicts, 'new laws ... simply political', 'severe penalties which have never yet been put into practice in any place in Christendom'. The indirect link between monarch and subject, mediated through ministers, magistrates and fallible and changeable laws, was contrasted with the link between man and man, between King Louis XIII and his Comte de Bouteville. For the nobility and gentry the great actions of the latter in the King's armies were more important than his infringement of an edict.

The distinction between King and law and the insistence on Bouteville's personal services indicate that these arguments around a few duels fit into the wider debate on the relations between the monarchy, which was becoming absolute, and the traditional aristocracy. Far from being an individual case, Bouteville's duels were one element in a trial of strength which lasted for about two years. During these two years Bouteville fought the most sensational of his duels; it was also during this time that the King's brother, Gaston d'Orléans, drew the 'Party of Aversion' together, and that Vendôme and d'Ornano, core members of this party, were arrested. Chalais, another member of Gaston d'Orléans' entourage, organised his conspiracy to murder Richelieu during these two years, and was then arrested and executed. Chalais was himself an ardent duellist and Bouteville seconded him on 1 March 1626. This drew him into a series of further quarrels in which Chalais friends were always involved (as both opponents and seconds).

More important than his association with Chalais, Bouteville was one of Gaston d'Orléans' familiars. When Monsieur learned of Bouteville's arrest, he interceded in his favour with the King, the Queen Mother and even the Cardinal, but to no avail. In fact 'it was whispered to him that the King was more angry with Bouteville for having been attached to his service than for his duels and his contempt for his edicts'. This was an exaggerated suggestion. Bouteville was not a man to engage in conspiracies and no such accusation figures in his trial. On the contrary, both his supporters and his detractors praised the way in which he had loyally fulfilled his duty in the army. None the less, the trial of Bouteville and Des Chapelles was in one sense the trial of the whole nobility, who were disconcerted by the way that French society and the royal institutions were developing.

The *Grands* confusedly saw the trial as a symbol of a crisis of conscience on the part of the nobility, while the *noblesse de robe*, traditionally opposed to the *noblesse d'épée*, had a fairly complex attitude to the two duellists. As royal magistrates, they wanted to see lawbreakers punished and the Paris Parliament had already sentenced Bouteville to death twice in his absence. A year earlier, when the King had promulgated his latest edict on duels, Parliament had been prepared to ratify it only with remonstrances because it judged the penalties it set to be too lenient. The capture of the two accused was in fact made possible by the initiative of a parliamentary family. The mother of Bussy (Des Chapelles's victim) was President de Mesmes' second wife, and while the Grand Provost was organising a search for the fugitive duellists in the Montmorency estates on the River Oise, the knights sent out by President de Mesmes caught them many miles away in Champagne. In all this the parliamentarians were following their traditional vocation as servants of the royal will and champions of written law against the expeditious, oral and bloody procedure of the nobility. In the symbolic system inherited from the Middle Ages, the Robe was opposed to the Sword.

But at the same time the parliamentarians lent an ear to the nobility's arguments. According to the diarist Arnauld d'Andilly, they were touched by Des Chapelles's eloquence; moreover they did not forget that condemning the accused meant condemning the memory of President de Mesmes' stepson. In fact all those involved in the duel of 12 May 1627 were put on trial, including Beuvron in his absence and Bussy's dead body (which the family took back from the police). When it came to voting, some members of the court were of the opinion that those accused who were present should be imprisoned for life, but the majority enforced the edict providing for the death penalty. However, Bussy's memory was pardoned and the court decided to defer execution of the sentence until the next day, thus leaving the King a final chance to pardon the condemned. Thus also disavowing the law punishing duels, while at the same time enforcing it. In a furious note to the Garde des Sceaux, Richelieu exclaimed: 'It's a fine thing to be a relative of M. de Mesmes!' and added, after this purely personal explanation: 'Yesterday it was publicly said in the Queen's antechamber that Parliament had made the King and that if the execution went ahead the King would make Parliament.' In this trial of upholders of the point of honour, the magistrates wanted to show – despite the King if necessary – that generosity was a greater virtue than obedience to the letter of the law. Arnauld d'Andilly states: 'The Court knew that there was no black wickedness in the condemned men's crime, but simply an excess of unruly courage.' In this sentence, the attitude of the *noblesse de robe* merges with that of the *noblesse d'épée*.

It would seem that magistrates in the provincial parliaments had a similarly dual attitude to those in Paris. In Aix they showed satisfaction with the sentence. Peiresc, who circulated a copy of the judgement, declared: 'The gentlemen of our Company were gladdened to see it.' But Tallemant des Réaux tells us that 'the councillors of that region are mostly gentlemen. . . . The soutanes of some of them are attached with only one button and they are always fighting, even though they are senators.'

The lawyers, who grew up with the monarchy, became members of the nobility and gentry when the monarchy became absolute. Having long been instruments of the King against the feudal lords, they began to see themselves as a privileged group when they started to distance themselves from the King. But this new aristocracy could affirm its character only by allying itself to the old families (as President de Mesmes did by marrying a Bussy d'Amboise) and respecting those values of the traditional nobility which were in fact most foreign to it. It could not really condemn such an archaic symbol of aristocratic freedom as the duel.

The bourgeoisie and the urban and rural working classes were not involved either directly or indirectly in the duels and trial of Bouteville and Des Chapelles. This did not mean that they were indifferent spectators, at least to the extent that they knew of the events; however, before assessing commoners' attitudes, we need to know how far they were informed.

In Paris, after two years during which Bouteville's duels had been the main topic of many conversations, everyone knew about his trial, if only because of the deployment of forces to which it gave rise. There was a great crowd outside the Conciergerie at the Place de Grève on the day of the execution and 'rooftops and windows were auctioned'. Parisians' interest in the trial went beyond the curiosity felt by all the capital's onlookers for any *cause célèbre* and any execution. Certainly it was a 'spectacle', and, as was traditional for spectators at an execution, they sang 'Salve regina'. But otherwise on the Place de Grève on 22 June 1627 there reigned a silence unusual for such a time and place, 'such a silence that you could hear yourself speak, and as though pity had called for modesty, as seldom happens in the world of men, and stopped the constant flow of people in and out. . . . It was seven o'clock when the bloody deed was done: Paris turned in on itself, continued to pray with tears in its eyes. . . .' At the moment when the execution was carried out, the spectators seem to have been struck by a stupor mixed with fear, seeing the condemned men less as monstrous individuals stained with the crime of *lèse-majesté* and more – from a point of view close to and doubtless temporarily informed by that of the nobility – as innocent victims of an incomprehensible political power.

But the execution was merely an instant of ephemeral unanimity. It was the only point when commoners in Parisian society were on the side of the two duellists. In saying this we are leaving aside the servants, lackeys and coachmen who appeared as witnesses at the trial. Whether or not they were bribed, as the prosecution claimed, it was in their interests to uphold their masters' statements. Furthermore, even if they were disinterested, they were still part of the ideological clientèle of the nobility and reflected the noblemen's point of view (there were duels between lackeys at the Pré aux Clercs). Let us listen instead to a journeyman stonemason, Robert Godefroy. He did not know the duellists, but he was working on the repair of a façade at the other end of the Place Royale when their fight took place and saw it from a distance. His testimony lacked precision in the eyes of the judges; but for us it supplies an essential element, the spontaneous reaction of a journeyman artisan who saw men fighting a duel in the middle of Paris without any preceding quarrel or any other immediately apparent reason. 'He said that the day before Ascension day, at quarter-past three . . . he was astounded to see six people with swords and daggers in their hands fighting three against three.' Duelling belonged to a world that was foreign to him, one which, though it could still amaze, was no longer marvellous.

The amazement of this artisan was a completely passive reaction. The bourgeois merchants manifested an active hostility (apart from their sentimental sobs at the moment of the execution) with regard to these two duelling noblemen who disturbed public order. On 24

April 1624, to prevent gentlemen coming to take down the gallows on which Bouteville had been hanged in effigy, Parliament employed the bourgeois militia and 'charged the inhabitants of the said city to keep weapons in their shops'. The duel put the Paris of the shopkeepers in conflict with the Paris of private mansions.

In the sources we consulted to get an idea of the repercussions among the provincial bourgeoisie – newspapers and *livres de raison* (household account books, in which notable events were sometimes mentioned) from 1627 – only very local events are usually considered worth mentioning. Three extra-regional events are mentioned, however, once each: Monsieur's widowhood (noted in La Rochelle), the siege of La Rochelle (noted in Agen) and Bouteville's trial, cited in an Anjou newspaper. The clerk of the Angers court makes a very brief mention of the execution in a résumé of a satirical pamphlet, and this brevity contrasts with his earlier vituperations against jugglers, the idle and the poor. It seems that for this Angers bourgeois, duellists condemned to death were neither subjects for commiseration nor a social danger; they were rather a spectacular anomaly, merely a nuisance in relation to society as a whole. This single mention is not enough to formulate a theory about the attitudes of the provincial bourgeoisie, but it is important in that it signifies that the execution was a sufficiently exceptional and sensational event to force its way into the usually very restricted scope of provincial curiosity.

There was one region apart from Paris where the repercussions were felt by even the rural population and that was Brittany. François de Rosmadec, Comte des Chapelles, had been born in Cornouaille and had studied under the Jesuits in Rennes, remaining very strongly attached to the province of his birth. His tragic fate touched almost all sections of society. For those who could read French, a genealogy of his family, which was in fact a panegyric on his person, was published in Rennes two years after his death. Laments in Breton spread among those touched by oral literature, expressing an attitude as favourable as possible regarding the prisoners and unequalled in its severity regarding the King. Thus the Cornouaille peasants, those of Tregorre and probably other parts of Brittany, were touched in their deepest sensibilities.

So, among those who knew about the trial, the great majority and most of the ruling classes supported the view that the duellists should not be punished, or at least that a degree of mercy should be shown to them. The parliamentarians' hostility towards them was extremely qualified and ambiguous. The petty bourgeoisie showed more determined opposition, although not inside the Place de Grève. And yet Bouteville and Des Chapelles were condemned and executed, and there was no rebellion.

So we need to look more closely at the group of men who decided on and carried out this 'bloody act'. It was a very small group, consisting of Richelieu, his administrative personnel and the men of letters whom he employed for his propaganda. Their point of view, or at least its public expression, is striking in three respects: their concern for moderation with regard to the accused, their desire to show that the sentence passed on the duellists did not call into question either their integrity or that of the men in power, and the none the less indisputable exigency of their death, as though it were an imperious necessity.

Let us consider their moderation with regard to the accused. The desire to be impartial is striking, whether in a confidential document like Richelieu's 'Advice' to the King, or in an official paper aimed at influencing public opinion, such as *Le Mercure françois*. Two gentlemen cannot have their names sullied and care is taken to make no complaint against them other than that of their disobedience to the edicts on duelling. Arguments in their favour are stressed, particularly those of their qualities as men and their bravery in the face of the King's enemies. The *Harangue given by the Count Des Chapelles to My Lords of the Court of Parliament* was printed 'by permission' and *Le Mercure françois* published letters from the *Grands* in Bouteville's favour, as well as the King's reply. In his 'Advice' Richelieu lists, in skilfully chosen order, but with apparent objectivity, the points in favour of mercy, followed by those justifying severity. 'I prefer', he says, 'to report than to judge.'

Large sections of the public, as we have seen, disagreed with the sentence. This would explain why the case might have been presented in a prudently qualified manner, but does not totally explain the great respect shown for two men who were being sent to their deaths. Government personnel indicated that they were not responsible for these deaths, imputing them to a sort of superhuman fate above the power even of the King. The 1626 edict provides for death by hanging (as if duelling degraded a gentleman to the status of a commoner) and the abandonment of the bodies without burial; however, the King authorised decapitation for Bouteville and Des Chapelles and gave the bodies to their families for funereal honours. The following day, Richelieu addressed his condolences to Comtes de Montmorency and d'Angoulême. In both cases he used the expression 'the accident which has happened to M. de Bouteville'. With this expression and the tone of his letters he signifies once again that he is not a 'judge' in this affair; furthermore he expresses his personal esteem for the deceased and lets it be understood that no one, not even the King, is responsible for their spilt blood. The leaflets produced by official sources at the time went even further. Their immediate aim was to justify the deaths of the accused. To do this they exalted their memories and extolled their virtues. These men, they suggest, were too perfect to remain long in our world; they could no longer find opponents worthy of their courage. There was nothing left for them but to confront death itself, and the vile death they suffered has turned them into heroes, with the scaffold as the instrument of their apotheosis. They conquered death, which will no longer demand from the nobility a bloody tribute of duellists torn from both life and the King's service. Far from being insolent subjects, as they could have been considered as long as they remained unpunished, they served and exalted the King with the death which they accepted and in some sense desired. He is forever in their debt.

From the point of view of the government, Bouteville and Des Chapelles had to be undisputed heroes. They also had to die. 'It is a question', said Richelieu, 'of slitting the throat either of duelling or of Your Majesty's edicts.' In the Cardinal's view it was necessary to perform an almost ritual act through which the nobility would come to understand that what was best in it must disappear for the good of the King's service, without the nobility initiating the holocaust themselves. Richelieu declared that the duellists' blood would be shed 'happily if it can confirm and cement royal authority and extinguish the burning frenzy of duelling'. The extinction of duelling was not the only aim, for in itself duelling was a symbolic means of affirming that the King was not absolute ruler. It therefore required another symbolic act of equal worth, the decapitation of two gentlemen of merit, to impose the new idea of the absolute state. In a pamphlet addressed to the nobility, Bouteville's shadow declares: 'Let my race not take offence that I have died for reasons of state.' The execution of two noble duellists was a founding sacrifice at the birth of that state.

The two gentlemen have left little idea of their own attitude to themselves. The transcripts of their interrogation show them oscillating between confessions and retractions: first one insists on denying the most obvious accusations, then the other magnanimously tries to take all responsibility for actions they performed together. They go through phases of despair, careless light-heartedness, fear and pride. This experience of a criminal trial for which nothing had prepared them reveals in them a fundamental absence of calculation, consistent reasoning and self-control. It shows them to be unstable people.

This instability is like that of adolescents. At the age of about fifteen these men had gone from school to battlefield and duels with no period of transition, and although they had reached the ages of twenty-seven and twenty-eight, they none the less display a lack of maturity which contrasts in the courtroom with the learned wisdom with which the parliamentarians cloak themselves. Youth is an essential characteristic of duellists. Twenty-one of the participants in Bouteville's duels were under twenty-four. According to Bouteville's cousin Montmorency, he had 'the sickness of his age'. Hence, on the one hand, the ludic character of these merciless fights. Arnauld d'Andilly tells how, for their 1624 duel, Bouteville and Pontgibault lacked daggers and so decided to use knives. 'But as one was sharper and a little bigger than the other, they tossed a coin, and the better one fell to Bouteville. The other which fell to Pontgibault was sharpened on a stone by his gentleman while waiting for Bouteville's second; during this time they amused themselves playing leapfrog.' Duelling was a game whose participants did not consider its tragic consequences. Many, Richelieu recalls, had thought that Bouteville 'would have been cured of it by the time he reached the maturity of the age he was'.

A second characteristic linked to youth and illuminating the duellists' instability is that of blind intrepidity. In war as in duels, Bouteville and Des Chapelles never calculated the risks and hurled themselves recklessly into the most dangerous situations. And when, having exposed himself to danger, Bouteville had the upper hand over his opponent, he was happy to let him live. For a gentleman, a man's life had no value: he had no interest either in sparing his own or in taking that of another man.

In an ever more bourgeois world, where economics was increasingly providing the framework for even ethical thinking, the wasteful generosity of duellists was becoming out of place. Such an uneconomic conception of the value of life made duellists into abnormal beings, ill-adapted to the prose of the world and destined for a brief existence. With duelling seen as a type of madness, duellists were pathological cases. Richelieu, considering this view, notes: 'If it is true that this gentleman's crimes are the result of an illness, his proper punishment should be prison, since it is true that, as the scaffold is the proper punishment for the wicked, so prison should be for the mad.' Here the Cardinal's thinking is in advance of his time. The idea of imprisoning duellists as a particular category of madmen would be current in the eighteenth century, but under Louis XIII it was premature and Richelieu did not dwell on it. Chivalric values were still sufficiently powerful for him to prefer capital punishment, which cut short a destiny that was ephemeral in any case and had been herocially accomplished. The autopsy confirmed for the public that nature had itself condemned Bouteville to an early death with an incurable illness.*

After 1624, Bouteville himself seems to have accepted that he was destined for a singular, excessive and ephemeral life. On returning wounded from a duel, he wanted to send out another challenge at once. 'When M. d'Elbeuf told him that he was mad and bedevilled, he replied that he knew very well that his life was extravagant, but that having started off like that he had to finish in the same way.'

We have already noted two elements in the relations between a duellist and his opponent: an atmosphere of juvenile play and an absence of bitterness in victory which did not require the death of the loser. These attitudes are clarified by an examination of the motives for the fights. Bouteville fought a duel against La Contour because he placed doubt on the truth of a story told by the latter, and against Pontgibault because he criticised him 'for pretending that he enjoyed complicated affairs'. Against Luppes it was because he was 'annoyed because a woman called Du Plessis had told him that Luppes was more skilful than himself'. During the trial the court reminded him of his 1626 duel against Thorigny: 'Asked what their fight was about, he said that it was because of a quarrel between their friends.' In this fight (which was fatal for Thorigny), the opponents were not really enemies. So that they could be at their chosen field early in the morning, 'all went together to sleep in an inn called the Galley in the suburb of Saint-Jacques. Comte de Thorigny and Bouteville spent more than four hours in the same bed. Speaking to the Comte, Bouteville told him he had always held him in great esteem and wanted to be his friend.' Bouteville's 'frenzy' for duelling was an effect of aggression without hostility. With him it was a case of fighting not against an opponent but for his reputation.

When he granted the loser his life, Bouteville also gave him his esteem and friendship. In 1625 Des Chapelles, having dispatched Luppes' second, went to help Bouteville finish with his opponent: 'Cousin, do you want me to kill him?' Bouteville replied: 'No, he is a brave man.' Two years later, Bouteville had a fight with La Contour: 'When Monsieur de La Contour fell, Monsieur de Bouteville was very civil about his advantage and they became good friends.' In his last duel, Bouteville behaved in the same way. According to Arnauld

---

Le Mercure français, 1627, p. 454; 'Bouteville's liver was found to be seriously damaged, indicating that he had not long to live.' *The Shadow of My Lord the Marquis de Bouteville . . .*, p. 10; 'My misfortune did not greatly shorten my life, for those who opened up my body found that my noble parts were so damaged that my natural life would not have continued longer than six months.'

d'Andilly, 'he said to Beuvron [over whom he had the advantage]: I could kill you easily if I wanted. – Beuvron said: that's true. – Bouteville replied: I would rather be dead. Saying this, he kissed him, threw down his dagger and ran to separate the others.' The most apt expression of duellists' feelings for their opponents is to be found in Des Chapelles's last *Letters* (whether or not these are authentic is unimportant for our purposes) to Beuvron, who managed to escape, and to his victim Bussy's mother. To the former he wrote: 'My dear friend . . . I am sorry not to have served you better, and perhaps you will think that I did not cherish your friendship enough. But the truth is quite otherwise. I have never had a stronger passion.' Of the Presidente de Mesmes he asks 'pardon for having taken from you your dear and only child, through neither *hatred* nor *vengeance*, as I only ever had reason to *honour* him, but through vain and false *honour*'. For Des Chapelles or Bouteville, duelling was less an experience of hatred and more a school for friendship. The real state of relations between the opponents can be seen in the pointlessness of their quarrels, the ease of their reconciliations and the solidarity they frequently showd in putting the police off the scent. For Bouteville an opponent was not an enemy, he was an accomplice in an initiatory trial for a secret brotherhood of young gentlemen.

Although in its essence duelling was not a confrontation with an opponent, it was a confrontation with the monarch. Certainly, as we have seen, Bouteville was nowhere officially criticised for his relations with Gaston d'Orléans and Chalais: on the contrary both his supporters and his opponents insisted on his military zeal in the service of the sovereign. Why was it so necessary to prove this zeal? Had not Bouteville failed in his loyalty as a subject by ignoring royal edicts? Was he analysing his behaviour sufficiently when he mentioned 'the respect that my actions have violated almost beyond my intentions'? The choice of the Place Royale as the site for a duel weighs heavily against him.

At the beginning of 1627 Bouteville and Des Chapelles were exiled in Brussels. Beuvron jointed them there to settle their quarrel. At the request of the French Ambassador, the Infanta had obtained a reconciliation, but this was simply for show. Once he had gone back to France, Beuvron corresponded with Bouteville and managed to get the two cousins to return to Paris in secret. They stayed near the Place Royale and accepted (or proposed) that the duel should take place on that square. Such a choice for a place to fight a duel was in itself a challenge. The judges asked Des Chapelles 'if he had not chosen that square the better to demonstrate the contempt that he and the man named Bouteville had for the laws and authority of the King'. That square certainly 'was a public place, a place of passage where others had fought before'. However, there was a great difference between such a geometrical, urban space, at that time the largest in the capital and the centre of elegant society, and those places which were the usual theatres for duelling: 'countryside', 'fields', away from inhabited places, undefined spaces beneath the civilised world, close to the beasts and the immediate life of the land. Louis XIII's statue was not put up in the centre of the Place Royale until 1639; but the name of the square already made it the place most explicitly dedicated to the sovereign in all Paris (apart from the palace). The regular layout of this quatrilateral of stone, brick and slate was a representation in the townscape of a social order centred on the monarch's will. The *True Account* indicates that Bouteville and Des Chapelles were 'condemned to death for having sullied and bloodied the Place Royale, which was a venerable place designated for jousts, tournaments, triumphs and spectacles of public jubilation'. Such sublimations were alone compatible with the dignity of the place, and were organised like ballets for the pleasure of the King who presided over them, then reabsorbed into cavalcades in which gentlemen, instead of confronting each other 'one against one', fell into hierarchical rank behind the monarch. To fight a duel on the Place Royale was to reject the conception of a French society made up of orders subordinated to the King; to expose oneself to death and to kill on the Place Royale was to affirm (and, through an extravagantly symbolic act, to arouse) the strength of a society dominated by an aristocracy of equals.

Throughout the trial, Bouteville and his second placed responsbility for the choice of place where the duel occurred on their opponents; but at the very least they agreed to fight there. Even if they did not clearly understand all the implications, this signifies that they had adopted a particular position in relation to royal power which went far beyond the infringement of edicts. They never gave up this position. They, who constantly protested their loyalty to Louis XIII, never expressed any remorse for having disobeyed him. They asked forgiveness from God, their opponents and their families, they did not even forget their creditors, but they never expressed a word of regret to the King. Arnauld d'Andilly records a last prayer that the Comte de Bouteville was supposed to have addressed to God from the scaffold. It is fairly lengthy but contains only one brief mention of the King, which comes at the end, as though it had been added as an afterthought: 'He also commended the King to God.'

This silence with regard to the King is as revealing as the choice of the Place Royale. Like the noblemen who interceded on their behalf, the two duellists made a distinction between the person of the King, whom they served in the traditional way, and the King's edicts, new laws of a new order which they did not approve of. The Place Royale duel was a public repudiation – indeed a negation – of absolutism by the traditional cadres of the realm.

The laborious insistence with which it is repeated that Bouteville and Des Chapelles were loyal subjects is surpassed by an even greater insistence on showing that they were good Christians, or at least that they died as good Christians. The accounts of their last moments are filled with edifying details. In the report of the execution, the clerk of the court records that when he announced to the prisoners that it was time to leave for the scaffold, 'These words were spoken by my lord the Comte Des Chapelles: "You are the angel Gabriel announcing to us the good news which is that of death and we shall pray to God for you." Then he prostrated himself and kissed the ground and prayed.' It is certainly likely that, following the religious attitudes of the time, the condemned men, having no hope left of pardon in this world, did prepare themselves for a good death. They were moreover guided towards a pious end from the beginning of their imprisonment by three Oratorian priests[*], Condren, Gordeau and Fautrat, and by an Oratorian bishop, Philippe de Cospéan. They enriched the ritual of the execution with a nocturnal adoration of the holy sacrament. But such deployment of religious talents and the quantity of almost hagiographic accounts of their end make one suspect that, besides a concern for the eternal salvation of the accused, there was a need for their death to be edifying, and publicly so. It seems that from a religious point of view this spectacular execution would have been useless if the condemned men had not demonstrated an excess of religious fervour. The event had to show whether duelling was simply a sin – serious no doubt, but one which, in isolation, did not challenge the Christian conception of the world – or an intrinsic sign of profound impiousness.

The attitude of the condemned duellists was different from the one they had before they were caught and punished. If we are to believe the Oratorian Séguenot, in their last days they were impregnated with a 'victim's devotion' and accomplished a real Imitation of Christ's Passion for the redemption of duellists. But Séguenot is obliged to admit that Bouteville and Des Chapelles differed in their style of devotion in the face of death: 'The Comte des Chapelles died like a saint, and Bouteville like a Christian.' Richelieu, for his part, says: 'Bouteville seemed sad at this last act, and the Comte des Chapelles joyful.' But Séguenot, Richelieu and the leaflets all insist that, if their styles differed, the condemned men's piety was the

---

[*]The Oratorians were a liberal and rationalist order, founded in 1611. (Ed.)

same. For there had been a rumour that only one of them made a pious end, while his companion 'died like a philosopher ... because he neither moved nor spoke [as he went to his death]'. This rumour was not unlikely. Séguenot admitted that Condren had to work hard at the spiritual preparation of Bouteville, who received:

> things that were said to him with the strength of his mind and his courage and behaved more like a philosopher than a Christian; for his mind was naturally of a rare and excellent cast, he was firm in his reasoning, relying on his own maxims and distanced from common and popular sentiments, and he seemed to have something of the ancient philosophers. All these are qualities that are not very favourable to that grace which is only given to the small and humble.

For the society which saw Bouteville as a paradigmatic duellist, that duellist was (except for miraculous cases of intervention by divine grace) a gentleman who placed all his confidence in his own virtue, a superbly magnanimous man, closer to Epictetus than to the *Imitation of Christ*.

More worrying was the choice that Bouteville made throughout his career to fight on days sacred to the Lord. His two duels against Vaillac were fought on a Sunday. On another Sunday (and the day when Louis XIII signed his last edict against duelling) he seconded Chalais. But his most scandalous duel was the one against Pontgibault, which took place on Easter Day 1624. There was even a rumour, which came up again in the trial and which Bouteville unconvincingly denied, that he had challenged his opponent in church during a service in which the latter had taken communion. Arnauld d'Andilly even adds that, when they drew lots for the knives with which they were to fight and Bouteville got the better one, he shouted: 'I'll take it in the name of the devil!' In his contempt for the sacred nature of divine time as for royal space, and in his recognition – even if only in jest – of the element of devil-worship inherent in duelling which preachers had been emphasising for the last twenty-five years, Bouteville shows himself to have been an impious man. As well as an archaic form of opposition to the monarchial order, duelling was a new attitude of religious rebellion. This implication, which Bouteville incarnated without perhaps perceiving it very clearly, was very lucidly understood by the Catholic elite of the Oratory. The link between duelling, impiousness and free-thinking is suggested in a passage in which Séguenot records the ecstasy that Des Chapelles was supposed to have experienced a month before his death, when it was revealed to the duellist that 'God was taking him as a victim for the expiation of duels ... that

God wanted him to pray on Earth and in Heaven for ... the extinction of duelling, Atheism, the Court's free-thinking practices, and Heresy in France'.

As an unstable person, lacking maturity and unaware of the value of life, lacking in hatred for his opponent, obedience to his King and fear for his God, the image of the duellist that Bouteville offered to his contemporaries was one which had something of both Don Quixote and Don Juan about it.

The radical themes hidden under the debate over whether the two duellists should be punished or pardoned are perhaps best revealed in the Breton language laments entitled *The Comte des Chapelles, Bodeillo* and *Louis XIII's Page*.

Unlike the other documents we have studied, these laments are of uncertain date and the facts they portray are heavily overlaid with fantasy. They were transmitted orally until the middle of the nineteenth century, and were then collected by folklore enthusiasts who were sometimes more imaginative than scrupulous, so we do not know the circumstances and social setting of their composition, nor the ways in which they spread and the changes they may have undergone. The three versions which we have are quite different in detail and in poetic form. However, the structure of the story they tell is sufficiently similar for them to show us a common archetype.

Let us briefly analyse the content of the three versions we have. Bouteville, a gentleman from Ile de France, is totally absent from them. The Breton Des Chapelles is the sole hero, with his sister-in-law the Marquise de Rosmadec. With his sword Des Chapelles has killed the King's favourite 'page', his 'favourite'. This 'senseless action', this 'misdeed', this 'crime', either accomplished in the presence of the sovereign or not, arouses the latter's anger. He throws the Comte in jail and intends him to be put to death. But Des Chapelles's female jailor gets a message through to the château of Bodeillo, where his sister-in-law is giving a ball. The latter interrupts the dancing, has her horses harnessed and hurries to Paris, where she intercedes with 'her cousin' the Queen, or with the royal couple, on Des Chapelles's behalf. She offers the monarchs a ransom: the condemned man's weight in gold; they refuse, on the sole ground that the death warrant has already been signed. The supplicant then changes her argument. In one lament she faints and the King's heart is softened. In the two others she flies into imprecations against the 'treacherous' Queen and the councillor Pierre Moquet, or against the King himself, whom she threatens with war. As a result of an almost miraculous chain of events, Moquet is defeated and the King besieged in his palace. In all three versions, and contrary to the reality of the story, the King pardons Des Chapelles. His sister-in-law brings 'the most handsome man walking in Brittany' back with her to Bodeillo, 'far from the throne where there is nothing but treachery'.

Besides the events of 1627, this depiction draws on the chivalric romances with their two essential themes, single combat between noblemen and the conflict between the sovereign and one of his gentlemen (the role of the hero usually going to the latter). Vulgarised forms of these romances were sources of history (or a mythical representation of history and society) in popular culture; so the laments on the Comte des Chapelles were recent (if not contemporary) reactivations of a traditional theme of peasant legend.

In the specific context of the Breton countryside, this reactivation was not simply a literary phenomenon. The laments express a political stance. Without denying the guilt of the noble duellist, they reject his condemnation to death. They portray the King as an abstract being, without first name or qualifying adjective, against whom they do not permit themselves to pass judgement, but who can be besieged in his own palace. The Queen (like the throne) is given her share of treachery. But hate is chiefly concentrated on the 'lawyer' and the absolutism of the signed document, of impersonal and formalist power. For the peasants who listened to and sang them, these laments signified a choice in favour of their feudal lords and local freedoms as opposed to authority centralised in Paris. From the time of the Revolt of Stamped Paper, through the opposition to the Farmers General and the anti-bourgeois *Cahiers* of 1789 to the revolt of the anti-revolutionary and royalist Chouans, Des Chapelles' home of Cornouaille was a place of conflict between people who lived in cottages and châteaux on the one hand and those who lived in cities and/or supported the King on the other. For the peasantry of a marginal region, impregnated with aristocratic and traditional ideals, the laments which denied Des Chapelles' execution and defeated royal power in vengeance for his death on the level of the imaginary, encouraged and expressed resistance. They were battle hymns.

In the Bouteville affair a whole people saw 'a bloody tragedy for the state': in it the fate of absolutism was symbolically at stake, both in its monarchial aspect as far as the gentry and nobility were concerned, and in its centralised aspect for the peasants.

At the end of this chapter, we should ask ourselves what were the consequences of the sensational Bouteville affair. It is traditional to repeat with Richelieu's *Memoirs* that a 'salutary effect ... followed'. But it must be admitted that this conclusion is at the least an exaggeration. There was no increased fear of punishment on the part of duellists, nor was there a stricter enforcement of the law against duelling on the part of the authorities. Three weeks after Bouteville's execution in Paris, Malherbe's son was killed in a duel in Aix-en-Provence. A few months later in the royal army besieging La Rochelle, Jacques Du Puy states that 'among the gentlemen in the camp there were a number of duels which were very difficult to settle. That shows that the recent examples have not borne the fruit it was said that they would.' Royal severity did not last. Beuvron, Bouteville's opponent, who had managed to flee to Mantua, obtained his pardon two years later. In 1628 Richelieu in person prevented the prosecution of a gentleman who had fought without his permission. The practice continued unchanged of prosecuting only absent duellists and obtaining letters of pardon for them after a few months or at the worst a few years of retreat to their estates or abroad. The execution of Bouteville and Des Chapelles was only an isolated event.

However, it had considerable consequences for collective attitudes. The feeling it caused split French society in two, forcing people to stand up and be counted. On one side were the servants of the monarchy (from Richelieu to the clerk of the court from Angers), the world of civil servants, the bourgeoisie and, to a certain extent, the urban working classes; on the other side were the old aristocracy and its peasants as well as, if somewhat reticently, the *noblesse de robe*. Bouteville's duels, his trial and his death formed the three acts of a socio-drama which made manifest the conflict between the traditional, aristocratic, rural and provincial structures and the new centralising and hierarchical power that in the next generation Saint-Simon was to call 'the reign of the vile bourgeoisie'.

The choice was difficult enough for magistrates who were transforming themselves into gentlemen; but it was devastating for the man who found himself on the very point of the split, King Louis XIII. He already knew that he was the state and he could not forget that he was the first gentleman of the realm. Neither severity nor mercy towards the two duellists could fully satisfy him. He could not be sure whether he would be more of a king by enforcing the law against a subject, or by showing mercy to a peer. By publicly proving – even if it was only once – that duelling was no longer tolerated and that a duellist had no greater prestige than any other lawbreaker, he made a revolutionary and irrevocable choice in favour of the arguments of the state, and against the relations of man to man and chivalric values. He sealed with blood a fundamental choice in the evolution of the monarchy.

The Bouteville affair highlights duelling as a profession of free-thinking faith in man, a rallying cry, an initiatory ordeal for young aristocrats who were not satisfied with the new structures of the state, and a symbolic act which halted the establishment of the new political order of the monarchy. In the execution of the two duellists it shows us an expiatory sacrifice for the lives which duelling had removed from the services of God and the King, and a ritual murder necessary to the foundation of absolutism.

Des Chapelles, in his juvenile generosity, was able to express to his judges both the impossibility of dialogue and the confused but sharp feeling of the fundamental significance of the debate. We shall leave the final words of this analysis to him:

> The said Lord says that, young as he is, he is ashamed to speak in front of grey-haired magistrates, and begs, my Lords, to tell you that if the King has to establish his realm with blood, he will sacrifice himself. But it is true that the Lord de Bouteville is a man full of virtue and that he is full of courage ... and that in ancient times men fought, and this has continued until now, and the Kings of France tolerated it and King François even sent out a challenge.

PART III

After 1650:
The Wane and Its Limits

Chapter 14

The Fronde, or
The Beginning of the End

There will be frequent duels. In relation to this a marriage
must be interrupted.

(M. Questier, Almanach for 1652)

Duels will reign, causing the death of two great captains.
(M. Questier, Almanach for 1656)

A peak reflecting decadence. When a custom is taken to
such extremes, it is because it is under threat.
(J. Berque, *L'Egypte, impérialisme et revolution*, 1967, p. 54)

In the France of the years 1650–2 we appear to be seeing the restaging
of a drama that had already been played out in 1614–15. On the
stage, gathered around the Child–King, the Foreign Queen and the
Perfidious Minister are gesticulating. Around them, captains and
braggarts, all prospective saviours, are exchanging mighty sword
blows. In the wings the people are groaning or complaining, while
the three-voiced chorus of the Estates is chanting its grievances.

As in 1614–15, the general uncertainty has made duelling blossom
and unleashed the fervour of its opponents. As in that earlier period,
much is expected of the meeting of the Estates General. And, also as
before, a devout gentleman proposes setting up a chivalric militia to
fight against the 'frenzy' of single combat.

But even when history repeats itself, it never reproduces itself
exactly and duelling had a different significance in the society of
the time of the Fronde from the one it had in the time of Marie
de Médicis. True, the tone of the chroniclers is similar to that of
L'Estoile forty years earlier. 'Duels this month, and before and since,
very frequent and unpunished', notes Dubuisson-Aubenay in March
1651. And as late as 1654 Guy Patin notes: 'Here all the talk is of
duels in which men have been killed or injured. . . . Among the
nobles there is a great ardour for such cruel fighting over trifles.' The
importance of duelling which they express, in spite of the
multiplicity of events in politics and society, proves that at this time

the phenomenon was an essential component of the social landscape (at least in the capital, courts and armies).

On the level of images and symbols, duellists' heroism was exalted with renewed ardour, in relation, of course, to the political opposition sheltering under the banner of the *Grands*. It was not for nothing that Vulson de La Colombière published his *True Theatre of Honour and Chivalry* in 1648, or that a portrait of Bouteville was engraved and offered to the public in 1650. And we should recall the heroic status duelling conferred on the Duc de Beaufort, royal bastard and 'Protector of the People'. Lastly, we should not forget the associative complex attached to the image of the young David, who killed Goliath with a catapult (*fronde*) in a duel. Frondeurs and duellists, or supporters of duelling, are not synonymous terms. However, they were held together by a very strong link in the socio-political imagination of the generation of the middle of the century.

So interest in duelling, which had gradually decreased over the years 1630–40, was greater than ever. The Church's efforts had come to nothing. Those of the state, which had never had much effect, seem to have been completely abandoned. As Coligny-Saligny, who had five duels to his name, observed, Mazarin 'had plenty of other things to do at the time besides ensuring that the King's edicts were observed'. Gaston d'Orléans, combining as always his political ambitions with chivalric daydreams, wanted to organise a judicial duel and to 'grant the field' to Beaufort and Candalle, while the queen, Anne of Austria, was doing all she could to reconcile them either voluntarily or by force. The Paris Parliament, which was gracious to the princes and rebellious towards the King, acquitted Beaufort, who had killed his brother-in-law Nemours in a duel (not to mention the two seconds killed and one seriously hurt). Indeed the sovereign court ratified without batting an eyelid the 'unsealed' pseudo-letters of remission which the rebel Duke presented to it 'on his knees' as being signed by the King.

This resurgence of duelling and the negligence of the authorities gave rise to counter-offensives.

From 1639 to 1648 nothing was published on duels and points of honour but between 1648 and 1659, six new titles came out, some of which ran to several editions. Certainly this accords with the increasing number of duels. But more than this, it indicates a will or desire to orientate public thinking on duelling in the direction of rejection. For all but one of these writings are explicitly, plainly and unrestrainedly hostile to all forms of single combat. The exception is La Colombière's *Theatre of Honour* and we should recall that this monument to the glory of a defunct chivalry stigmatises contempor-

ary forms of fighting and is always careful to stress the difference
between the prowess of gallant knights and the yen of its readers. In
the last analysis this book is a cathartic rather than an exemplary
exercise.

Popular works on aristocratic ethics, which nevertheless neglected
to mention duelling, were republished at this time, with additional
warnings on the matter. After 1650 René de Menou's *Knightly
Practice*, which had been reprinted unchanged since 1612, was given a
sixth part entitled 'Treatise on ways of preventing duels and banishing the vices that cause them'. From the sixth edition (1653) of his
Testament, or Good Advice from a Father to his Son, Fortin de La
Hoguette inserted an additional chapter, 'On duels, and the remedy
which may be used against them following reason'. In it this ir-
reproachable Catholic, who frequented the circles of the clever and
witty rather than those of the pious, 'confesses' that he has 'twice
been carried away by the torrent of our combats, *like others*'. Injured
the first time and a murderer the second, he owed it entirely to 'a
[victorious] fight with himself' that he had not fought a third duel.

Texts emanating from the civil or religious authorities were also
published: a royal edict of 1651 (with a promise to include the
struggle against duelling in the coronation oath), a declaration by the
Marshals of France, warnings from the doctors of the Sorbonne, a
resolution from the prelates of the Assembly of the Clergy.

There were also individual cases of effective punishment. In
August 1652 the Archbishop of Paris, while allowing the Duc de
Nemours to be buried in consecrated ground, forbade 'public
prayers for him, in his parish ... saying that it was forbidden by the
Church to pray to God for people who had died in this way'. At the
end of the winter of 1654, the authorities prosecuted in a most
spectacular way one of the participants in a fatal duel. Comte
d'Aubijoux fought on the Place Royale; one of the seconds died.
Aubijoux withdrew to Blois and his friend Gaston d'Orléans. The
King gave orders whose severity surprised the marshals themselves.
In spite of solicitations in high places, justice took its course.
Parliament passed the death penalty on the absent accused on 18
March and had him executed in effigy two days later. Much to the
confusion of Monsieur and the King's cousin Mademoiselle,* Aubi-
joux had to go into exile in England.

This relative severity against Aubijoux and the clear return in 1654
to a policy of punishing duelling, in spite of pressure from certain
Grands, can be explained only by the fact that other pressures were

---

*Mademoiselle was the title given to the oldest daughter of the King's brother or
uncle. (Ed.)

being exerted in the opposite direction: 'Messieurs de Fénelon and d'Albon went from door to door turning judges against them,' wrote Mademoiselle, 'almost weeping for shame.' In doing this, Fénelon and Albon were not acting as isolated individuals. They were delegates of an association of gentlemen who were against duelling. Antoine de Salignac, Marquis de Fénelon was the driving force of this association, which was called the Brotherhood of the Passion.

The Brotherhood of the Passion was the chief weapon in the arsenal opposing duels in these troubled years and during the period of return to order which followed them. It was a group of devout men, in many respects a specialised branch of the Company of the Holy Sacrament, and like the latter a secret society. In its earliest form the devout militia was 'a group of a few gentlemen in Normandy' gathered round the Baron de Renty. A lay mystic, who had become a soldier out of filial duty and a duellist against his will, Renty proclaimed: 'My condition is that of a commoner in Christianity.' In the parish of Saint-Sulpice, and with the support of the parish priest Jean-Jacques Olier, he formed a Parisian company. It had six members, one of whom was Fénelon (another of Olier's friends), and was consecrated to St Louis, the King–Crusader and first legislator against duels, who had previously been joint patron with Mary Magdalen of an earlier, unsuccessful anti-duelling chivalric order founded by Jean Chenel de La Chapperonaye.

After the siege of Paris and Renty's death, Fénelon reformed the group and brought in a few new recruits, without the number of members at any meeting ever rising above ten.

At this point it becomes more obvious that the Company of the Holy Sacrament had taken up the group. Patronage passed from St Louis to the Passion – which gave the group a significance that was less political, or differently political, more pious than Gallican, referring more to the piety of the late Middle Ages than to dynastic fidelity. The group's programme of action was extended. The first list of regulations gave as the company's sole aim: 'to discredit and destroy ... the practice of duels'. In the final version of the regulations, 'to abolish the accursed practice of duels' remained the 'first employment' of the Brotherhood, but it had gained others: to fight against blasphemy and new and suspect doctrines, and to prevent disorder at Court and in the army. The Brotherhood members were to use reconciliation as a weapon against duels, of course, but they were also to obtain a commitment from 'those who carry arms by profession' that they would solemnly renounce duelling, and furthermore that they would second or even forestall the secular arm, 'so that no duel of which the Company is aware shall go unpunished'. Provision was made for provincial subsidiaries, but they were to recruit only a small number of members (about fifteen) and were to be ignorant of each other's existence and of that of the mother cell in Paris, with only one or two members maintaining discreet links. For, like the Company of the Holy Sacrament, 'this company will be entirely secret, secrecy being the foundation without which it cannot exist'.

The reduced numbers recruited and the secrecy of the meetings and actions went hand in hand with the amount of publicity given to the results. Fénelon and his noble companions publicly took a solemn oath to renounce duelling and to turn others away from it; this on the Sunday of Pentecost 1651 in the church of Saint-Sulpice, and in the presence of Olier, who was their spiritual director. A few months later the gentlemen of the King's Household were signing a similar text and, here and there in the provinces, gentlemen were making public renunciation of duelling, either in groups or individually, in the presence of their bishops.

In 1655 all the deputies from the nobility and gentry gathered at the Estates of Languedoc did the same thing. A little later the noble order of the Estates of Brittany followed their example and, as in this province every gentleman had the right to a seat, it was made clear 'that in the future no gentleman will be admitted to the Estates nor will deliberate there before he has signed'. A few years later, the Governor of Brittany gathered another 172 signatures.

This result was certainly due to the work of the Marquis de Fénelon and the Brotherhood of the Passion. But who were these men? We have a few definite or probable names in the subsidiaries of Normandy, Quercy and Dauphiné: little-known characters, even when they are definitely identified, and about whom there is nothing to say except that they were gentlemen and doubtless devout. It is easier to get an idea of the Parisian group, the 'brains' of the affair, without, however, being able to satisfy all our curiosity.

Whether famous or obscure, all fourteen members of the Brotherhood of the Passion were gentlemen, and at least four of them of very ancient families. And although the Maréchal de Fabert was lacking a few quarters on his coat of arms, he made up for this by his personal glory. Five of the members we know to have been aged between thirty (Fénelon himself) and fifty-three; so there were no hotheaded young men among them who might have been too quick to speak or to draw their swords, even if their zeal had been devoted to the right cause. At least seven had, or had had, a military career; this was indispensable if they wanted to eradicate duelling from the milieu in which it had taken deepest root. However, we do not know whether they had all accomplished the feats on the battlefield which were indispensable to prove that renunciation of duelling was compatible with courage. Fabert certainly had and Fénelon almost certainly; but we do not know the service records of the others. Apart from Renty and Fabert, there is no proof that any of them had a duelling past.

On the political level, none of them was an out-and-out Frondeur; but, apart from Fabert (and perhaps Montbas), none of them was an unconditional supporter of Mazarin. On the other hand four, or even five (one of which was Fénelon), 'belonged' to Gaston d'Orléans. Halfway between the extremes then, but with support from differing quarters, the group was sufficiently unmarked to act throughout the nobility and gentry without being a hostage for one party. On the religious level at least seven are known to have been members of the Company of the Holy Sacrament, four were actively involved in foreign missions, and at least four – one of whom was Fénelon – had Jansenist friends or sympathies. Their religious involvement was undeniably less vague than their political affiliations, although the former could be seen as a different form of political involvement.

Variety, cohesion and prudence characterised the actions of these fourteen men (and the powerful Company which supported them). Rebelliau eloquently described an example of a local action by the Grenoble brotherhood:

> We use Lesdiguières against and on the town; on Lesdiguières himself we use the King – we should like the government to come down harder against duellists. . . . So M. du Ferrier, Vicar-General of the diocese of Albi and member of the Company, whom we met during a trip of his to Grenoble, will be asked to write to our friends in Paris. And these will induce Louis XIV to write to M. de Lesdiguières, whose zeal will thus be miraculously increased.

The Parisian group used similar tactics. It needed the support of those high Crown officials, the Marshals of France, who had prodigious authority among the aristocracy and in the armies. Fabert represented the marshals in the Brotherhood, and another marshal, Schomberg, was a sure ally. Thanks to their efforts a declaration written by Fénelon was adopted by the Marshals of France: it reiterated the condemnations of duelling, approved all individuals who had solemnly renounced it, and encouraged all the nobility and gentry to do the same. After this martial endorsment, the approbation of the ecclesiastical authorities was sought. Olier worked to obtain a decision from the theologians at the Sorbonne. A few weeks later Solminihac, who was both Fénelon's bishop and one of his close associates, and like him a member of the Company, carried the decision at the Assembly of the Clergy.

It still remained to turn the private, individual step of renouncing duels into a law of the land. To manoeuvre the Regent in that direction the Company had the services of Pierre Paulin, the confessor whom Olier had given to the young King. But his intervention had to be neither premature nor too tardy: it was part of an overall strategy. Olier wrote him the following words: 'M. de Fénelon and I thought it of the highest importance to beg Your Reverence to put off until this Sunday coming his talk with the Queen on the matter of duels, so that, in the meantime, something can be done that is most necessary to make it succeed for the glory of God.' Three months after the oath he had sworn at Saint-Sulpice, the King proclaimed an edict against duels and announced that his coronation oath would engage him to fight them in the same way as heresy. And Fénelon himself collected the promises of the gentlemen of the King's Household.

And when, two years later, Louis XIV's majority was proclaimed, it was the Company who orientated decisions on duels and organised their enforcement: 'King Louis the Great, who has, since his earliest youth, been inspired with an aversion for this great disorder ... entered so strongly into agreement with the Company on this subject' that in his inaugural *lit de justice* he renewed his edict against duels. At the same time he organised the Tribunal of the Point of Honour in the provinces. All that was left was to appoint the personnel. The Parisian group 'took on the task of writing to all the companies so that gentlemen in each province could advise them as to whom MM. the Marshals of France could trust to execute their orders when the need arose'.

A few years later, while Fénelon and his companions were pursuing impenitent duellists one by one, it was a manoeuvre by the same group that obtained the unanimous renunciations of gentlemen in the provincial Estates. In Languedoc the operation was led by the Prince de Conti, Governor of the province, whose 'most intimate friends were members of the company', and who at that time dreamed of nothing but of having himself admitted to it. In Brittany, it was orchestrated by Lamoignon, Royal Commissary and member of the Company of the Holy Sacrament. At the Estates of Béarn, it was obtained by the Governor, the Duc de Gramont; it seems that he was a member neither of the Holy Sacrament nor of the Passion, but as a Marshal of France he had been for several years a *de facto* executor of their decisions. He had even agreed a few years earlier to prosecute Aubijoux, for whom he had 'all the esteem and friendship imaginable'. So he was a sure agent.

When Louis XIV and Mazarin became more reticent with this group of men who used the wheels of the state to advance their policies, the Pope's support was sought. St Vincent de Paul was charged to write to Rome to obtain pontifical blessing for Fénelon's work. Meanwhile the support of that other power, public opinion, was constantly being solicited. *The Destruction of the Duel* was published in 1651 on the initiative of Fénelon's group. Its author, the Carmelite monk Cyprien de la Nativité, was an old friend of Renty's. His work contains the text of the Saint-Sulpice oath and reports of the actions taken by the different authorities during the summer of 1651. It is also a vehement exhortation to gentlemen to make 'holy links between themselves for these exercises' and to join with 'all the brave gentlemen who have crossed themselves as their predecessors did, saying, *God wills it*, to destroy duels'.

Among other publications very probably initiated by Fénelon's group was *Christian and Moral Arguments Against Duels*, which first appeared in 1653 and ran to several editions. This text was signed 'Vantadour, canon ... of Paris', but at the time everybody knew that this clergyman was none other than the Duc de Levis-Ventadour, who had been the King's Lieutenant-General in Languedoc. And the initiated also knew that since its foundation he had been the man in charge of the Company of the Holy Sacrament.

What an impressive orchestration of capabilities, aspirations and responsibilities! Let us try now to assess this collective and concerted effort against duelling in terms of its two essential achievements: the renunciation campaigns and the setting-up of Brotherhoods of the Passion.

When looking at the renunciation campaigns, we should beware of being fooled by spectacular events. Group decisions are not necessarily the most sincere and lasting, even less so unanimous ones. Pressure and manoeuvring reduced their spontaneity and out of the hundreds, maybe thousands, of gentlemen who renounced duelling between 1651 and 1656, it is more than likely that a certain number later accepted a challenge, challenged others and even fought duels. After a few years, obstacles to the actions of the Company of the Holy Sacrament blocked the efficacy of this gesture.

That said, the oath of renunciation, although not a supreme remedy, was certainly a very effective medication for the state of mind of people who carried arms by profession. To men for whom being called a liar was unbearable and for whom truth always manifested itself in terms of an ordeal, swearing an oath, or giving their word, were very constraining acts. After 1651 the shame of an insult was possibly preferable to the shame of perjury. And this was the case even outside the restricted circles of activists which had been set up by the Marquis de Fénelon. The Duc de Navailles, who was challenged in 1660 by the Comte de Soissons, 'as a Christian refused to fight, and also did so out of the respect he bore for the memory of the late Cardinal', Mazarin. And in her *Memoirs* Madame de Motte-ville stated: 'By the grace of God and the efforts of the King and Queen, the most valiant men no longer held it shameful to refuse a duel, and he who did so on that famous occasion, a man whose worth cannot be doubted, gave abundant proof of this.' It was now possible to refuse a duel for reasons of conscience without being considered a coward. Nevertheless, it was necessary first to have a well-established reputation for valour.

The groups affiliated to the Parisian Brotherhood of the Passion deliberately had very few members. We do not know how many of these groups there were in the kingdom, nor how active they were, and they were gradually extinguished along with everything else connected with the Holy Sacrament. During the summer of 1659 the subsidiary of Bas-Quercy still held monthly meetings, but there were never more than two or three members present. However the most important thing was that a small, hard-line group of gentlemen were sufficiently convinced and fervent to proclaim publicly not only that they would work to reconcile quarrellers, not only that they had forbidden themselves to fight duels, but that they were ready to fight against the practice by every means they could, including informing on duellists.

The 'holy conspiracy of these Christian heroes' first consisted of casting aside all those things that were marks of heroism, not just in aristocratic or military circles, but in society as a whole. They preferred informing to challenging and masks to plumes, they put up with incomprehension, mockery and contempt and they were pre-pared, if necessary, to pass for spineless hypocrites. Condé was said to have given Fénelon the cold shoulder as a result of his early efforts, while Mademoiselle, outraged by the implacably meticulous steps taken by Fénelon and Albon against Aubijoux, wrote: 'People were surprised that gentlemen of quality should thus insult an unfortunate and no one thought that there was any charity in treating him as they did.'

The actions of this tiny group of men involved daring to cause a scandal and being sufficiently self-confident to compromise the public authorities at the same time as oneself. They were a tiny minority of the aristocracy, but an 'active minority' if ever there was one, and their difference testified to a change of attitude which was gathering pace at the time. The charity which they claimed inspired them was not to be confused with generosity. They claimed to be inspired by the Crusades, but this in order to carry out policing operations. These valiant men who would have nothing to do with valiant actions – like the Port-Royal saints who would have nothing to do with miracles – these society men who were not priests but disregarded the sword, or Baron de Renty, who proclaimed himself to be 'a commoner in Christianity', were determinedly mixing together the three orders of society. They were erasing from the imaginary sphere (from their imaginary sphere, for the moment) the three orders of Christendom and exalting in their place the public order of the Most Christian Realm. In destroying 'the idol of duels', they were the prophets of the absolutist cult of Leviathan, as propounded by Hobbes.

In the short term, duels were an emblem of the Fronde. For the gentry and nobility (but also outside them), duels were still symbolic gestures affirming the proud vitality of an aristocracy resisting the direction in which monarchial order was moving. The Fronde was, among other things, an aristocratic revolution whose supporters drew their inspiration from – among other more or less vague ideals and doctrines – the exaltation of a mythical past of heroism and valiant deeds. As one historian today has said 'The Fronde remains a period of imprudence and exaggeration,' and, as a contemporary of the leaders of the Fronde said, 'With their courage, almost all of them would doubtless have beaten the twelve paladins if they had found something to fight about.' These times of trouble and contradiction, these times when chivalric romance sometimes took the place of political ideology, were bound to have been a golden age of duelling.

But this late golden age was the last. Like other periods of social and moral tension, the Fronde anticipated the future at the same time as it reanimated the past. In the long term what was significant was the Brotherhood of the Passion and the signing of public renunciations of duelling. On a deep level, history is not made with conspiracies, and attitudes are not changed by the waving batons of invisible conductors; but it is because attitudes change that conspirators can meet and conductors come forward. The actions of Fénelon and his companions has a revelatory role for us. It shows us changes which were not clearly perceived by those experiencing them: theirs was no longer the time of Etienne Pasquier's *Gentleman*, even less that of Castiglione's *Courtier*. Theirs was the time of Yves de Paris' *Christian Gentleman*; the times to come were those of Baltasar Gracian's *Courtier*.

From a long-term point of view, the fervour for duelling of those living at the time of the Fronde was like the pathetic last gasp of the dying. 'All the nostalgia of an end was contained in this exaltation.*

---

*The expression used by A. Dupront to describe the atmosphere of holy war engendered by events at Lepanto ('Le mythe de Croisade. Etude de sociologie religieuse', unpublished thesis, 1959, vol.3, ch. ix, p. 19).

Chapter 15

The Personal Reign of Louis XIV, or An End Which Is No End

Justitia regis optimi Singularum certaminum Furor coercitus

(Commemorative medal, 1679)

'This horrible custom lasted until the time of Louis XIV,' stated Voltaire. 'The eradication of duels was one of the greatest services rendered to the country [by the Great King]. His happy severity gradually corrected our nation, and even the neighbouring nations, who conformed to our wise customs, after adopting our bad ones.'

In saying this, the historian and philosopher was merely reiterating an opinion that was almost universal among writers at the time of Louis XIV. The poets vied with each other in repeating it. At the beginning of Louis' personal reign (1664), Molière wrote:

Un duel met les gens en mauvaise posture
Et notre roi n'est pas un monarque en peinture
Il sait faire obéir les plus grands de l'Etat.
Et je trouve qu'il fait un digne potentat.

(A duel puts people in a bad position
And our King is a real monarch, not a picture
He knows how to make the highest in the land obey him.
And I think him a worthy potentate.)

These enthusiastic poets had stipends from the King. However, the sentiments expressed by prose writers were no different. This impressive contemporary consensus can be summed up in two statements, whose sound basis needs checking: duelling died under Louis XIV; duelling died because of Louis XIV.

Certainly the King had a deliberate and lasting policy against duels, duellists and their accomplices, which manifested itself in the passing of laws. In 1679 Louis signed one of the longest and most detailed edicts to appear on the subject, with thirty-three pages and thirty-six articles. Prepared with great care, it breaks with all its predecessors in both tone and content. The preamble does not bother with moral and religious considerations and, in particular, the King does not appear in it as the first nobleman of the land, acting on the advice of his peers; he is the autocrat who decides after consultation with experts, 'on the advice of our Council and from our own certain knowledge, full power and royal authority'. The opinions of the princes of the blood or of the high officers of the Crown are no longer mentioned and the Marshals of France give theirs only when the monarch expressly seeks it: 'the King having asked [them] to meet'.

The 1679 edict roused the judges. It obliged the governors and prosecutors regularly to send information to the King on the state of quarrels and fights which had taken place in their *départements*. It insisted on the irremissibility of the sanctions: the duel was an infringement of the 1670 criminal law decree; it was not subject to limitation, and suspended limitation in relation to any other crimes committed by the duellist. But the edict was in no way innovatory in terms of the punishments set down for the different categories of criminals. It was in fact a detailed regulation of both judicial procedure and the management of the accused's property prior to conviction. Its aim was not to launch a new offensive against an action defying the authorities, but to clarify the legislation previously set in place and to harmonise with the provisions of the criminal law decree of 1670. So it is an empty question to ask whether Louis XIV was more or less severe in this edict than his predecessors. The only body of laws to which the 1679 edict belongs is that of the great juridical codes of the decade from 1660 to 1670.

Other legislative texts of Louis' reign relating to the point of honour and the prosecution of duellists are written in the same spirit. Basically they are about the allocation of the guilty men's property and – in an effort to build up a disciplined army – the sanctioning of one of the typical crimes of military insubordination. It was a carefully made effort, sustained over a long period, and Louis XIV recognised its effectiveness in one of the last texts that he signed: 'We have had the satisfaction of seeing these disastrous combats which used to be practised in our kingdom cease almost entirely.'

It appears from everyday administrative correspondence that the royal directives were impressively well enforced. Starting in 1679, the bishops were charged with 'sending notes' to Court 'of all duels and private combat' which took place in their dioceses, with a retroactive list concerning the ten or twelve previous years. Colbert, the King's Chief Minister, 'carefully and surely' saw 'that the edicts concerning duels were executed in all naval dependencies', and kept a close watch to ensure that all altercations between officers which took a form approximating to a duel were energetically prosecuted.

Where necessary he got his information from unofficial informers, and rebuked this or that intendant who had tried to minimise any such incident in his report. In 1666 Le Tellier, who was in charge of the army, sent out a circular to all the governors of frontier regions with the aim of arresting the author of a challenge and duel, although the latter had not been bloody. In 1688 Colbert's son Seignelay, Minister for the navy, gave written instructions to the First President of Parlilament to prosecute two duellists of very important families, 'not wishing the quality of the guilty men to prevent the execution of the edicts'. In 1700 and 1712 Pontchartrain, the Intendant of Finances, reminded public prosecutors that it was necessary to be severe 'on the simple rumour of a duel', without other proof.

One anecdote clearly shows how the King was backed by the whole state apparatus in a concerted crackdown on duelling. In 1676, two friends of Louis XIV's brother Monsieur, Chastillon and Fiesque, were generally known to have challenged each other, to have met 'by chance' and to have been 'happily separated before their valour had done them further harm'. They tried to hush up the affair. But Seignelay sent instructions to Harlay, the Public Prosecutor, authorising searches 'even in the Louvre and the Palais-Royal'. 'On behalf of the King' (*sic*), Monsieur required the Public Prosecutor to go to Saint-Germain to ask the King to suspend the proceedings; to do this Harlay insisted on an 'express order from the King'. The guilty men were apprehended and prosecuted. To make an example and to break Monsieur's arrogance without being disrespectful to the royal family, Parliament, in accord with the Chancellor, resolved to 'punish this fight more by the severity of a long investigation and an exact and rigorous inquiry than by that of a definitive ruling'. Meanwhile, Louis XIV was draping himself in the attitude of an ancient Roman: 'His Majesty was so convinced that his conscience, his honour and the good of the state obliged him to have his edicts against duels enforced, that if it happened that M. le Dauphin or Monsieur His Majesty's brother contravened them, His Majesty would not spare these persons who were so dear to him.'

Prosecutions for duelling were no longer exceptions. The prison registers of the Conciergerie, which are almost silent until 1650, reveal eight incarcerations for duelling in the second half of the century, the Paris Parliament, sitting in secret, turned its attention to this type of cause and the criminal archives of the supreme court show us sixty-three sentences for 'duel', 'challenge to a duel', 'adviser' or 'accomplice in a duel', which gives an average of four or five affairs a year.

Most of the sentences were passed on living, present defendants and those playing a minor role in duels no longer escaped prosecution. The majority of those charged were involved in duels in which no one was killed: some of these were *Grands*, like Prince d'Elbeuf, or courtiers like Chastillon and Fiesque, others were obscure soldiers, and even civilian commoners. All these observations – along with the relatively moderate sentences – tend to prove that the crackdown on duelling had now become an accepted part of life and that the law enforcers were vigilant and effective, justifying Voltaire's opinion with which we opened this chapter.

Not everyone agrees with this view, however. *The New Century of Louis XIV*, published during the French Revolution, states: 'This was a mistake due to Voltaire's enthusiasm for Louis XIV. The only thing this Prince really put an end to was the practice of seconds. Gentler manners had diminished ardour for duelling: but this barbaric practice still lives on throughout Europe.' We shall bear this in mind as we continue our investigation of the three agents of the crackdown: the judges, the ministers and the King.

First, below is a table of sentences actually enacted at the end of trials begun between 1661 and 1700, some of which, as we have seen, were begun in a style of implacable severity.

Acquitted and released	15
Absent or in effigy	14
Corpses and memories	3
Convicted and executed	1
Insufficient information	1
Remission	3

These figures overturn our first impression: although proceedings were started mainly against present and living defendants, they were seldom concluded according to the severity of the decrees. And the single convicted man to be executed 'with a sign in front and behind bearing the word duellist' was an obscure painter who had murdered a groom.

Next, a nineteenth-century investigation into the activity of the judiciary in a garrison town found that 'in the dossiers of the senechalsy of Brest one comes across a fairly large number of cases of duelling, but incomplete proceedings lead to the suspicion that they were abandoned or had a negative outcome, even in the cases of the most humble combatants'. And after 1695 the Paris Parliament seems to have preferred to drop charges on the grounds of 'insufficient information', rather than proceed to the conviction without proof required by law. Public knowledge, without proof, was sufficient to begin a duel trial, but the supreme court was loath to convict or acquit a man accused in such conditions; it preferred to release him and bury the affair. Practices which might be expected to have become outdated were still current. In duel trials prosecution of any dead men was often omitted. A corpse which had not been removed by friends or relative (which was therefore supposed to be dragged along on a rack, hung by the feet and thrown on to the rubbish dump) was taken to the Conciergerie, and without any further form of trial was buried in the cemetery of the Innocents. Those convicted in their absence stayed on their estates, or came back to Paris without proceedings against them being reopened. Defendants in cases of fatal duels found themselves convicted of unpremeditated, and indeed involuntary, murder and, while the legislation put encounters in the same category as formal duels, judges were eager to reduce a duel to a chance encounter, so that even when the trial ended in a death sentence the way was left open for a pardon.

Though less indolent than the judges, the ministers were equally lenient, sometimes more so. It was Colbert who advised an intendant to hush up an old affair which had been revived by 'the violent proceedings' of a provost. It was Seignelay who, while ordering a search of the musketeers' residence to find a duellist's corpse, refused to authorise their valets to make statements. It was Pontchartrain who put the brakes on the Breton magistrates' ardour when a duel trial seemed about to become a political incident: he wished the court to decide that it had been an encounter and not 'a real duel'.

These instances of indulgence on the part of the ministers did not undermine their judgement of the crime itself; their leniency favoured only those criminals with whom they had links, or else it was dictated by consideration of the overall circumstances. As for the King, his indulgence contradicted his much vaunted resolution, and possibly went further than that of his collaborators. Louis XIV, who appeared inflexible over the matter of the Prince d'Elbeuf's duel in June 1688, 'judges' in September that the proceedings, in spite of 'all the necessary diligence', have not found 'any evidence against him' and therefore 'that there [is] nothing which prevents [the judges] from deciding in favour of his acquittal'. Unlike his predecessors, he did not grant batches of pardons to mark the victories, weddings and births dotted throughout his long reign and even refused the entreaties of a pope to break his oath never to pardon a duellist; however, he granted individual letters of remission to duellists of all social positions. He did not tolerate duelling within the army; however, according to the Comte de Toulouse, he did not accept in his own regiment officers who placed discipline above honour. And to settle international conflicts, he let it be understood that he was prepared to meet the Emperor in single combat.

So behind the official façade of rejection and intransigence there were still duellists at Court, in the army, in Paris and even in the trade associations. Some still went unpunished, others still found lenient judges and sometimes a conniving King. Have we in our turn become the victims of a gigantic illusion? Have we been, to use anachronistic language, intoxicated by government propaganda, by the psychological action departments of Versailles?

Not exactly, or rather not solely. We are beginning to see that, in the period between the end of the Fronde and the Revocation of the Edict of Nantes, the opposition did not give up their arms so totally and order did not reign so undisputedly as the Bourbon Leviathan proclaimed. All the same, the latter's repetitive language was an excellent example of political pedagogy. When aspirations towards peace and order became generally widespread, and when the King went round repeating 'all's well everywhere' like a master of auto-suggestion, people paid no attention to dissonant signs and felt a deep sense of peace. So duels no longer existed because it was proclaimed that they no longer existed.

The result was more convincing because government action (or government language) against duelling was only adding to a trans-formation of manners, a moral evolution which both preceded and overtook it. People were no longer interested in duelling as a concrete and articulate reality. Let us recall here the attitude of the casuists after 1650: either they smartly condemned duelling in an unqualified sentence, or else they did not even mention it. The narrative sources which tell us of 164 affairs of honour in the first forty years of the century show us only 42 for the years 1661 to 1700. In the same period *La Gazette* and then *Le Mercure galant* do not mention them once: they were no longer a subject of interesting news or of sensational jurisprudence. Duel and honour disappear from the booksellers' titles, manuals of aristocratic savoir-vivre hardly mention them and only Courtin devotes a slim volume to the *Point of honour* (1675) in the guise of a sequel to a *Treatise on French Civility*, which he had sucessfully published three years earlier, while Guillet de Saint-Georges does not give a single line to duels and honour in his *Arts of the Swordsman, or . . . Gentleman's Dictionary* and the playwrights abandoned this previously commonplace mechan-ism of dramatic action. So even if single combat was still practised, and concerned the administrators, it was no longer of any real interest to the public. In the words of *The New Century of Louis XIV*: it was not the Sun King, it was the 'gentler manners [which] diminished the ardour for duels'. Duels no longer existed because no one talked about them any more – except for those who proclaimed that they no longer existed.

Louis XIV was hardly more successful than his predecessors in his action against duelling. Perhaps he did not really want to be so. But he appropriated the beneficial effects of the duel's great loss of importance during his time. Whatever the statistical importance that it retained, duelling, in the eyes of those who created and proclaimed social values, was nothing more than a fossilised phenomenon. Bourgeois men were less and less interested in dying like gentlemen; and gentlemen were thinking more and more like members of the bourgeoisie. From La Rochefoucault to Saint-Simon, a new type of aristocrat was becoming established: an aristocrat who had not been invented by Versailles, who moreover did not lack greatness and courage, but who had given up ardour, impatience, the immediacy of appearance and a certain generosity.

One author who resembles a French Baltasar Gracian, the Capuchin monk Yves de Paris, gave this new elite a bible, his *Christain Gentleman*. In it he advises the young man who arrives at Court not only to flee the 'pernickety hotheads', but also to be reserved in speech and to find a powerful protector 'who looks after his interests and shows he will defend them like his own; [this person's] reputation will shelter his own from a thousand quarrels'. He even advises him, if he receives an insult, not to avenge himself or to forgive, but to wait and dissimulate.

'If you are certain of your valour,' the Capuchin goes on, 'do not fight duels!' In these times the truly valiant saved their valour and the man who knew his own worth did not believe what others said about it. It was of little importance whether or not men fought duels, if they got no recognition for it.

Chapter 16

After Louis XIV, or An End Without End

It would be a shame for France if the practice of duelling were completely eradicated.

(Coustard de Massi,
History of the Duel in france, 1768, p.39)

French society must stop preventing duels that have just causes.

(Guizot, *Speech*)*

On 22 April 1967, the military coup by which the colonels had just seized power in Greece had to compete for the front pages of the French daily papers with a duel: 'The duellists: Defferre wins by two touches to none' (Paris-Presse, L'Intransigeant); 'Duel in Neuilly: G. Defferre touches R. Ribière twice' (France-Soir). Having been printed the night before, *Le Monde* reported the duel only on page 24, under the heading 'latest news', but gave three full columns to the fight, which was the conclusion of a rather heated parliamentary debate. However, a private radio station boasted that it had transmitted the echoes of the fight 'almost [*sic*] live'.

The scenario put forward by the press was not very different from those of the time of Balagny and Bouteville. There had been a public 'quarrel' and an 'insult': the Mayor and Deputy of Marseilles, who was a member of the opposition, had twice called a former Prefect who was now a deputy for the majority an 'idiot' (*abruti*). The President of the National Assembly, like a point-of-honour judge, tried to reconcile them; but he 'failed'. The offended party chose the weapons; this high-ranking civil servant, when reminded of sections 309, 310 and 311 of the Penal Code, said, 'Honour is above the law'.

The protagonists were accompanied not by seconds, but by two witnesses and a doctor. One of the witnesses said nostalgically, 'I should have liked it if the witnesses had fought too, like they did in the time of the musketeers.' Another witness, an important member

*Cited by Juverger de Saint Thomes, *Nourean Code du duel*, Paris, Dentu, 1887.

of the Council of State, 'climbed over the wall' round his home to make the material preparations for a fight which had to be discreet as it was against the law. 'Rivière eluded the police' and 'M. Defferre left his house hidden in the boot of his car'. The fight took place outside the city walls of the capital 'on the lawn of a Neuilly garden', 'in the garden of a large, derelict house'. 'They fought in white shirts, with open collars and rolled-up sleeves', 'without ties'. The point of Defferre's sword touched Ribière's arm on two occasions. The second time 'blood flowed; the insult had been washed away'. 'Two scratches, and each was satisfied.' The combatants were separated at once. 'They run the risk of between six days and five years in prison,' 'but in practice the public prosecutors almost never act in such cases'.*

This review of the press, taken from *La Croix, Le Figaro, France-Soir, L'Humanité, L'Intransigeant, Le Monde* and *Paris-Presse*, shows that nearly three-quarters of the way through the twentieth century there was still an audience for the story of a duel, a story whose framework – if not its heroes – had been fixed for centuries. It was the story of an extremely rare event in normal contemporary life, a tragicomic story, but one whose 'ridiculousness' is emphasised by only two newspapers (*France-Soir, La Croix*) with an abundant supply of adjectives. For us the main significance of this story is that it demonstrates the long-term survival of duelling. This social phenomenon resisted Church condemnations and state prosecutions. It lost its moral virulence and political audacity in the change of values, or rather the new balance of values, which was established in the middle of the seventeenth century; but it never disappeared from French society, or ceased to interest that society.

The last three centuries show us three stages in the ever more tenuous, but never ending survival of this wear-resistant, anachronistic duel. We shall begin with the eighteenth century, which appears as a very faithful, but considerably weakened echo of the seventeenth.

At their coronations Louis XV, Louis XVI and even Charles X took the anti-duel oath that Louis XIV seems to have avoided at his own coronation. Again at his coronation, Louis XV promulgated a final edict. And as late as 1784 the First Lieutenant of the Con-

---

*Most of the newspapers stress that the loser had brought 'filed down' swords, which his opponent had substituted with good blades. And also that the winner had refused to shake hands with the loser. Only *Le Figaro*, in a jocular tone, and *La Croix*, in an embarrassed style, mention that Ribière's wedding ceremony, scheduled for the day after the duel, had been cancelled: the Church could not give its public blessing to a duellist, who had been *ipso facto* excommunicated a few hours earlier!

stabulary published a body of legislation on duelling, challenges and insults. The point-of-honour court was honourably if not abundantly active: it began at least 624 trials between 1725 and 1790. Half the jurisconsults of the time devoted a few lines or a few pages to this 'crime which is most contrary to Christian religion, and among the most disastrous to civil society and to the state'. The courts often prosecuted duellists, but hardly ever punished them. The most famous philosophers condemned 'this horrible practice' and from time to time the academies, both Parisian and provincial, devoted their debates to this outdated and irrational, but still current phenomenon.

Anecdotes abound of obscure and famous people who faced each other in regulated fights. Many of these people were gentlemen and most of them were soldiers. But duelling never became the preserve of any one order, caste or socio-professional group, while its prestige and the glory of the duellist always overflowed outside the circles in which duels were practised. In the Paris of *la douceur de vivre*, the Opera audience gave a hero's welcome to two princes of the blood who appeared in their box after fighting each other in the Bois de Boulogne. In a small Languedoc town people began crowding at their windows several hours before a fatal duel between two local notables. Here let us quote Nicole Castan: 'No one wanted to separate them, as would have happened in an ordinary quarrel; moreover, the old criminal judge in person shouted "Don't go near them, leave them alone" . . .; their audience, by their silence, showed that the two of them had an imprescriptible right to settle their quarrel in this way.'

One reason for the strength duelling retained in the eighteenth century was that it was an obligatory part of the life of a knight. Knights were an essential social type in the high society of the time and the most celebrated of such knights, Casanova, owed almost as much to his success as a swordsman as to his success as a seducer. Indeed he wrote a short work, *Il duello*, the only autobiographical piece he published in his own lifetime.

In the nineteenth century, the duel was primarily linked to military practices. 'It is part of the moral inheritance of the army,' said one connoisseur. It was present in every arm, even the infantry, which was the least prestigious; career officers of all ranks, even commoners, practised it. However, duelling was also alive and well in another section of society, that of men whose profession was public speaking: lawyers, journalists and above all members of Parliament. There were a fencing room and masters at the Palais-Bourbon, just as there were near the barracks, and it was not rare for politicians to go from a debate in the House to a combat on the field. Lamartine, Cavaignac, Gambetta, Clemenceau, Déroulède and Jaurès were among the most famous. A man who performed brilliantly in a fight was assured of the esteem of his companions-in-arms and a flattering reputation in the salons. However, he also had to leave the fight unscathed. At this time duels were more often fought with pistols than with swords and were potentially fatal. Although it was generally agreed to call a halt at the first blood, still men did die in duels.

Although between the wars of the Empire and the First World War duelling seems to have been far more marginalised than before, it gave rise to a literature on codes of honour which had never previously existed in France and had disappeared in Italy after the middle of the sixteenth century. The quantity of titles and the sometimes luxurious quality of production prove that this literature was very successful. The military and political worlds to which duelling was then confined had such moral and social prestige that it could not fail to reverberate through the rest of society.

After the 1914–18 war, formal duels became rarer in the French army and then disappeared from it altogether. Parliamentary duels put up more successful resistance, but lost their frequency. Although Defferre, the Minister, fought two duels, a great number of the Chamber's leading lights had long political careers without a single cartel. The record for duelling – a low one moreover – passed to another social group, that of the entertainment world. In this world challenges were almost a professional obligation and individual susceptibilities a publicity tool. Men were called to duels and they sometimes went to fight, but they never killed each other. The most widely publicised fight was that between the dancer Serge Lifar and the Marquis de Cuevas in 1958.

However, the duel still lives in forms which may be bastardised and vulgarised, but which retain the essential elements. As an illustration, we should like to recount the following true story. There was once a private in the marines who was displeased with the attitude a captain showed towards him. He challenged him with the ritual: 'Take off your stripes and come outside!' The Captain took off his shirt, which bore the insignia of his rank, and went outside to 'explain himself' to his subordinate with his fists. For the spectators this confrontation was, as always in such cases, a joyful and serious test of *esprit de corps*. Hierarchy and obedience were neither contested nor abolished, but they were suspended. Need we add that the man who came out on top was the officer? He was a calm giant and keen rugby player, while his opponent, a veteran of the colonial wars and an inveterate alcoholic, was just a little runt senile before his time.

The duel also lives on in the collective memory, that conservator which recreates as much as it transmits. Let us recall Comte des Chapelles' fights, which, historically speaking, ended tragically in 1627 but which, in the sung memories of Brittany peasants, lasted until the middle of the nineteenth century. The story of another, much less famous duel, involving an Agen nobleman of Louis XV's time and attributed to one of the latter's decendants, a peer under Louis-Philippe, was still being told by old men in the 1930s, at which time a local scholar collected the story and its variants and transmitted this past to a new future.

Finally, the duel still lives in and through works of the imagination, such as swashbuckling historical novels, or the epics of the American West (in the form of books, serials, cartoons, films and television programmes). This output maintains and strengthens images of single combat and a general understanding of circumstances in which it is the only possible outcome, of the need it fulfils. It is also a response to public expectation and nostalgia, and doubtless to a similar need secretly felt deep within. The duels shown and related by present-day means of communication may be referring back to a golden age of French chivalry which is gone forever, or to the exotic birth of a tough nation whose culture dominates the horizon of our world. But whatever the distance separating the mythical image from the viewer's everyday life, a link still exists at a fantasy, and therefore privileged, level between these scenes and their audience.

So since the time of Louis XIV duelling has been an increasingly buried phenomenon in France; but it has had sudden periods of revival which have brought it to the surface of society for a few years. The time of the Regency, during Louis XV's minority, and that of the Revolution were two such periods.

Duels came back into fashion during the Regency. The Duc de Richelieu, among others, carved himself a fine reputation from them. The numbers dealt with by the Paris Parliament swelled, but were treated no more severely than before: there were fifty between 1715 and 1724 as opposed to thirty-two in the previous decade. According to Saint-Simon, the revival was due to two captains who had fought near the Tuileries, and to the Regent, the Duc d'Orléans, who did not punish them in an exemplary way. As always, the intellectual counter-attack was not long in coming. Comte Maffei's *Chivalric Pseudo-Science* was internationally successful, and the Abbé de Saint-Pierre published two *Memoir*[s] *on Perfecting Police Action Against Duels* in succession.

This revival can be explained by the political ambience: the King's minority, theories of aristocratic government, the public practice of discussions in councils. There is no shortage of analogies – as Montesquieu stressed – between the time when the long monologue of the old dead King ceased and the time of the Estates General of 1614 and the Fronde, those blessed times for duels.

More interesting, and more unexpected, is the renewed favour enjoyed by duelling during the Revolutionary and Napoleonic periods. These were supposedly times when a new era was beginning, one which had even overturned the thousand-year-old continuity of the calendar. Feudalism was abolished and the symbols, emblems and rites of the nobility and gentry and of chivalry were suppressed and despised. One might have expected duels to have been swept away, and indeed the new penal code which was sketched out and took shape between 1790 and 1810 did not, in any of its successive reworkings, mention the crime of duelling. But the new legislators proved fearsome duellists. Many were the deputies of the Constituent who took debates begun in the House to the field: Mirabeau against Beaumets, Montlosier against Huguet, Barnave against Casalis, the Duc de Castries against Charles de Lameth. Meanwhile Mirabeau the Younger grandly postponed his response to twenty-two cartels until the end of the parliamentary session, and strollers on the Champs-Elysées complained that this fine promenade was cluttered with 'prowlers, beggars, tarts and duellists'. Neither concern for the 'country in danger' nor the Terror could totally calm the itch. Two drapers fought in 1792 and two members of the Convention challenged each other to fight with pistols in 1793. It was not until imperial order was established and parliamentary life put on standby that the spectacle of challenges and duels between deputies came to an end. But the enormous military society, set up in the name of France the 'indivisible' and consolidated by the Empire, proved to be at least as fertile for duels as the old royal army. In 1793 the decimation by duelling of the volunteer force assembled to fight the Vendée uprising was deplored and in 1812 a military doctor who was keen on anatomical studies admitted that the raw material for his work was provided by duellists' corpses.

In fact, this renewal of duelling had begun with the reign of Louis XVI. We can see this from the type of affairs arbitrated by the point-of-honour court: between 1725 and 1775 the court dealt only with questions of hunting rights, quarrels over gambling or reputation between aristocratic heirs; but between 1775 and 1790 the word 'duel', which had been strangely absent until then, figures frequently. At the Carnival of 1778 Monsieur openly acted in a way that the brothers of Charles IX and Louis XIII had never dared, challenging a man to fight, then meeting and fighting him. At that time, aristocratic attitudes were more important to the Comte d'Artois than dynastic solidarity.

To situate the duels of the Revolution and the Empire in the context of this wider chronology is to place them between Herder and Walter Scott, between pre-romanticism and the 'troubadour style', between the meeting of the Estates General in 1789 and the coronation of Charles X in 1824, those two acts of political archaeology. The generation that was born into the Enlightenment and reached adulthood at the end of the eighteenth and beginning of the nineteenth centuries lived through the return of much that was repressed. We can see this in the interest that some of these people showed for 'French monuments' and popular folklore and we can be sure that there was a similar interest in aristocratic folklore, of which the duel is an essential monument. The return of the collective repressed made its mark in these times of crisis, hope and bitterness, for this generation in whom the passion for freedom went hand in hand with hero-worship.

Collective awareness in the twilight of the century of the Enlightenment was rediscovering certain traits that we have seen in the attitudes of duellists at the end of the sixteenth century. The attraction of duels betrays a fascination with death, which other historians have come upon by other routes. In Chanu's words, 'The end of the eighteenth century went through this fascination with death. . . . Between the end of the eighteenth century and the beginning of the nineteenth there was a short moment which was once more favourable, during which heroism was in fashion, during which heroism was possible.'

Other returns of the repressed but never forgotten duel certainly occurred (with less strength, it is true) in the nineteenth century. Perhaps there will be others in the future. In our world duelling exists mainly in stories and images and not as a reality in our lives. However, its history has shown us that it was from stories and images, from *exempla*, that the duel long drew its formidable strength. Although the only place left to it in our civilisation is that of dreams, we have to acknowledge that this is a prime position.

PART IV

Towards a Definition of Themes

In which, having tried to understand the 'total social phenomenon' of the duel in its development, its victories and retreats, we shall to try to define what it represented in the vision of the world of both the duellists and anti-duellists with whom we have rubbed shoulders through two centuries of French history.

Chapter 17
Tangible Themes

The Sword

> I have no words
> My voice is in my sword....
> (Shakespeare, *Macbeth*, V, viii, 6–7)

Duellists did not wait until the nineteenth century to use pistols. From the sixteenth century onwards any personal weapon, be it blade or firearm, was used for their purpose. However the sword (alone, or in conjunction with a dagger held in the other hand) was by far the most frequently used.

This was because a sword was always within the reach of every man's hand. Gentlemen and soldiers wore one at their side all the time and, in spite of the ban on carrying weapons (as oft repeated as it was inefficacious), many others did the same. As the chronicler Claude Haton wrote for the year 1555: 'There was no mother's son at this time who did not carry a sword or a dagger.' The commoners, he added, drew their swords like gentlemen, and the clergy often did so as if they were laymen. As the weapon widely used in brawls and 'ambush murders', the sword was naturally the favourite instrument for duelling.

But there was more to it than that. In the public mind the sword had a particular relation to single combat. This was understood by the erudite magistrate Jean Savaron, who wanted to extend the privilege of carrying a sword to all Frenchmen (thus bringing the law into line with the true state of things), 'commoners, merchants, workers and peasants ... the sword suits them well, although they have such respect for it that they are careful not to misuse it'. Four years after writing these lines, Savaron moved from theory to practice. He was a Deputy of the Third Estate at the Estates General, where he insulted a deputy from the nobility by declaring that the second order was the 'older brother of the third'. The other man wanted to put him in his place by having him beaten by lackeys. Savaron drew his sword: 'I have carried arms, and I have the means of answering to anyone.'

To democratise the duel and to generalise the wearing of the sword was the same thing. For the sword's role in duelling was more than just technical, it was symbolic.

Different hyper-significant gestures, all of which refer to the sword in relation to the duel, will help us to understand this symbolic function.

- The gesture of the duellist who, before the fight, meditates in front of his sword as before a sacred object. 'He said: I wish to pray to God before beginning. Then, having made a cross with his sword and his dagger, he knelt down. . . .'
- The gesture of the kiss given to the sword before it strikes and wounds. 'When Captain Jean had undressed . . . he took his sword in his hand and kissed it. His lackey was on his horse, and so the fight began.'
- The gesture of the victorious duellist who takes no spoils from the loser but his sword and who, if possible, makes his opponent, who is lying on the ground but still alive and still conscious, give it to him by his own hand, thereby assuring him that he will no longer use it against him, and recognising the winner's superiority.
- The more magnanimous gesture of the victor who refuses to take the loser's sword, or who gives it back to him.
- Lastly, the gesture of the repentant duellist who breaks his sword, the instrument of his past sins and future temptations. St Vincent de Paul watched M. de Rougemont, one of his first converts, make this gesture. This man was involved in all the duels in Bresse, where he came from. He was led to examine his conscience and felt himself ready to give up all his earthly ties: his château, his hat, his wife, 'every other creature', but not his sword. 'What, he cried, a sword which has saved my life so many times? Oh, I must keep it!' Then the saint showed him that this piece of iron was a 'chain that held him captive'. Renouncing both duelling and the world, 'he got down from his horse and broke the sword against a stone'.

When it was not simply being used as a weapon, the sword appeared as a material object endowed with moral virtues.

First of all, the sword was a *sign of nobility*, the 'gentleman's faith': 'the Nobility and gentry wear it as the instrument of their profession, which is to be always at the service of the Prince'. And the Prince, when he wanted to appear as a gentleman, and challenged an opponent to fight him in a closed field, preferred the sword to any other weapon. Charles V reminded François I of this in his cartel. François had suggested fighting him with a whole arsenal of offensive and defensive weapons. Charles V replied that 'they could not fight with finer or more noble weapons than the sword, which was usually worn at the side as a most signal mark of nobility and worth'. The jurists even imagined that it would be possible to put an end to duelling by threatening lawbreaking gentlemen that they, like commoners, would be forbidden to wear a sword.

The sword was also an *emblem of justice*. Vendramin explains in his treatise *On the Duel* that it is the knight's preserve to 'defend the oppressed, assist the Prince [and] repel insults to ourselves and to others; all these being things which can often be done only by putting one's hand to one's sword'. This is why the sword was the 'weapon of justice'. Half a century later, Alberto Pompeio declared: 'the sword in the hand of justice is a symbol of peace; as it is in the hand of the sage'. When the justice of monarchy and state was opposed to aristocratic 'private' justice, the kingly right to the 'sword of justice' was distinguished from the aristocratic right to wear a sword. From this point of view, whoever used his sword to administer justice was a usurper. In such a case it was required by single and indivisible justice that the most ignoble sword, that of the executioner, should win out over a sword which was quite possibly heroic and generous, but unqualified. Richelieu's comment on Bouteville's execution is in this vein: 'All of France saw in this action killed by the most loathsome sword in the kingdom those who had always had such good ones that no one could take offence if it were said that there were none better in the world.'

Lastly, in France the sword was the *insignia of the Constable*. During the coronation, the Constable, who was both a high official of the Crown and the supreme member of the *noblesse d'épée*, carried the royal sword. Although his role as leader of the armies was fictional, he did in practice preside over military justice. In the matter of duelling, it was traditionally his role to grant the field in the King's name and he arbitrated in judicial combats until the middle of the sixteenth century. After this it was he more than anyone who dealt with settling quarrels between gentlemen and running the jurisdiction of the point of honour.

Why was the word 'iron' (*fer*) often used in preference to the word 'sword' (*épée*)? And not just in Corneille's poetry, but in the prose of the moralists. Furetière notes in his *Dictionary*: 'Iron is used absolutely of a sword, or of weapons.' This preference for the name of the raw material over that of the manufactured object leads the imagination towards the work of the blacksmith, and that of the miner. It has connotations of obscure chthonian powers, powers seen as malevolent by wordsmiths contemptuous of duelling, but – we can be sure – seen as benevolent by the duel's silent admirers.

To speak of 'iron' instead of 'sword' in relation to duelling is to liken single combat to an alchemical operation. Indeed iron occupied the central place in the traditional classification of the seven metals. Its astrological analogue was Mars, central planet of the seven. A series of analogies takes us from iron to the warrior god Mars and to the young and vigorous fighter, from the iron reddened by fire to the blood spilled by iron. This metal that mediates between life and death makes its user an arbiter between the just and the unjust, truth and falsehood. In baroque France the duellist, like the blacksmith in other societies, had a taboo function.

We shall conclude this discussion of the theme of the sword by presenting three antithetical couples: sword and robe, sword and hand, and sword and stick.

Sword and robe. Within the same aristocracy individuals whose career involved the wearing of a robe were distinguished from those who carried swords by profession, although a single individual might pass from one role to the other, each time adopting the appropriate behaviour.

The robe of the lawyers (*robins*) did not permit the wearing of a sword, and therefore also forbade recourse to duelling, a taboo they shared with other wearers of long and ample clothes (cymar, soutane or habit): priests, monks, women, little boys. All these people had a 'horror of blood', and were unable to avenge themselves for insults and challenges. To use and extend a distinction made by Scipion Dupleix, all robe-wearers came into the category of 'venerable', which had nothing in common with that of 'honourable'.

For some of them, such as Camus, the Bishop of Belley, wearing a robe was a safeguard which gave them welcome shelter from challenges and *démentis*, thus allowing them to tell those 'meticulous about honour' a few hard truths with impunity. For others, this irresponsibility in the matter of honour was in itself dishonouring and became unbearable if they received an insult. In such cases insulted magistrates would ask to be relieved of their office in order to avenge themselves. Sometimes young magistrates, high-born clergymen and even women would forget the reserve which their clothing obliged them to maintain and would use a sword while wearing a robe. This shocking mixture is revealing: for a long time active honourableness often had precedence over passive venerableness. The man who was responsible for his own honour cut a more imposing figure than a dependent person – even if the latter incarnated the most sacred values.

Sword and hand. In the formal duels of the Middle Ages a challenge was made by throwing one's glove at one's opponent. The glove taken from one's hand was the token of a challenge. This gesture was no longer used in the ritual of the point of honour in the sixteenth and seventeenth centuries, nor was the complex symbolism of the glove. But the ritual had become simpler without becoming weaker. There is a rich opposition here between the ungloved, naked hand and the sword held in the hand like an artificial extension of the arm.

For a duel to be fought, the two opponents must each carry a weapon. A fight with naked fists would be nothing but a brawl. Hand-to-hand fighting, direct contact and the opponent's touch without the distance imposed by a weapon removes respect, both for oneself and for the other, and the sense of justice. Strangulation is a vile thing; stabbing is a matter of brute strength; but to defend oneself with a sword, looking one's opponent in the eye, is to consider him (in both senses of the word), it is to salute and honour him as one strikes. To defend oneself with one's hand, to slap him or deal him a blow with one's fist, involves taking one's eyes off him, or closing one's eyes the better to concentrate one's brute strength, it involves denying him his honour. It means adding moral contempt to physical strength.

Indeed, because the fist, that natural club which is an integral part of the body, is outside the domain of human industry, when it knocks the opponent out and flattens him it simultaneously reduces the attacker to the rank of a brute beast. In a far more conscious and deliberate gesture the open hand does less harm physically, but it humiliates the other and only the other; it is a way of stating that the attacker has a moral superiority called authority on top of pure strength. The hand opens to slap just as it opens to greet, to forgive, to take an oath, to bless. There is an ambivalence about the meanings carried by the open hand which is culturally expressed in the distinction between left and right. If the hand closes on the pommel of a sword, it is once again closed like a fist, but its 'nails are turned towards the sky'. It is no longer a stiff and crude mass; it is the supple and subtle place where a man's mind animates the sword of iron. It belongs to an order which remains conflictual but is deliberately human, an order in which the opponent is invited to participate: the frequent requirement that the duellists' swords be of the same length and the compulsory invitation to place oneself 'on guard' are forms of dialogue and the beginning of a recognition that each has equal dignity as a man.

In fighting with swords there is a serious chance that one man will mutilate or kill the other, much more so than if he strikes him with a naked fist. But that man accepts the same risk for himself, from the other. And if at the end of the fight the two opponents are alive and conscious (at this point it matters little whether there is a winner and a loser), then the hands let go of the weapons and open once more, this time to be held out, to be given to each other, no longer as a pledge to fight, but as a token of peace and reconciliation.

Sword and stick. The stick is held in the hand like a sword. However, it is never used in duels. Although two individuals may confront each other with sticks in a formalised fight, this is simply for entertainment.

The stick or rod is an instrument of punishment which a single individual uses and to which the other is simply subjected. A superior uses it to strike an inferior: the teacher canes the pupil, the master thrashes the valet. It is not, like the sword, a tool of reciprocal punishment. It does not reinstate a lost equality through the common trial. It leaves wounds and lumps, even bruises; it does not make the purifying blood spurt forth.

The stick is the mark of superiority to such a degree that it often ceases to be an effective instrument and becomes the badge of power, for example, the king's sceptre, the marshal's baton, the herald's caduceus and even the bailiff's rod: 'a bailiff with his rod carries the authority of the Prince'.

Like the iron sword, the wooden branch is one of the attributes of justice, but it signifies an essentially superior justice. The sceptre-bearer is the supreme mediator of all conflicts. Duellists can re-establish peace between themselves only by the bloody mediation of iron, of metal; but by throwing down his baton in the closed field the Prince recognises the valour of both of them and imposes on them the unbloody mediation of wood, of the vegetal. He alone is the complete arbiter, for only he has a completely free will in judicial matters: his authority alone is arbitrary.*

Henri II did a grave deed during the fight between Jarnac and La Châtaigneraye when he hesitated to throw down his baton, then threw it down too late. For a long time after that, while in England Elizabeth was continuing to grant the closed field, and to throw down her baton, no authority could impose itself on French soil that was above the justice of arms,

Blood

> Il faut que de mon sang je lui fasse raison.
> (Corneille, *Mélite*, IV, 6)

> Ce n'est que dans le sang qu'on lave un tel outrage.
> (Corneille, *Le Cid*, I, 6)

---

* Here I am not, of course, using the word 'arbitrary' in the pejorative sense which it has acquired since the Philosophers of the eighteenth century.

The sword is the chosen instrument of ritual combat because it makes blood flow. For the effusion of blood is the most certain sign that satisfaction has been obtained, that the duel is finished: more so than the neutralisation of the opponent, more than his death.

This can clearly be seen in the practice of the *duel to first blood*. A simple scratch, one single drop of blood, and the duel could be ended with honour. 'The opportunity is taken to separate the combatants or to infer a kind of satisfaction when one has drawn blood from the other, however slightly he is hurt.' These words of Pierre Boissat's date from 1610: so this practice was not a late development that appeared in a phase of decline when duels were seldom fatal and were reduced to a simulation for public show. The duel to first blood was even noted in the middle of the sixteenth century by Muzio and La Noue. To be victorious in a duel did not mean killing; it was a question of 'drawing blood', of manifesting by an unequivocal sign that one was capable of taking a life by exposing one's own.

The idea of duelling gave rise to an obsession with blood, either fascinated or horrified, depending on the individual, but always poignant. We shall consider four essential connotations of the insistent link between duel and blood: *lustration*, *sacrifice*, *rite of alliance* and *mark of vengeance*.

To spill blood, to make it flow, is to say in a tangible manner that a duel cleanses outrage, purges insults and wipes away the stains on a man's honour. Like holy baptism, this symbolic bathing requires only a few drops of purifying liquid. 'Disputes can also be settled at first blood: in such cases it is a question of cleansing the stain from the insulted party, not of taking the life and honour of the wounded man.' Spilt blood even washes away the collective blot shared by a whole network of relations when the blood of one of their number is dishonoured (according to extra-biological laws, since not only descendants are stained by impure blood, but ascendants and collaterals as well). This is why the Duke of Medina-Sidonia felt obliged to challenge the Duke of Braganza in 1640. The former was loyal to the King of Spain in the Portuguese uprising, while the second accepted the Portuguese crown. This 'traitor' was related by marriage to Medina-Sidonia: 'the chief subject of my displeasure [said the cartel] is that his wife is of my *blood*.* Which, as it has been corrupted by this rebellion, I wish to spill in single combat.'

'Human blood abundantly spilled on the ground' is an image of sacrifice. It is a frequent, obsessive image in speeches (and even legal texts): a holy immolation in which the duellist is both priest and victim, the field is an altar and the gods are human vanity, the idol of

* Italics FB.

honour and lastly the infernal vampire who 'loves the effusion of blood and the loss of souls'.

Even more significant is the use of the verb *égorger* ('to kill', literally 'to cut the throat of') in the language of challenges, judicial inquiries and anecdotal tales. These hardly ever speak of men piercing each other's sides, breasts or hearts, but always of 'cutting each other's throats'. 'When so many places on our bodies can be pierced', it is surprising that the only gesture to stick in the imagination is that of the sacrificer slitting the jugular vein so that the blood spurts out and away from the victim's body in a powerful jet, to wet the earth around it.

Behind the particular and momentary meaning of the individual oblation of each duellist who offers himself and his opponent for destruction, the phenomenon has a global meaning. The collective holocaust of the 'blood of the most generous nobility' was a kind of destructive potlatch in which the warrior aristocracy pushed generosity to the point of sacrificing its youth and future the better to affirm its being. One is reminded of the practices of republican Rome, such as the *devotio* or the *ver sacrum*. But in monarchial France, such costly initiatives by an elite of equals could only be subversive.

The blood that two brave men draw from each other, spill and mingle is also reminiscent of the archaic contract sealed by two warriors or two clans with a libation of the liquid of life. Of course we are not claiming here that duellists were clearly aware of the barbaric customs reported by Herodotus or Tacitus, nor even that an intimate knowledge of the Bible might have given some of them the idea of imitating the blood covenant of the ancient Semites. We even know that 'the mingling of blood had a purely literary existence in the fourteenth and fifteenth centuries'. But we suggest that a kind of tacit tradition existed, in which the gentlemen of modern France participated, and which helps us understand the kind of companionship which was established between two of them when they measured themselves against each other in a combat *ex condicto*.

Whether lustrative, sacrificial or contractual, the duellist's blood gave his engagement the value and virtue of a decisive, definitive and final act. It ended a quarrel, re-established esteem, reconciled men, parties and indeed peoples. But blood has too rich a symbolism and the duel is too complex a phenomenon for a bloody duel not simultaneously to signify the opposite of all this. It recalls 'that all blood draws other blood after it'.

Blood purifies, but it also stains. Innocent blood silences hatred; it also calls for vengeance. Many fatal duels were fought only to avenge the victims of earlier duels. For the group to escape the bloody fatality of an eye for an eye, illustrious duellists had to spill their blood on the scaffold of royal justice; otherwise, it would have been the monarch's blood that paid for all the blood spilled on the field.

The paralysing fascination of duels can be explained by the underlying notion of sacrifice, a notion whose fundamental importance in the construction of the cultural edifice in which we have lived for centuries has been described by René Girard. This observation helps us to understand that before the time of combat for a point of honour other forms of single combat existed which carried the same meaning as the duel. It also explains why the duel proper, though banned, disavowed and outdated, has never completely died.

But why was there a sudden peak in the number of duels between 1550 and 1650? We can answer only by noting that at this time and on several levels the craze for duelling coincided with an obsession with blood. French tragedy, from Jodelle to the pre-Cornelians, was, like Elizabethan theatre, a 'theatre of blood, sensuality and death'; medical science, from Servet to Harvey, was discovering the repellent idea of the circulation of the blood; in the Catholic Church, the chosen objects on which devotion was focused were the Five Wounds and the Sacred Heart,* and while Spanish society was haunted by the idea of the purity of blood, 'Frenchmen full of blood and consequently of heat [gave themselves up to] the infernal dragon, which took their souls from their bodies and breathed the scent of the most generous and pure blood.'

Speech and Dialogue

> Posuit os meum
> Quasi gladium acutum.
>
> (Isaiah, 49: 2)

> Tout homme de courage est homme de parole.
> (Corneille, *Le Menteur*, III, 2)

Fencing and duelling provide a series of metaphors for designating a certain type of conversation or debate. French has the expressions 'oratory duel' (*duel oratoire*) and 'verbal jousting' (*joutes verbales*), during which the protagonists exchange 'sword thrusts' (*passes d'armes*). Stichomythia, a literary procedure in common use among tragic poets, where alternate speakers utter single lines, is defined by one specialist as 'the threatening click of dialogue between heroes

---

*In this context we could also note that at this time images of the death of St Sebastian were much in vogue.

expressing their mutual hatred'; and another sees in it 'the equivalent of alternating blows delivered by two opponents in single combat'.

Conversely, language and dialogue have provided a series of terms and metaphors to designate duels and the events surrounding them. The French expressions for 'to give and to receive a cartel' are, literally translated, 'to give and to receive the spoken word' (*porter* and *recevoir la parole*). The challenger is called the 'caller' (*appelant*); his challenge is a 'call' (*appel*) with which he 'asks for an explanation' (*demande raison*); he asks his opponent to answer for his honour, his integrity and the truth of his utterances. 'I have', said the author of one cartel, 'a just desire to speak to you . . . in the manner to which good men of my profession are accustomed.'

This relation between the language of duelling and that of dialogue was possible because in practice there is a successive substitution of duel and dialogue: the duel is substituted for an interrupted dialogue, then a re-established dialogue is substituted for the finished duel.

At the moment when the insult and challenge are given, dialogue ceases, each refuses to listen to the other. The English expression designating two individuals who have fallen out – 'they are not on speaking terms' – puts it very well, particularly in relation to quarrels of honour, since here the supreme insult is the *démenti*. Once A has said to B, 'You are lying', he no longer listens to him. For A such a suspicion takes away all guarantee that anything that B says is true, even if the accusation of lying refers to a precise and limited instance. At this point there is only one sentence that B can utter: 'I will uphold the truth of those words that you say I spoke against any man in the world, except him to whom I owe respect.' No further arguments or negotiations are possible between them; any word they spoke would be delaying chatter, 'as some do who settle their affair with arguments and words'. For both of them the only way out is the path of arms.

It is not only between the appellant and the *appelé* that dialogue ceases. As long as the injured party (or the insulter whose attitude is inconsistent) has not fought, he has no right to speak among his peers. Because he is accused of lying, or has lightly accused another of lying, he is publicly condemned to silence. He who refuses to fight, even if it is in obedience to his Prince's order, 'would not be worthy to converse with knights'. As Castiglione, author of *The Art of Conferring*, puts it, 'We are only men, and we only treat with others, through speech. . . . He who speaks falsely betrays public society.'

The completed duel re-established dialogue between the champions. This is true to such an extent that if some incident interrupts the combat, or even postpones it, once the opponents are on the field and have proved their determination to fight, they may exchange calm, lively or even amicable words.

The completed duel brings the duellist back into the social circle of conversation. He can now be listened to; what he says can be believed. There is nothing like a fine duel to obtain an audience with the ladies, the powerful and even the Prince himself. As François de Sorel says at the end of the tale of his duel with Bajamond (a more than victorious, generous duel): 'The King showed me more affection than ever on this occasion. He thought all the speeches I made in his presence were good, and gave me permission to speak both good and ill of anything I liked, since he well knew that I would not criticise anyone who did not deserve it.' To fight a duel is to defend one's word of honour; to fight well is to win the honour of speech.

The analogy we have noted between 'to speak to each other' (*se parler*) and 'to fight each other' (*se battre*) becomes comprehensible when we consider the duel's place as one from which speech was banished, and the duel itself as the only act which could re-establish dialogue. We can also understand Brantôme's scruples about fighting a man who has been excommunicated, 'for, according to the doctors of the clergy, a man's soul is at stake if he fights, or indeed speaks and confers with an excommunicated man'. To come to the point of duelling is not to reach the point of rupture, it is to finish a journey to the extreme, it is to try out a metalanguage. It is to use a sacred language which takes over from profane language in a discontinuity which is not an end.

This is a sacred language in all its ambivalence. The duel has connotations of both forms of oath, blasphemy and the sacred vow.

Blasphemy. 'This abominable habit of swearing and that of fighting duels have almost always gone together,' notes Delamare in his *Treatise on the Police.* At the moments when the challenge and the mortal blow are given, a sacrilegious imprecation is often uttered (both by the giver and by the receiver). For men of the time there was more than an association between the two, there was an analogy between blasphemy and that particular type of profane act, the duel.

Vow. The formal duel of the high period was preceded by 'oaths of loyalty'. As we have seen these oaths had atrophied and disappeared even before the duel was transformed from a public to a private practice.

In fact this development consisted of casting off the inessential elements. For, like the oath, the duel is a form of trial. An anecdote from 1490 will illustrate this. A character who was suspected of dishonouring crimes 'of which he denied himself guilty' was to go before the Parliament of Grenoble; by order of Charles VIII he was told to 'purge himself of them by means of an oath upheld as true by

twelve supporting witnesses'. We find the same thing in the definition of the oath given by an eighteen-century jurist: 'affirmation of a
fact by imprecation, that is to say in taking God as witness and judge
of what one has said, one subjects oneself to his vengeance if one
takes him as witness to a falsehood'. The obsolescence of the
supplementary oaths in the procedure of sixteenth-century duels
underlines all the better the fact that the armed combat was itself an
oath. A silent oath, beyond all speech, which 'would tell the truth',
made by the reciprocal and decisive touch of two living and mortal
bodies. The duel took on the most profound meaning of the oath at
the very time when the latter was developing in the opposite
direction. The law and custom were increasingly turning against the
gesture of placing a hand on a sacred object (not only relics, but also
the daily bread, wine and salt), and preferred the oath taken 'tactis
Evangeliis', giving the human word no support other than that of the
divine Word. This was a greater humanisation and abstraction; but
there was always the possibility of more concrete transcendence in
single combat.

The humanist and rationalising attitude which was then reshaping
the oath was that of the classical casuists in their analysis of duelling.
For them, this phonomenon was essentially a tacit understanding
between two individuals who were deaf to all speeches and to society
and dumb when they were asked to explain their action. When the
duel can no longer be understood as an impious metalanguage
mixing together the sacred and the profane, it is condemned as an
extra-legal paralanguage which confuses private and public.

Historical phenomena can often be seen in their purest forms at the
point when they are about to come to an end. It is in the army and
the political assembly, those two sanctuaries of its late survival, that
the duel demonstrates the full extent of its link with speech.

The army is an essentially hierarchical society, disciplined and
obedient.* No one in it is quite the equal of anyone else, as there is
always some difference between two officers of the same rank which
prevents their being on the same level: one will have been in the
service longer, have fought more campaigns and won more medals.
On the emotional level, the spirit of 'off-duty' comradeship counter-
balances the constraints of this entirely vertical organisation of
human beings. The army is also a great place of silence, a world in
which once a decision is taken there is no room for discussion, where
orders must be carried out 'without hesitation or murmur'. The only

---

* Plato's *Laches* is the best analysis I have seen of the military spirit.

words uttered (but not exchanged) are orders and the report that they have been carried out. In this society the duel has the function of a safety valve, as an agonistic complement to the solidarity which is born of the spirit of comradeship. The duel is something that resembles discussion, but sidesteps contention; it offers a relationship equality which avoids insubordination (it is an ephemeral and ritualised relationship: one 'takes off one's stripes') and an event resembling disorder, but one which is still regulated. It is one of reason's ruses, separating individuals the better to bind them together in the same *esprit de corps*.

In comparison with the laconic* world of the warrior, parliamentary (derived from the French *parler*, to speak) politicians are professional speakers, chatterers even. When members of Parliament take to duelling, they do it not as a substitute for discussion, but as a prolongation, a new dimension to the spoken debate. 'From oratorical duelling ... to just duelling' (*Du duel oratoire ... au duel tout court*) ran the headline of the newspaper *Le Figaro* to report the combat which brought two parliamentary deputies to blows on 21 April 1967. In fact both the speakers in the previous day's debate and the newspaper commentaries had constantly used metaphors of single combat: '*Skirmishes* in the general policy debate', 'M. Pompidou throws down a *challenge* to the opposition', and the final words of the Prime Minister's speech: 'The weapon that you have so brilliantly waved is merely a wooden *sabre*. If you want to use *iron*, I am ready!' Such obvious continuity in the most recent of parliamentary duels reflects the way in which the legislative assemblies have been islands of the duel's survival since the beginning of the nineteenth century. It also helps to explain the dates for previous peak periods of the phenomenon: 1614–15, 1651, 1789–90. These were years of elections and meetings of the Estates General, points when the political life of the realm was linked to the life of deliberating assemblies. The duels were carried on the tide of debates.

There is continuity and discontinuity between the dialogue and the duel because there is a change of register between these two languages. The quarrel (be it serious or petty) uses contemporary expressions in the vernacular: the language of reason and passion, of Aristotle's logic and Descartes's common sense, or that of chicanery and legal disputes. However, armed combat returns to an archaic language in which the blade retains the power of the master words of sacred speech, 'power over reality' and 'power over others'.

---

*It is not for nothing that the same adjective applies to the model armed city and a defiant disdain for long speeches.

Every duel arouses both fascination and disapproval. It is easier to understand this once it is accepted that the duel is a metalanguage. To parody Carl von Clausewitz, or rather to make explicit the presuppositions of his famous phrase: the duel is a dialogue continued by other means – which are not the words of the tribe.*

---

* A few lines after the too-famous phrase, Clausewitz clarifies: 'Do political relations between peoples and between their governments ever stop when diplomatic notes are no longer exchanged? Is war just another expression of their thoughts, another form of speech or writing? Its grammar, indeed, may be its own, but not its logic.' (*On War.*)

Chapter 18
Ethical Themes

Honour

> A man who knows how to
> die cannot be dishonoured.
>> (J.-J. Rousseau, Letter to Abbé M., 1770)

We shall confine ourselves here to discussing the honour of duellists, sketching out its characteristics (which often refer to more global conceptions of honour). We should remember that honour has collective, individual, feminine and masculine forms. It is primarily masculine honour which is at stake in duelling. We should also bear in mind the expression 'point of honour', which belongs to the sphere of duelling (Brantôme calls it the 'dot [*pointille*] of honour', copying the Italian phrase, *puntiglio d'onore*). For its detractors, the honour which is defended in duelling is merely a dot, 'a certain *je ne sais quoi*', an almost nothing that lacks both surface and depth, a vain illusion. For its upholders this honour is a fine point, a pointed and tangible summit in which the very essence of the purest, most refined and most demanding honour is distilled and concentrated. For both upholders and detractors, the point of honour is a standard which men regard as superior to the more respectable values of life, the state and religion.

Loss of honour in the chivalric ethical code is 'a kind of civil death'; it confines the individual to so unbearable an existence that death is preferable. Fear of death is lifted by an insult to one's honour. Life without honour is so devalued that it can be risked in a duel, which offers a simple way to reach an end that is infinitely superior to such life. The death to which one may put the other man in a duel is simply a secondary result of the essential re-establishment of honour. 'Homicide is not the end of the duel, its end is the recovery of honour, and when homicide comes into it, it is by accident.'

Perhaps all forms of honour are linked to violent killing, like the crime of honour in some Mediterranean societies, or the voluntary death of the virtuous woman who has been dishonoured in the manner of Lucretia. But their relation to death is always more partial than that offered by the duel for a point of honour; this homicidal and suicidal experience combines vengeance against a man who has committed the sin of shame, with the refusal to outlive one's honour and the regeneration of a failing honour. This brings us to the paradoxical point that, of the living winner and the deceased loser, it is the second whose honour is the more assured: no future quirk of his now finished destiny can take away this secular and warlike variant of the state of grace; his opponent, on the other hand, keeps his honour only by perpetually putting it at stake, paying the exhausting price of a risky continuous creation.

There is a sliding of sense here that gives the duel its full meaning. It is the mortal trial which reveals honour; it is also the mortal trial that creates honour. One might, with Falstaff, see this in a sad light: 'What is that honour? Air ... who hath it? He that died a-Wednesday.' But one can also, with the Prince de Condé, exalt 'the custom that makes honour consist in perilous actions'.

The twentieth-century duellist Defferre told journalists: 'Honour is above the law.' He was only repeating, without knowing it, the words of a sixteenth-century 'doctor of duels': 'Not understanding that this [honour] should be subject to any human law'. Of course a man who knowingly adopts a forbidden procedure automatically places himself outside the law; but it was no different in the days when duelling was legal and authorised: by granting the field, the sovereign proclaimed that he did not have the power to make a judicial decision. The Prince, or the magistrate, thus announced the limit to his powers, and defined a space beyond the law. 'The Prince', said Bodin in his *Republic*, 'disposes of the subject's life and property, but he had no power over his honour'.

True, political authorities could use the polysemy of the word 'honour' to their own advantage. Loyalty to the sovereign and courage in defence of the country were indisputable deeds of honour and the praise and titles given out by the sovereign to his worthy servants were a way of honouring them. This is why legal bills and the texts of laws often proposed that duelling gentlemen should be humiliated, so that their crime should be seen as one that brought with it infamy and loss of status. In France, the guilty were threatened with loss of their rank, responsibilities and coats of arms, death by hanging and the reduction of their families to the state of commoners. In England, the Chancellor, Bacon, summed up the situation with his usual felicity of expression: 'The fountaine of honour is the king, and his aspect, and the accesse to his person continueth honour in life, and to be banished from his presence is one of the greatest eclipses of honour that can bee.'

But the great mass of gentlemen, when they found themselves appellants or *appelés* in a duel, rejected such arguments and drew a distinction between 'honours' and 'honour'. The Prince can bestow only honours: these are concrete rewards, or responsibilities, or material symbols. Honour is a spiritual value; it is a mode of the very substance of these exceptional subjects who are called knights, men of worth or gentlemen. Honour is an intrinsic, indivisible part of the man of honour, which can be challenged only with a *démenti* by another man of honour. It can be taken away only by the individual himself if he does not respond to the *démenti* according to the laws of honour. In the land of chivalry, honour has no sovereign other than free will.

It is free will which means that the sphere of honour is beyond both loyalty to the Prince and obedience to the Church. For its adherents, the duel is not, as its opponents would have it, a sign of atheism or idolatry. It belongs to a different (and equally demanding and exalting) value system from that of clergymen. Honour, for those who 'profess' it, is not a counter-religion; it is another religion. On condition, of course, that the word 'religion' is taken not in the sense of a community professing the same credo, but in the old sense of a group of exceptional human beings brought together in obedience to the same rules of living. There is a state of knightly perfection which is different from that of monastic perfection. Our duellists might echo the reply that Cervantes gives to Don Quixote when Sancho Panza speaks to him of the paths to sainthood:

' . . . it's better [said Sancho Panza] to be a humble little friar, of any order you like, than a valiant and errant knight. A couple of dozen lashings have more effect with God than a couple of thousand lance-thrusts, even against giants, or hobgoblins, or dragons.'

'All that is so,' replied Don Quixote, 'but we cannot all be friars and many are the ways by which God bears His chosen to heaven. Chivalry is a religion, and there are sainted knights in glory.'

This is what all men think who fight each other in duels – all of them, even though in the seventeenth century their conviction became increasingly unconscious and inarticulate, expressing itself only in the bloody act of single combat.

The duel for a point of honour was the final and most tenacious form of resistance of the *noblesse d'épée*, who were themselves the last believers in a tripartite conception of Christian society, morality and religion. To place honour above all the rest – and even above the ordinary path to Salvation – was, under Henri II and even more so under Louis XIV, to swim against the tide. It was to resist the totalitarian enterprise of the clergy, whose aim was to impose their norms and to control the lives of the faithful, the different social groups and the Christian states. It was also to resist the way in which mass Christianity was turning the religious model into something ordinary and banal, reducing different forms of behaviour to a uniform type and encouraging the mediocre and the gregarious. Such resistance was a struggle lost in advance, as its champions well knew; but this in itself meant that it was a manifestly disinterested struggle, a struggle forever marked by the unique finality of honour.

Uncomprehended by the vulgar, condemned for the crime of *lèse-majesté* against God and King, the duellist glorified a free will which neither the discipline of a hierarchical society nor the conformism of the plebeian world could wear away. He aspired only to the satisfaction of recognising himself (in his intact honour) and being recognised by another man of honour who went through the same trial with and for him: his opponent. Doubtless also, in a confused way, he was aware that his cult of honour inspired general respect and that his calm and mad determination undermined those over-confident authorities whom he dared to resist.

Blaise de Montluc, a personal enemy of Brantôme's, who nevertheless resembles him like a brother, gives us the final word on the honour of duellists: 'Our lives and our property belong to our kings. Our souls belong to God and our honour to us.' Thus speaks the man of honour in his haughty autonomy. He has no business with the powers of heaven and earth; but he cannot be himself if he is alone. He needs a peer against whom he can measure himself; he needs another to recognise him.

Justice

> And by the grace of God and this mine arm
> To prove him....
> (Shakespeare, *Richard II*, I, iii, 22–3)

'God will be our conscience's judge and witness, and not us,' proclaimed François I in his challenge to Charles V. The idea of God's judgement, which went without saying in the judicial duel, never really disappeared from the duel for a point of honour. Churchmen could not help thinking duels had an element of trial and in the outcome of any duel ordinary mortals could not help seeing or seeking a more or less subtle and more or less mediated sign from God the judge by virtue of the simple fact that there was a winner and a loser, one man an executor and the other executed.

In 1610 Boissat noted an empirical statistic of 'eighty quarrels in which it was manifest that those who were in the wrong were beaten'. For him 'divine judgement' often extended to making the innocent party suffer handicaps only to make his victory at the end of the combat shine more brilliantly.

His contemporary, Dupleix, qualifies this idea, but retains it. His reasoning is psychological, or, as he would say, 'physical': the man who is certain he is in the right believes in his cause and draws from this the strength and courage which help him win. There may be cases where the wrong man wins, but this is because Providence is passing sentence not on this quarrel alone, but on all the sins committed by both opponents during their lifetimes.

After the Council of Trent, the pious tried to reconcile a rejection of duelling with the maintenance of the role of Providence by displacing the notion of God's judgement. Some considered the more guilty of the opponents to be the man who initiated the fight by giving the challenge: he is the man who should die. Hence the title of a paragraph by Balinghem the Jesuit: 'Ordinarily those who challenge another to a duel are killed in it ... as proved by several old stories.' For others, the guilty man was the one who killed, since he had committed the crime of homicide. In such cases the supernatural sentence was not apparent in the duel itself: it was deferred, but would be executed with sufficiently obvious signs to edify witnesses and inspire them with a horror of duelling. The mark of celestial justice would be a violent death, in war or in an ambush, supplemented by predictions where necessary, and perhaps met with on the very spot sullied by a fatal duel.

Towards the middle of the seventeenth century, when the edicts were becoming particularly severe concerning challenges given to persons of unequal rank, the death in a duel of a combatant of inferior rank could be seen as a punishment for scandalous insolence. In his *Memoirs* Goulas reports that a simple gentleman died on the field 'as if in punishment for having attacked a Prince and to mark his difference of condition'. God's judgement is only suggested; He does not intervene in a quarrel between His creatures; His judgement is pronounced as a guarantor of the social hierarchy.

The mysterious presence of God is felt all the more when human understanding cannot decipher the sentence of Providence as expected. Thus it was felt by all the spectators and commentators of the duel in which Jarnac killed La Châtaigneraye.

Even when the duel is seen as a purely human phenomenon, it still remains bound up with the notion of justice. And its unfolding is described in courtroom terminology, with analogies of court procedure. Two accounts from different periods will illustrate this state-

ment. The first was written by Rondinelli at the end of the sixteenth
century: 'In justice proper, three persons are necessary (the man who
is lodging the complaint, the defendant and the judge); and in the
duel, there is only the appellant and the *appele.*' The second is by La
Grasserie, dating from the end of the nineteenth century. He defines
the duel as 'the clash of two parties who each claim to be in the right,
in the absence of an ordinary judge, judgement by force replacing
that by law'. Such texts show us that the duel is described as a trial, a
trial whose specificity rests in the fact that all the roles (from accuser
through to executioner) are represented by the two champions alone,
and that all the action (witnesses, evidence, pleas, sentence and
execution) are confounded in their hand-to-hand fight. Although the
duel may come down to earth from heaven, it appears as an act of
human (too human?) justice, simplified to the point of caricature, or
concentrated into its essentials.

Juridical concepts, like the very notion of justice (perhaps even
more than that of honour) have a rich history, and have reached their
present form in a gradual development over time. We shall consider
only one of them here, for it is central to thinking on duelling in the
period in question, and also lies at the changeable heart of juridical
science at that time: this is the concept of *proof.* The duel contains all
the different notions of proof:

– trial by ordeal in a matter where there is no clear proof: 'when the
  truth of the matter cannot be known';
– proof-test which re-establishes a suspected individual, so that
  afterwards it becomes superfluous to continue considering the
  crimes of which he was suspected;
– an experimental method practised by gentlemen to demonstrate
  their virtue: 'to try out one's courage with someone'; but in which
  the intellectual elite refuse to see anything but a variation of
  probatio vulgaris, popular superstition, in which neither men's
  reason nor God's will is made manifest;
– finally, an act of *proving oneself* in front of a jury, in front of one's
  peers: either all together or in succession: a rite and examination of
  passage leading to approbation and enthronement. The gentleman
  upholds a *démenti,* just as the cleric upholds a thesis.

This mirroring in the meanings of the duel–trial is given its own
meaning in the general legal conjuncture of the first centuries of the
modern era. Throughout Europe the written, so-called 'inquisitorial'
procedure was coming to dominate more and more, for which the
chief form of proof was the confession, extracted where necessary by
torture. Meanwhile in the kingdom of France (unlike procedure in
England) legal powers tended not to be the preserve of juries of the

defendant's peers but were concentrated in the authoritarian hands of a hierarchy of professionals.

A learned contemporary of the young Louis XIV, Guillaume Ribier, considered the point-of-honour court to be a departure from 'ordinary justice'. He saw in it an exceptional aberration, a gratuitous concession on the part of the King, who sympathised with the erroneous 'imagination and fantasy' of the *noblesse d'épée* according to which they claimed access to a jurisdiction of 'lords of the military profession'. He thus excludes the idea that one can make one's own law, with an opponent–accomplice. The author takes care to avoid seeing this court as one island in an archipelago where one finds, among many others, consular and ecclesiastical courts, as one constituent part of a conception of justice which is more archaic, but no less respectable or logical than that of the *noblesse de robe*.

The same Guillaume Ribier tries to draw a parallel between duels and torture. His aim is retrospectively to justify the duels authorised by François I. 'These were acts of justice, which were used to bring an illumination and revelation of truth when this could not be hoped for by ordinary means, just as the censures, imprecations and curses of the Church, and the torture of the accused, are now used to the same ends.'

The judicial duel was an archaeological phenomenon in the middle of the seventeenth century. Nevertheless, it could be understood and justified by the contemporary and – all things considered – wise practice of inquisition. In both procedures violence is used and the victim is not necessarily guilty. But when all else fails and given the poor results of ecclesiastical moratoria, they have to be used. 'One is often obliged in this way to deal with one evil using others and there is neither law nor police which are without drawbacks.'

A good half-century before Ribier, and speaking of the duel in the present, Scipion Dupleix had already sketched a parallel between torture and combat used as a trial. In serious cases, where proof was lacking against gentlemen whom it was forbidden to interrogate, 'kings and sovereign courts have sometimes permitted duelling to manifest the uncertainty of the matter'. With the precautions inspired by respect for sovereign decisions, the author permits himself to expound his personal opinion. 'For myself, I do not doubt that to live in a Christian manner (as we must) it is much better to use torture, or to put off judgement completely, when there is uncertainty as to who is the author of a wicked act, than to seek proof by such oblique means that are so foreign to good manners, which do not permit the life of an innocent to be thrown to chance in order to convict the evil-doer.' The advantage of torture (and thus the justification of the modern practice of extracting proof) is not that it makes judicial error impossible. It is that this procedure has only one victim (innocent or not), whereas in a duel there are potentially two victims (one of whom is always innocent). In the name of Christian charity, and without really daring to push his idea to its limits, Dupleix dreams of a levelling common law which would extend torture to affairs of honour and to which gentlemen would be subjected.

Between the criminal law decree of Moulins (1566) and that of Saint-Germain (1670), the French penal system underwent a profound change. At that time many concepts were being defined, distinctions were being made between them and separations established. One result of this process was the impoverishment and restriction of sense of the notion of Justice. Differences were being clarified between increasingly opposing ideas: public and private, civil and criminal, legal courts and courts of peers, sentences of transaction or arbitration and sentences of sanction or of conviction, compensation and punishment. In both institutions and attitudes the divide between the justice of men and the justice of God was growing.

The duel is an invention of this time. Even if it imitated venerable precedents and borrowed elements from ancient traditions, at the end of the sixteenth and beginning of the seventeenth century the duel was a new, modern and in many ways unprecedented phenomenon. It was like a house built on a faulty base and its function was to fill, or at least to camouflage, the cracks into which its foundations were sinking. It was not an archaic relic, but the creation of a wilful archaism. The duel was a compensation, a reply, a resistance to a general observation of the crumbling and impoverishment of the notion of justice. It proclaimed, and not only for the *noblesse d'épée*, the immediate (and tragically nostalgic) plentitude of single, indivisible justice. It proclaimed this with an action in which men dispensed their own justice, but it was God who pronounced, with an action in which the equity of authoritarian restitution went hand in hand with an agreed transaction involving an invaluable property, that of honour. For the French contemporaries of Don Quixote, to fight a duel was to try to prove that on earth as in heaven justice and truth were the same thing.

Generosity and Fraternity

> Give praise that is hearty and fair, even
> to one's foe.
>
> (Pindar, *Pythian Odes*, IX, 95–6)

Il n'est forcénement si grand
Que d'une rancoeur fraternelle.
(R. Garnier, *Antigone*, 11.1513–14)

For both Bouteville the swashbuckler, who loved duels, and Pascal the philosopher, who was hostile to them, such combat was characterised by the absence of bad feeling between the fighters, who were indeed united by a mysterious bond of sympathy.

Of course it would be easy to gather anecdotes contradicting such a definition. We could recall that no duels were fought without a quarrel, and therefore without a desire for vengeance; it is hard to see what a desire for vengeance could consist of if it were stripped of all thirst to avenge. Or we could draw up a list of duellists who were acrimonious, envious, vindictive or simply irascible. But one cannot go from a sum (however impressive) of real individual cases to the very essence of the total social phenomenon.

No statistics can alter the definition of the duel implicit for both Pascal and Bouteville. All they could do would be to prove that individual reality was impure and imperfect in relation to the theoretical model and that many men claimed to have confronted each other in a duel who had managed only to fight each other in a brawl (as they admitted, moreover, if a court tried them for the 'crime of duelling'). Nor would they take account of the massive numbers involved in the role of seconds, those men who fought to the death with 'neither quarrel nor spite'. The duel, asymptotic with all forms of single combat, brings together men without anger or hatred and free of everything in vengeance that is stained with emotion.

In practice, as is abundantly apparent in the French sources, this requirement produced two attitudes: respect for the opponent (before the fight) and the absence of any intention to kill him (even if a duellist did his best ot kill his opponent, and succeeded). First, real duellists owed it to themselves to honour their opponent in order to honour themselves. For it was the worth of the loser that gave the greatest proof of the worth of the victor. This is an aristocratic argument related to that which leads Corneille's Chimène to praise her enemy Rodgrigue's success: the more he covers himself in glory and demonstrates his heroism, the more worthy a victim he becomes of her inexpiable resentment.

Respect for the other was taken to the point where the desire to cut short his life and, arguably, the responsibility for his death were removed – not only in the case of the guilty man who obtained letters of remission, or in the eyes of the casuist juggling with direction of intention, but for any individual, duellist or not, who accepted the logic of the duel. The true duellist was he who, like the Duc de

Beaufort, mourned his victim. Although he killed, he was merely a tool; it was the man who was killed who had brought about his own death.

This meant that the death which hovered over the execution of a duel did not represent its inevitable end. By leaving an opponent his life, by making up with a wounded or disarmed opponent, the victor proved all the more that he was a man of honour. He did so above all if he did not allow the loser to make his defeat obvious by pleading for mercy. For, according to Vulson de La Colombière, 'the goal of generous courage should be not to kill but to win. And there will always be more glory in being famed as merciful than as cruel, even towards one's most mortal enemies.'

Even more than esteem or respect, the opponent could/had to inspire a feeling of *fraternity*. Not only after he had demonstrated similar valour to that of his opponent in the duel, but from the very moment he accepted the proposition. Two opponents who had quarrelled over a hurtful satire nevertheless showed such attitudes: 'As soon as La Garde and Bazanez saw each other they would salute one another, and going forward with their hats in their hands, would embrace with the same courtesy and compliments as would have been exchanged by two good friends, smiling always.' The ritual of the formal duel as described by Champier makes this feeling explicit: after the oaths the 'actor' and the 'defender' 'took each other's hands to demonstrate the trust there should be between human beings who are brothers'.

The duel is like a purified version of other bloody fights in which soldiers who have been insulted feel equal and bound together by a common inheritance of values to which ordinary mortals have no access. The Crusader and the Infidel, or the French paratrooper and the American marine, experienced or dreamed of the chance to 'clash [with] affectionate curiosity'. For such men to fight each other in an isolated place is to set the seal on a complicity which places them apart from, and disturbs, other people.

The duel permits the realisation of a deep theme at the imaginary level of our cultures which has been called the theme of the 'brother enemies' or 'antagonistic complementarity'. A duel is not a Manichaean struggle which pits good against evil, the just against the unjust, leaving the stake to the man who deserves it. Often the stake is derisory; it is only a pretext. It is desired and demanded only out of mimicry, because the opponent desires it. In its essentials the duel pits an individual against his double. A double who is also a monster, who has taken on the guise of a monster. But who, in the duel, is stripped of almost all monstrosity once he and his opponent speak in the metalanguage of arms. Here the individual and his double have an equal share of monstrosity, which for the combatants themselves is wiped away by their familiarity. However, for those who do not share their secret, that monstrosity is reinforced (as is shown by the expression common around 1610 of the 'monster of the duel'). They are together in their foreignness.

In the sixteenth century the practice of using armour and emblazoned liveries (helmets and masks) fell into disuse; men now faced each other in their shirtsleeves and with bare faces. It was no longer a question of confrontation between the champions of a heraldic bestiary (infra-human monsters incarnating groups which transcended the individual); the confrontation now was between an almost naked individual and his fellow man, his brother. Profoundly fragile, men no longer displayed any sign of belonging to any society or family, they had no totems; each was the most insignificant and at the same time the most irreplaceable of creatures. More masked than ever from ordinary mortals, stripped of his character, he was visible and recognisable only for that other person whom he met on the field, as unprotected and frail as himself, but caparisoned in the same sense of honour.

Complicity was woven between them and by them, beginning with their armed encounter. Theirs was a private and egalitarian society which ridiculed the norms of society as a whole. In the eyes of the Church every duel was the foundation of a satanic sect. In those of the magistrate it set the seal on a conspiracy. In those of the whole collectivity duels created a secret society. And – as Goethe said in a text condemning duels – 'what is fascinating in every secret society, its essential attraction, is the transgression of a ban, is the setting up of laws against the law, and where possible of power against power'.

These manifestations of fraternity help us to understand the other characteristic of the ideal duellist, *generosity*. Allowing the opponent to pick up his sword or to get up after a fall, leaving him his life and giving the loser back his weapon were all elements in the scenario of a fine duel. They proved that the combatant who had the advantage was not dominated by his passions, that he was still in control of his urges.

Descartes defined generosity as 'the empire that we have over our will'. This control of oneself was not the same as domination of others. Victory in a duel worthy of the name attributed superiority not to the winner but to 'the luck of arms'. And where the winner treated the loser well, this was not done as a gift, or pardon. For the right to pardon belonged to the sovereign. Royal grace (like the divine form) was an invaluable and undeserved gift, and the person who received it was forever in the debt of whomever had granted it. Generosity, which was a power belonging to the gentleman, was different. The liberal King maintained his position over his subjects because of their gratitude. In a duel the generous gentleman made his equal a gift which simultaneously required an equally invaluable gift in return. He did not subject his opponent, he did not abase him. He gave him recognition as a free agent, by using his own freedom in relation to him. Here it would be apposite to cite in their entirety the two or three pages in which Descartes describes generosity, but we will content ourselves with selecting two or three sentences:

> true generosity, which causes a man to esteem himself as highly as he legitimately can, consists ... in the fact that he knows that there is nothing that truly pertains to him but this free disposition of his will, and that there is no reason why he should be praised or blamed unless it is because he uses it well or ill.... Those who have this knowledge and feeling about themselves easily persuade themselves that every other man can also have them in his own case, because there is nothing in this that depends on another. That is why they never despise anyone ... they are for this reason always perfectly courteous, affable and obliging towards everyone.

Armchair Cartesians have gained the impression that there was no place in the master's system for the problem of how we can know others. This is because they were not gentlemen, and had not, as Descartes had, practised duelling. The latter had no need for discursive proof when he had an experience of the other which was as immediate and as obvious as the *cogito*. To challenge, meet and confront one's equal on the field was to test out another free will without which the ego could not be revealed, against which the ego must both clash and lean to proclaim *I am*.

The individual can recognise himself only by recognising another of such worth that his worth is affirmed to the point of suppressing his own life. There is a fundamental solidarity between these men, who are at once both fellows and strangers, each magnificently autonomous.

Perhaps this sentence, written on the fight between Jacob and the Angel, applies to every duel: 'the goal of the combatants is not separation from one another, but union'.

Chapter 19
Theologico-political Themes

War

There are many links between duelling and war.

First, there is the negative link, stressed by some moralists. According to these fencing is neither a military exercise nor a kind of art of war and the skill and audacity of duellists has nothing in common with the courage and strength of the warrior; it is 'a trick of valour'; the personal point of honour is a diversion from patriotism, as proved by the Italians, incomparable masters of arms but hopeless soldiers: 'They think only of their glory and disdain their country's honour.'

But above all the links are positive, and contemporaries were very aware of them.

The sociological link. The men who had a vocation for duelling were 'people who carried arms by profession', the *noblesse d'épée* and military personnel in general. When duelling became obsolete elsewhere, it kept all its importance within the army. So the professional warrior, the man 'meticulous about honour' and the man who fought duels were all the same.

The chronological link. The frequency of duels, or their importance in the collective mind, seems to reach its peaks in the years and indeed the months which immediately precede or follow a civil or foreign war. Contemporaries were well aware of this, although they attributed to it a causality which was rather too simple, seeing the proliferation of duels as a pure consequence either of the state of war or of the state of peace. A more pertinent explanation, all things considered, was given by an Italian prelate who saw the wars ravaging the Piedmont as effect of divine anger, itself engendered by duels.

There was also a *relation of substitution*, when departure for a war was the only possible path for a man of honour who was prevented from fighting duels. Reconciliations imposed by indisputable authority and, later, the quibbling arbitration of the point-of-honour judges made life unbearable at the scene of a quarrel where a point of

honour was at stake. The appellant or *appelé*, frustrated in his desire
to fight a duel, had no way out but to enlist for what Brantôme called
'the fine journey of war'. In this he was seeking neither military
discipline nor the conventional aspect of the conflicts of the period,
but a distant and hazardous adventure, beyond the constraints of an
everyday life that could permit neither an insult nor its avenging.

The conceptual link. At least two authors devoted a whole treatise to
the related themes of duels and war. For the old etymologists *duellum*
was a doublet of *bellum*. And although the cauists often defined
duellum as *pugna duorum*, the persistence in French of the expression
'duel combat' (*combat en duel*) proves that there was an 'analogy of the
duel' with war, rather than with combat, or the battle (which is only
an element of war).

It is possible to lose a battle without losing the war; but a man
cannot lose a duel without settling his quarrel. Certainly for anyone
who understands duels as simply elements in rivalries, vendettas or
more or less lengthy, more or less eventful and bloody private wars,
they would seem to resemble a battle involving a small number of
men. But for the duellist himself, or for the witness who accepted the
logic of the point of honour, the finished duel formed a whole, as a
war forms a whole. And, like a war, it was intended definitively to
resolve a pre-existing conflict, which was more or less complex and
long-lasting. Between societies and between individuals, wars and
duels were respectively the final confrontation which violently ended
rivalries and obliged each to recognise the other.

This was not really a recognition of where right lay, however the
stubborn tradition of the ordeal would have it; nor was it even a
recognition of failure on the part of the man who admitted defeat. It
was a recognition that the other existed, that he had the dignity of
existing, and that this irrevocable dignity could only be saluted (even
in the defeat and death of the opponent).

The analogy between duelling and war was so strong that it
supported the idea that international conflicts and military struggles
could be resolved by single combat between captains or champions
designated by them. The exchange of knightly cartels between
François I and Charles V was a major episode in the European
context and later Henri of Navarre challenged the Duc de Guise
during the Wars of Religion, as Christian IV of Denmark did
Christian IX of Sweden in the Northern War. Louis XIV himself
asked 'if in all conscience he would be allowed to fight the Emperor
Leopold'. This type of duel, never realised but always envisaged,
occupied an important place in the thinking of the casuists – who
were certainly not visionaries.

The great Dutch jurist Grotius himself devoted a paragraph of his

De jure belli et pacis to this type of duel; all things considered, he justifies it out of a concern to spare human life. He bases his theory on references to Herodotus, Plutarch, Strabon and Livy; but in contemporary eyes what really authorised the duel between champions was, as we have already seen, the biblical example of the combat between David and Goliath. War and its miseries were avoided; but blood flowed in a confrontation between man and man in which the outcome was decided by God.

The duel, like war, is a kind of ritualised violence. Like war, it developed from a fundamentally religious liturgy into a contractual practice. Like war which became 'conventional', the formal duel became a fight *ex condicto*, it became in some sense secularised. But this did not mean it was desacralised.

The Crusade

Although every war was sacred, the war of the Christians against the Infidel was a holy war. This was why duellists' careers often followed the path of the Crusade.

We can see this in a random investigation of their biographies. Sometimes we come across a gentleman greedy for honour, who has been reconciled with his opponent without drawing his sword; or else we find a homicidal duellist who has a long period to wait for his pardon. He goes off to fight in Hungary, in Candia or on the galleys of Malta. At first glance his choice does not seem very different from enlisting for an expedition led by his natural sovereign, or under the banners of the Stuarts or the House of Orange. If it were possible to draw up statistics it might even be that the holy war was not the one most frequently chosen. Yet it is the one most in harmony with the duellist's logic of catharsis. Instead of immediate reintegration into the social order through military discipline and participation in a war between states (a war in which what is at stake, even if most worthy of respect, is only human), this choice offers a reconciliation of the individual (excluded by dishonour or by murder) with the most all-embracing, the most perfect society of Christendom. It matters little to the outlaw who has withdrawn from his world and entered the Other World with his drawn sword whether or not he ever returns to his native land. As late as the beginning of the eighteenth century we still find duellists who were unrepentant, but transfigured by holy war.

Looking beyond these individual choices, planners often saw departure for the Crusade as a salvation from the temptation of duelling, for two reasons. The first starts from an observation of the high numbers of victims of duelling. Why did these men not sacrifice themselves instead for the just cause: the deliverance of the Holy Land by Christendom and the conquest of the Eastern Empire by the King of France? One of Richelieu's apologists perhaps gave best expression to this first view, saying, 'It is unbelievable, Théopompe, how many men this disastrous calamity [of duelling] has lost us since the time of Henri II. Today a bridge could be made of their bodies which could be used to conquer the Levant.'

The second argument is presented as a grand operation of social policing: if they are to be forbidden the sterile release of duelling, gentlemen's combative urges should be put to use against the Turk and the Infidel.

Protestants advanced these two similar and often merged proposals as frequently as Catholics did, often adorned with prophetic references. Such appeals to the glory of the beyond were necessary to make men who were hungry for honour listen to those who were trying to dissuade them from 'cutting each other's throats'. For it was the same ardour that sent gentlemen into duels as sent them to the Turkish front. Dupront lists the years when 'the urge to leave' was the most felt, after the peace of Cateau-Cambrésis and just before the Thirty Years War. These are also the periods when we found peaks of duelling.

It was precisely during one of those peaks that Chenel de La Chapperonaye proposed his Order of the Knights of the Magdalen, the most polished example of a plan for combating duelling by having men enlist for the Crusade. This Breton nobleman had an example of a famous formal duel in his family tree: he boasted of being descended from Beaumanoir, hero of the 'combat of the Thirty' during the Hundred Years Wars. His life, or the image of it that he wanted to leave behind him, was an endless movement between three poles, one negative – the duel – and the two others positive: holy war and the life of a hermit. He enlisted with the Knights of Malta following a duel and met a hermit in Calabria who told him the story of his life and described to him his revelations. The hermit had himself been a French gentleman and furious duellists, who had been cured by the loss of a close relative whom one of his friends had killed in a duel. He had wanted to 'find war in Hungary', but had arrived there at a time of truce and, disillusioned by this sordidly temporal hitch, had retired to a wild part of Italy. However, he still dreamed of death at the hands of the Turks, in the Holy Land this time. On leaving for Rome to obtain the necessary dispensations, he had heard a voice telling him to return to his hermitage, where a series of allegorical visions had given him his real mission: to prophesy an order of French knights dedicated to the Magdalen who 'would renounce duelling and other vices by oath', and would wear the cross on their coats. Filled with enthusiasm, Chenel gave up his plans for an individual crusade and returned to France 'since God wills it': there he proposed to Louis XIII that the revealed order should be set up, with himself as its first Grand Master.

Like many utopias, his proposal minutely weaves together concrete details, dates and limitless eschatological dreaming. Ultimately the 'knights with red crosses possessed all of the Holy Land ... and the Palace of their Grand Master was built on the ruins of the Castle of Magdalon'. Young Louis XIII had 'Empire's seat at Constantinople, and the whole of the Levant had come under his rule by virtue of these knights'. Had not 'the dying Mahomet' himself predicted that his sect would be flattened by the French?

But in the shorter term the Knights of the Magdalen would be patriarchs from the depths of rural France. On Sundays, after mass, they would see that the peasants of their respective domains practised the use of arms, and in the evening they would dispense justice to these same people. This was a prefiguration of the dreams of the party of the 'rurals', the agrarian party which is one component of contemporary France, remaining silent and unnoticed most of the time, but coming to the fore at times of national catastrophe: in 1815, 1870 and 1940.

For the moment, the Order of the Magdalen was to run an academy for well-born but poor young men, providing assistance to those gentlemen who needed it and a school of moral worth. Young men would be accepted on the 'attestation of their bishop and three notable gentlemen'. They would have to give up blasphemy, duelling, gambling, forbidden books and lascivious songs. But to prevent idleness they were to have a games room, a tennis court, pall-mall and billiards.

This plan was printed 'with privilege' and its author received encouragement and perhaps some funds from Louis XIII. But the planned Parisian academy was never built and Chenel de La Chapperonaye imposed the cross on no one. Condemned to remain alone, he was once more thrown from the life of the Crusader to that of the hermit. For a while he camped in a tent emblazoned with the fleur-de-lis in the great gallery of the Louvre, then he retired to Samois, on the edge of the forest of Fontainbleau, to a place which still bears the name of the Hermitage of the Magdalen. After 1625, all trace of Chenel was lost: 'he disappeared, without anyone ever learning what became of him'. A mysterious end, in keeping with his character, and which does not prevent us from imagining that he died a heroic death fighting the Infidel.

Chenel de La Chapperonaye's work has the kind of perfection that only belongs to failed enterprises. The Marquis de Fénelon's Brotherhoods of the Passion, which existed and acted, do not tie together the fight against duelling and the fight against the Infidel so neatly. However, there were links between the two which, though indirect and buried, were still numerous and strong.

Certainly at the *symbolic* level, the Passion did not have the same emotional charge as the Cross. The first was a sign of victory, an emblem of conquest, imperious in its superhuman geometricality. The second was a moving scene in which the Man of sorrow was crushed by the weight of evil: an emotional and individual form of religiosity, pathetic rather than tragic, and much less warlike and virile than the exaltation of the Cross.

In *publications*, the link is explicit in the work of only one author, the Carmelite Cyprien de la Nativité. In his *Destruction of the Duel*, he recalls the prophecy which reserves for the French the crushing of Turkish might, and celebrates 'the declaration of all the brave gentlemen who crossed themselves like their predecessors, saying "God wills it" to destroy duelling'.

But the link is implicit, we think, in another short work, beginning with the title page: '*Christian and Moral Arguments Against Duels* by Vantadour, canon of the Church of Paris'. For a quarter of a century Canon de Ventadour had been the man behind the Company of the Holy Sacrament; he published nothing apart from this pamphlet, and this in itself gives weight to his writing. But what gives it its full significance is this man's past, and the tradition of his family. Henri de Levis, Duc de Ventadour and the King's Lieutenant-General in Languedoc, entered holy orders only after he had brought about the military defeat of the Protestants. His Levis ancestors had been given the title of 'marshals of the faith' and the fief of Ventadour after conquering the lands of Oc in a Crusade against the Cathar heretics. This background of the Crusades was obvious to the nobility and gentry, to whom his pamphlet was addressed, and who were fascinated by great deeds and genealogies. A text against duelling signed Ventadour was a text in support of the Crusades, a call for a new Crusade: this time against the Enemy within, the Infidel lurking in the heart of Christian society and in Christian souls.

We can also see the link in the work of members of the Brotherhood of the Passion. In their actions, they often combined the theme of the fight against duels and quarrels with that of the conversion of non-Christians. In 1653, three of them, Fénelon, Albon and Dufour, signed a letter with St Vincent de Paul advocating foreign missions, which was addressed to the Roman Congregation of the Propaganda. A few years later, we find many members of the Brotherhood are shareholders in a commercial company providing financial cover for a mission to Tonkin; and the fight against duels, the ransom of prisoners in Barbary and missionary work all appear on the agenda of the same meeting of the Company of the Holy Sacrament.

This work for the propagation of the faith in infidel or pagan countries was a transposition of the spirit of conquest, no doubt aimed at satisfying the archaic drives of the *noblesse d'épée*, while integrating them into the changing times. The quest for spiritual glory justified and compensated for their active renunciation of the quest for the point of honour. After 1660 these exotic and purely transcendent conquests were also doubtless an attempt to compensate for the collapse of the dreams of political domination which Fénelon and his companions (consciously or not) had had. But would these men have been satisfied with such sublimations? It is certain that more than one of them preferred concrete and tangible chimeras to something so terribly abstract as the conquest of souls and – to use terminology unknown to them – propaganda of cultural integration. For those activists who had given up duelling but who did not want to and could not (indeed were duty-bound not to) give up their own values, especially that of the Brave Man, the archaic dream of the Crusade retained all its meaning.

Let us look once more at an example already cited, that of the Duc de Navailles. This Protestant who was converted by Richelieu, this devout soldier and faithful servant of the King and his ministers, made a profession of modesty before the Court.

In 1660 he refused to fight a duel 'as a Christian . . . and because of the respect he bore for the memory of the late Cardinal'. Four years later, he confessed to the priest of Fontainebleau 'his zeal for going to sacrifice himself fighting the Turks'. And five years after this confidence he embarked for Candia, at the head of the detachment of volunteers who served by permission of the King under the pontifical banner, to defend the last Christian place on the island. He had the shame of returning alive and beaten and the King thanked him by disgracing him.

Navailles was not an isolated case. We believe that this expedition to Candia should be reinterpreted in the light of the Brotherhood of the Passion's logic of combat. This sad venture, which progressed in an undistinguished way and ended in hopeless failure, would gain a kind of grandeur if it were taken out of the diplomatic context and interpreted in terms of the spirit of the gentlemen who took part in it, and who had, beforehand, been (or not) involved in an interiorised stuggle against duelling. We have undertaken no psychosociological study of the French contingent in Candia; but we know the leaders and principle characters of the expedition well enough.

First, there was La Feuillade. He was an old-style man of the sword, of whom Louis XIV is supposed to have said, 'As long as La

Feuillade grants that I am as good a gentleman as he, that's all I ask of him.' For this future Marshal who said that his titles came 'from God and his sword', the royal edicts against duelling carried no more weight than the pious condemnations of the gentlemen of Saint-Sulpice. He had a number of quarrels and at least one actual duel. He also challenged a gentleman who had retired to Spain and had dared to place inverted lilies in his coat of arms, thereby insulting the fleur-de-lis, emblem of the French royalty. Before Candia La Feuillade had already had a taste of holy war, having won fame in the service of the Emperor and Christianity against the Turk at the battle of Saint Gotthard.

There was also Beaufort. Beaufort has appeared several times in this study: a typical Frondeur and impenitent duellist, he was a brave man to whom the spirit of Bourbon absolutism and the party of the *dévots* (the religiously devout) were equally foreign. As a *Grand*, he would never have caused trouble under Louis XIV; but as a brave man he could only have found life difficult under the Great Louis. So he took command of an anachronistic venture which gave him the opportunity for a hero's end. Not only was he killed in battle, but his body, like that of the Emperor–Crusader Barbarossa, was never found.

Besides these leaders, who still believed in duelling and in the Crusade, there were those who wanted to believe in crusading because they had made a declaration that they no longer believed in duelling, such as the Marquis de Fénelon himself. This hotheaded officer, whom Olier had long ago dissuaded from pursuing a military career, returned to the service in the company of his son. Although he was not in charge of the expedition, he may have initiated it. His behaviour before Candia (where his son was killed at his side) is an example of heroic spirit, if not tactical skill. This opponent of duelling was in the same mould as Beaufort; for both of them what mattered was not winning a war condemned by the Chancelleries, but conquering a hero's glory and a martyr's crown. 'M. de Fénelon's zeal', said a witness, 'contributed not a little to maintaining the ardour of those who aspired to martyrdom.' Those to whom death on the field in a duel was refused, or who refused it to themselves, could die only on the field of honour.

From Montchrestien to Beaufort and from La Chapperonaye to La Mothe-Fénelon, from the challenge to a duel to the challenge of holy war, the same profound needs of the chivalric attitude are expressed – at least in France. Surveys of neighbouring countries in the sixteenth and seventeenth centuries have not shown that the idea of duelling was linked to that of the Crusade. France was the country in which the duel was most alive, most virulent; however, the Crusade was only experienced indirectly in that country which shared no frontier with the Infidel and where, since the reign of François I, official policy had been one of good relations with the Turks.

The relation between duel and crusade, those two forms of impossible and unavoidable combat, was keenly felt by a few generations of French gentlemen. But it disappeared from the clear – too clear – understanding of the men of the century of the Enlightenment.

As a counter-proof, their close connexion reappeared on the other side of the eighteenth century and the other side of Europe, with Kant, who wraps both phenomena in the same incomprehension and condemnation. 'The Crusades, and ancient knighthood, were *adventurous*. Duels, a wretched remnant of the latter arising from a perverted concept of chivalry, are grotesque.' Interestingly, the two phenomena, reduced to the absurd in the writing of this philosopher, remind us of a third: 'the *adventurousness* of the ancient hermits' solitary devotion'.*

So for the man of the Enlightenment there is a relation of aberration between duel, crusade and hermit: those three poles between which the destiny of Chenel de La Chapperonaye was split. These were also the three things to which the Marquis de Fénelon's son aspired and the three irreconcilable but inseparable ideals of the Duc de Beaufort. After his duel against Nemours, there was a rumour that he was going to become a Carthusian monk; after his disappearance before Candia, there was a rumour that he had retired to a hermitage somewhere in Crete or in the Holy Land. A solitary life in the desert, single combat *alla macchia* and confrontation with the Infidel on the outer reaches of Christendom; these three quests for an invigorating death in the confines of this world belong to the same imaginary whole. They are the three ways in which, for more than five hundred years, the chivalric world expressed its Mount Carmel complex.

The Page and the King

> Brassa Mignon en devoir ar'rove
> En deus lachet gante kleve.
>
> > (The greatest friend the King had
> > He killed with his sword.)
> > (Contrechapell)

---

*Italics FB.

Like love, as some would say, the duel needs three participants. Indeed, throughout the preceding pages, a third character has always been present between the two duellists, or at their side, above or behind them: the sovereign Prince, the King.

We have seen how the relation of King and duel changed over the period in question, from the days of the judicial duel, when the King had ultimate temporal authority over the proceedings, through the time when he oscillated between his role as 'first gentleman' and head of the state, to the still ambivalent but absolutist position of Louis XIV. We have seen how the duel represented a challenge to royal authority, and the importance of the image of David in this context.

To get a better idea of the relation between duelling and the person or role of the King, we shall now examine two powerful moments in a reign, the coronation and the murder of the King. The first was an inaugural rite which every new king underwent and to which he owed his legitimate power; the second was a bloody act, a brutal end, which did not come to every king but which haunted all of them more or less, and which many came near to before their deaths.

The Coronation

For Henri II, let us remember, a formal duel in which a champion represented the monarch was a preliminary to the coronation ceremony, and inaugurated his own reign. For his successors, who disapproved of duels, condemned them and sometimes prosecuted them, such a relation between duel and coronation was unthinkable. But another link was established. This was the inclusion in the coronation ritual of a phrase by which the new sovereign undertook to conduct a pitiless campaign against those who went against the ban on single combat.

After he had received the holy vial in Reims cathedral, the new sovereign uttered the *oath of the realm* (an undertaking to ensure the rule of justice and to pursue heretics). He then took the *oath of chivalry* (which made him the Grand Master of the Orders of the Holy Spirit and of St Louis). Immediately afterwards, he put on the gold spurs and sword of Charlemagne. It was at the end of the oath of chivalry that the words against duelling were to be uttered:

> To this end, We swear and promise by Our faith and word as King, to exempt no one in the future for any cause or consideration from the rigour of the edicts ... that no pardon or abolition shall be granted by Us to those who are convicted of the said

crimes of duels or premeditated encounters; that We shall have no regard for the solicitations of any Prince or Lord who intercedes on behalf of those guilty of the said crimes ... in order inviolably to uphold so Christian, just and necessary a law.

There is a history to this oath. When Henri IV was crowned at Chartres, he did not utter it, and with good reason: there were as yet no edicts which formally condemned the practice of duelling. Moreover it was important, so soon after his abjuration of Protestantism, not to drown the promise to fight against heretics in too long a text and he took the oath of the Order of the Holy Spirit the following day, in a different ceremony from that of the coronation. Louis XIII did swear not to pardon duellists. This promise was included with others in his declaration upon his coming of age, but it was absent from the text he spoke during his coronation (which included the oath of the Order of the Holy Spirit). In his 1651 edict Louis XIV promised that he would undertake to combat duellists in the coronation oath; however, accounts of the Reims ceremony make no mention of it and the most likely explanation for this is that he did not keep his promise. Doubtless this was deliberate; whether on the part of the young King, of Mazarin or of a pressure group close to those in power we cannot tell. But this unexplained backtracking certainly had effects on the relation between royalty and duels.

We must wait until 1723 and the coronation of Louis XV before the oath promised in 1651 is finally uttered, with a piously untruthful reference to 'Louis XIV of glorious memory, our great-grandfather, who solemnly swore on the day of his coronation to carry out the declaration of his coming of age'. In 1723 duelling was still practised, but it was sufficiently drained of political content and heroic prestige for an absolute monarch to profess that he would combat it pitilessly in his capacity as Knight of the Holy Spirit and of Louis.

In 1774 Louis XVI also took this oath, in a clear, firm voice, contrasting with the hesitant and almost inaudible tone in which he undertook to 'pursue all heretics'. These were times of reason and tolerance. France was as embarrassed at excluding the co-religionists of its leading financier M. Necker as it was enthusiastic at the condemnation of frenzied upholders of a cruel and barbaric practice.

The anti-duelling clause, included with some hesitation in the coronation oath, has a clear meaning for us. It branded duelling as a practice that stirred up discord and betrayed the unity of the realm. Like heresy, duelling tore the seamless robe of France. A king worthy of his title could not tolerate it without breaking the basic pact binding him to God and to his subjects.

The Regicide

The murder of the King, the most abominable crime of all in the minds of people around 1600 (unless Providence inspired it, transforming it into a tyrannicidal act of salvation), was not unrelated to duelling. We saw this clearly when the champion of the Paris Leaguers, Marolle, faced the champion of the royalist army, L'Isle-Marivaut, in single combat, the day after Jacques Clément's assassination of Henri III.

However, ten years later when duelling was becoming an act of rebellion against the royal will, the relation between the two bloody deeds changed; it was said at the time that it was because Henri III was too lenient towards duellists that he himself was stabbed to death. The Sieur de Chevalier stated this very definitely in a 1609 pamphlet: 'Before duels was blood seen so horribly spilled as since? . . . Was it said that a great King, very great, very magnificent, was driven from his house and then assassinated by one of those who preach peace every day?' As a warning to Henri III's successor Henri IV, he added: 'Consider this well. From the duel men go on to contempt for the laws and orders, from this to contempt for the sovereign, then to conspiracy against the state and after that to attacks on the sacred person of the Prince.' A year later François Ravaillac's knife proved him right. Richelieu and Arnauld d'Andilly repeated to his successors that Providence had wanted Henri IV to die in an assassination to punish him for having allowed duellists to kill each other without punishment: 'these words made a great impression on Louis XIII'.

An anonymous leaflet published in 1616 developed the same theme. It was supposed to be a message sent from the other world by Baron de Monglas, who had been killed in a duel, to his still-living murderer Vitry and to all those tempted by the point of honour. A description of hell concludes this edifying little volume. The place of those killed in duels is almost at the bottom of the world of the damned. There Monlas's shade recognises and lists celebrities of the time, devoting two pages to describing them. But he devotes three pages to the group after this, at the bottom, a group in which he recognises Chastel, Ravaillac and the 'good fathers' who were the theoreticians of tyrannicide. For the author, as for Dante before him, an attack on the monarch's life was the worst of sins. But the duel was the sin most closely related to this supreme crime.

Lastly we should note the chronological coincidence between, on the one hand, the peak of the 'frenzy of duels' and, on the other, the blossoming of theories justifying tyrannicide and the repeated attempts to put them into practice around the time of the successful actions of Clément and Ravaillac. The time of duels more or less began with that of regicides. But it lasted longer; perhaps taking over from the latter, to recall them without enacting them, symbolically replacing the unbearable act of striking at the sacred person of the sovereign. Britain, where there was a plurisecular tradition of royal murder (brought back to mind opportunely at the time by Shakespearean theatre), had a sufficient sense of the state to carry out two things which were then unthinkable in France: on the one hand duels ceased to flourish as abruptly as the vogue for regicide stopped in France; on the other, the authorities condemned Charles I to death and executed him by a procedure which was considered legal. In France duelling may have been a premonitory substitute, a warning of the impossibility of regicide. 'Et nunc reges erudimini!' the clicking blades repeated.

These combats in which the knight confronted his king and the oath in which the King-knight confronted his gentlemen call for three interpretations which interpenetrate and complete each other: the first psychological, the second anthropological and the third properly political, and even theologico-political.

Psychological Interpretation

This postulates that we accept the analogy between king and father. From this point of view, every duellist was to a greater or lesser extent the young men's champion against a king–father representing the older men. He kills his brother to show his father that he is capable of killing him, that he is only sparing him out of a respect in which there is no fear, and that in return he expects and requires that his father should recognise him as his equal. He is Rodrigue in Corneille's *Le Cid*, who can succeed Don Diègue because he has proved his courage by victoriously fighting his father's substitute:

Tout autre que mon père
l'éprouverait sur l'heure.

(Any man other than my father
would feel it at once.)

(*Le Cid*, I, 6)

The duel was a trial by which the *juvenes* gained admission and recognition among the *seniores*, while at the same time supplanting them.

As we have seen, the duel was an initiatory act, a rite of passage. This interpretation alone resolves the contradiction between the theoretical discourse, which saw duelling as exclusively the province of youth, and anecdotes in which duellists are often, indeed most often. mature, married men, fathers, with administrative or military functions and responsibilities. They were adults, or even greybeards. But in terms of the collective psychology they were – in their action, and again each time they repeated it – youths on an aggressive quest for integration. These men were perpetuated rather than perpetual adolescents.

Like all initiations, the duel is a rite of regression at the same time as being a rite of passage, it is a rejection of ageing and socialisation, a rite of return to an original state. This rejection was prolonged by the quarantine, the exile by which every man 'guilty of duelling' was punished; it was repeated and revived by each new armed encounter. Thus the purest duellists, collectors of quarrels such as Balagny and Bouteville, proclaimed that they had no place in this world in which they were none the less adulated by the ladies, imitated by men and fearfully admired by kings.

On the part of the combatants such regression is signified by the choice of out-of-the-way places and the rejection of armour and clothing. It is also signified by reference in writings of the time to a metaphorical bestiary. The animals in this bestiary are not those famed for the prestigious courage on which authority is based (lion, stag, eagle, cock), nor are they the sly and venomous ones that slither along the ground (serpents, scorpions); this bestiary is full of powerful, wild and solitary beasts (wolf, bear, boar). Bishop Camus invented the name 'lycanthropophagi' for these werewolves of the point of honour.

So the duel is a confrontation of father and son. In it the son both avenges and kills the father. He wins the status of father, while rejecting it forever. When necessary he excludes himself from this legitimate and sacrilegious succession by a self-sacrificial death. He is essentially *father* because existentially he is *son*.

Like Ernest Jones in his analysis of *Hamlet*, we can, in the scenography of a duel and the psychology of a duellist, observe 'throughout the tragedy the theme of the son–father conflict which shows through even the most obscure interlacing'. One can, as Jones does, see at work on that stage without an audience which is the field of a duel a psychic *process of decomposition* and a *process of doubling*.

Process of decomposition: every duellist is/represents for both his opponent and himself *both* his brother–enemy and the Father (familial, social or moral). And single combat allows the ego, which wants to affirm but is afraid to impose itself, to satisfy both its murderous and suicidal drives and, more profoundly still, its life and death drives.

Process of doubling: this 'procedure which consists in peopling the scene with pale supernumeraries in order to exalt the hero' is achieved in single combat by the use of seconds. The seconds repeat and amplify the duellist's action, but they do not betray it. Rather they enhance the implacably singular character of his fight.

In Shakespeare's tragedy, it is only during the final duel that the hero becomes generous towards the brother-in-law manqué, Laertes, whom he is going to kill; it is only then that he can both kill the King-neo-father (Claudius) and avenge the King–father (Hamlet I), thereby proving himself worthy to reign. But this murder of investiture makes him the equal of his rivals to the point where he accompanies them into death. The victorious duellist does not become King. He becomes the King's brother. He invests as King the son of the man his own father had previously killed in a duel. This man of words gives his 'dying voice' to Fortinbras. 'The rest is silence.'

Anthropological Interpretation

The duel seen as the murder of the King's substitute, or as the sacrifice inaugurating a reign, and the coronation oath seen as the duellists' *devotio* to ensure that the monarch's reign will be good, are solemn and bloody acts. In both manifest and latent representations, whoever spills blood regenerates and/or weakens the society and the individual or group which leads it. In a more abstract representation (that of the jurisconsults and 'politicologues', from St Thomas to Pufendorf), whoever spills blood holds or usurps the 'right of the sword' (*droit de glaive*), which both symbolises and completes political power.

To fight, causing and facing death, is to manifest or acquire energy deserving of prestige and to possess prestige is to have a right to power. The King cannot fight in person. He cannot risk himself in single combat. Even if the reason given is his royal superiority over any warrior he maight claim to equal, this ban can only be felt as symptomatic of a fundamental weakness of the individual wearing the crown. His life is too fragile to be exposed. In comparison the aristocratic heroes who 'rush' unrestrainedly into encounters 'in which death is seen to appear' seem invulnerable.

The young hero who pays homage to the old man on the throne manifests an insolent vitality. Each time it is the encounter between David and Saul: the warrior teaches the King a lesson. Even if this is useful and precious to the King, it can only be unbearable to him. The warrior is potentially a competitor, a rival, a usurper, even if he is only an obedient and loyal subject. But if the hero should for a moment free himself from his obedience (as is the case in a duel) and spill blood without receiving the express order to do so, if he disposes of his own life, he becomes an active rebel; he lays claim to being a legitimate successor and takes for himself the 'right of the sword'. The duellist may well be unaware of the meaning of his action, or not care what it is; this does not change the fact that his action is understood in such a way by both the King and the people.

Heroism is indispensable to the cohesion of the group it saves and incompatible with the order that the King guarantees to that group. It is therefore the hero's destiny to take power, as it is the King's vocation both to congratulate the hero–victor and to suppress the hero–transgressor. However, in duelling, which is suicide, the hero eliminates himself. He kills both his opponent, the King's substitute, and the King's successor, who is himself. This double murder can only doubly weaken the legitimate King. A tyrant like Tarquin might find it useful that the ambitious should mutually kill each other. A legitimate King knows he loses power each time he loses one of those who hold prestige. And the Valois and Bourbon kings well knew that every *Grand* in the kingdom was 'still greater dead than alive'. Prestige won in death cannot be diminished. The hero who is young in age or by his self-sacrificial act will age no more, while the King who outlives him, old by reason of his function, will age a little more every day of his reign.

The aristocratic duel is a potlatch of destruction and the most radical form possible, since in it its organisers destroy their own lives. Those who annihilate themselves – and the group they represent – in duels forever subjugate those who only watch, and primarily that individual who is condemned not to compete with them in this outlay of vital energy: the monarch. The more the population of gentlemen was reduced by duelling, the more noble values were reinforced; and also the weaker the other social values grew, for no one was so extravagantly affirming them.

When ancient Rome was in danger, the *ver sacrum* gave renewed strength and cohesion to Roman society in the face of the enemy from outside. But when the French nobility sacrificed its springtime, was it the nobility or the kingdom that was regenerated?

Political Interpretation

The question that ends the preceding paragraph leads to another: why did this transferred confrontation between gentleman and King that was duelling occupy a particular phase of a particular history? Why did this phenomenon particularly flourish in France, during the reigns of the sons of Henri II and the first Bourbons?

The duel against the King is an unacknowledged fight. In it the gentlemen's rebellion is accompanied by constant affirmations of loyalty which, overall, are sincere. In it the severity of the kings is accompanied by almost constant and comprehensive leniency. It is a confrontation in which neither wants to see the suppression of the other, nor really his subjection. What each is looking for in these duels and in their repression is a balance between a tempered monarchy (to which both sides are attached) and an absolute monarchy (which is proclaimed but not believed in). The duel was a privileged manifestation of these tensions which, in Montesquieu's analysis, formed the reality (and for him the value) of the monarchy in modern France. 'The fundamental maxim [of the monarchy] is: No monarch, no nobility; no nobiltiy, no monarch.' These tensions prevent the monarch from becoming a despot, and the nobility from sliding into oligarchy. They maintain the delicate balance which saves the state from both tyranny and anarchy.

Such was the political meaning of duels: both a violent challenge to the man in power, a refusal to submit to his orders, and a refusal to take power or to participate in his power. The duel is an injunction to the King to be the King and a warning to the monarch to behave like a gentleman. Although the peak periods of duelling coincide with those of political agitation, they are the sign of the latter, but not its expression. They do not propose the other solution in a political alternative; they profess that the only politics possible is that of alternatives.

The absence of political aims and demands on the part of duellists is striking. They have no programmes. They have almost no language. They have only examples, to which they add a new example each time they give a challenge, and cross swords. Their action is not one of opposition, it is one of resistance. Not a passive resistance, clinging to outdated positions, but one that invents a new symbolic strategy (the duel for a point of honour) to signify an autonomous counter-power within the contemporary political system. This is a balanced political system in which the power of the monarch cannot be hegemonic. Of course, the duel claims to be part of venerable traditions, but does not the King's justice do the same? Their confrontation is in no way a struggle between past and present.

Some have maintained that the French nobility and gentry went through a long crisis between the mid-sixteenth and mid-seventeen centuries. This much debated thesis is far from evident from the historian's point of view. Let us prudently say that over this century the aristocracy (if we can conceive of it as a whole) came up against the many different facets of a world that was changing, but which was nevertheless not rejecting or marginalising the aristocracy. The aristocrats adapted to these changes through crises and changes in awareness. For some duelling was a manifestation of these crises in awareness. The nobility and gentry were to survive the vogue for duelling, and the vogue for duelling was never limited to gentlemen alone.

In the relation between duellist and King the duel was therefore not a manifestation of a 'reactionary' political opposition. It did not mean that the duellists were becoming ossified in outdated positions, it was not a resistance in the passive sense of an attitude of a group which history would condemn. It was the arrogant affirmation that aristocracy and monarchy are fundamentally associated opposites in a coherent political system.

In the biblical 'duel' of David and Goliath, the two participants hide/reveal a third, King Saul. There is another combat in Holy Writ which is far more like a duel in terms of its procedure and what is at stake, but to which our sources never allude: the combat between Jacob and the Angel. This was a fair fight for recognition, with equal arms, and it also reveals a third character: God. But, at the period under study here, he was hidden by the duellists themselves and by those who wrote for them. Does this reflect 'forgetfulness' and unease, or rather silence and reverence before so formidable an example?

To be a duellist, on the political level, was to be drunk on equality and to have a passionate love of hierarchy. On the religious level, it was to proclaim transcendence and to make oneself equal to God. It was an extreme situation, a contradiction which, for the individual, could be resolved only in death.

Chapter 20

The Duel In and Beyond Time

And Jacob was left alone; and there
wrestled a man with him until the breaking
of the day. And when he saw that he
prevailed not against him, he touched the
hollow of his thigh; and the hollow of
Jacob's thigh was out of joint, as he
wrestled with him. And he said, Let me go,
for the day breaketh. And he said, I will
not let thee go, except thou bless me.
And he said unto him, What is thy name?
And he said, Jacob. And he said, Thy name
shall be called no more Jacob, but Israel:
for as a prince hast thou power with God
and with men and hast prevailed. And
Jacob asked him, and said, Tell me, I pray
thee, thy name. And he said, Wherefore is
it that thou dost ask after my name? And
he blessed him there.

(Genesis 32: 24–9, King James Version)

The Time of Duels

Although contested and attacked from its very beginnings, the duel
has a strength which it owes neither to the protection of a legal status
nor to a propaganda offensive. It has had long and undeniable
periods of calm, even of retreat, at least at the only level accessible to
our analysis, that of collective interest in it. But the meaning of these
periods is challenged by sudden and violent upsurges. It matters little
(in one sense) that in our eyes each of these revivals is less vigorous
than the preceding one; for those who lived through them, each
reduced previous developments to nothing and signified the inanity
of the efforts underlying them.

In duelling we can find a typical case of *resistance*. We watch the
edicts, decrees and synodal statutes pile up, we hear the voices of the
preachers superimposed over those of the moralists and poets, and

we note the derisory, illusory nature of the power and prestige of those in authority faced with the silent resolution of two individuals who are masters of themselves to the point of choosing solidarity and death. The duellists block that power without making speeches, without pride, but also without humility, as though they are indifferent to the Prince's actions, 'psychological' or otherwise. How much more exasperating and frustrating is resistance than opposition for *homo politicus*! A duellist who demonstrates his faithfulness to the demands of the point of honour does not shut himself away in a 'long-term prison', he places himself in the isolation of lasting freedom. How right were those who saw duels in terms of little David fighting the colossal Goliath!

Historical resistance is not a fixation on objects which become irremediably more anachronistic and outdated. Such an act would only be a rejection of passing time, and of the temporary rule of the present-day masters of time. A form of collective resistance like the 'frenzy of duels' is a type of inventiveness; it is a fabrication of an original system. In the sixteenth and seventeenth centuries the French duel was a new composition, even if it drew on traditional values, and not a bastion in which to take refuge and make an honourable last stand. It was a war machine which effectively influenced the course of history, a course which can only be the result of several forces in both contradictory and complementary relations. It was a 'positive defence', since resistance to a new order provides the means of participating in the future order.

In fact, in the historical role of duels, we can see three histories in the making at the same point. First, there is the history we can call authoritarian, which is often official history. We shall represent it here with a school textbook: 'The King forbade duels on pain of death. This did not prevent a great lord, Comte Montmorency-Bouteville, from fighting.... He was condemned to death for disobeying the King and had his head cut off.' Then there is sociological history, the history of reality rather than norms – at least of a certain reality which is not the only one, but whose weight is impressive. According to this second history, duels, which the action of the authorities could not eliminate, were marginalised sooner or later by an overall change in the way of life and by a slow and non-linear shift in values considered supreme. Lastly, a third history is symbolic history.

This third history designates, after the *forces from on high* (of ideology and active minorities) and the *forces from below* (attitudes, silent or chanting majorities, either conformist or in revolt), the *forces from elsewhere* (let us call them prophetic, or those of resisting minorities). The duel is one of these tenacious and stubborn forces, which has something different to say from official accounts, or their opposite.

To understand the function of the duel in monarchial, Tridentine France, we should like to draw a parallel with a phenomenon which has a place and role in the contemporary West: aeroplane hijacking. Both types of event end in the failure of their perpetrators, sometimes in their confusion and ridicule, always in their final neutralisation and often in their physical elimination, coupled with the loss of their victims (in the one case the aeroplane hostages and in the other the opponent and seconds in an encounter). On the level of 'reality', these are hopeless actions, ineffective strategies. But during the unfolding of such events neither side involved reasons according to the logic of 'reality', and, when the action is over, another, similar, soon occurs elsewhere, for other motives. These motives, it must be admitted, are sometimes futile, sometimes exorbitant, but never really in proportion to the tragic nature of the event. What is at stake is not, in fact, the acknowledged stake: the object of a quarrel between duellists or the ransom demanded by the hijackers (which may vary strangely during the negotiations, without thereby reflecting a change in the power relations in operation). In such cases everything unfolds according to a logic of the symbolic. Like forcing a jet to change course, accusing a man of lying and waiting for him in the field means drawing society and those who run it into a terrain which is not their own. It means, by a kind of intellectual fencing, avoiding reality's blows, its power relations and measurable violence. It means touching (without piercing) the chink in the armour of the authorities, forcing the armour's wearer to display this tiny but irreparable crack and to confess loud and clear that at this point he, the King, is forever naked.

It matters little that the system survives and the hero dies. Like the hijacker committing suicide, the duellist 'rushes' voluntarily into the duel which sentences Leviathan to live his vulnerable life. Obliged to live in reality, the latter is forever excluded from the paradise of symbols. He always lacks that additional being which belongs to the hero of the challenge.

So the duel was a form of resistance, a symbolic challenge, and not a form of political opposition or cultural fidelity. Although almost all of society was the fascinated witness and accomplice of duels, although commoners and civilians fought them in great number, it is clear that duelling was essentially the affair of the *noblesse d'épée*. Stone, in his study of the duels of English lords, sees in them a way of defusing the brutality inherent in the language and life of the times, a sublimation of private wars and – without those concerned being aware of it – a tool for the installation and acceptance of a modern monarchial order. A stage therefore on the road towards the monopolisation of licit violence, and even a stage in the process of the reduction of violence itself.

Whatever the pertinence of this interpretation as regards the British high nobility, it would be imprudent to apply it to France, and to extend it to all the 'duelling' population. Stone himself signalled the specificity of the French case in terms of the generalised French use of seconds (an almost non-existent practice in Britain). We would add that the French duel – whatever the pretensions of the theoreticians – did not put an end to the chain of vengeance and counter-vengeance. Often it was simply an intermediate stage (but heavy with concrete consequences) in collective struggles between families or factions. And nothing indicates that the practice of duelling eliminated or reduced that of brawling, of 'ambush fights', or of murder by paid assassins (even in the ranks of those who expressly regarded themselves as following the code of honour). Ferri's hypothesis according to which humanity is evolving from primal spontaneous violence towards deferred and calculated ruses receives no verification from the practice of duelling among the French nobility and gentry. We shall therefore leave to one side these interpretations which, surreptitiously, lead us away from the symbolic and towards 'reality'.

Those who inherited or invented the practice of duelling were the gentlemen who went through not a material crisis of the nobility nor a questioning of the social and moral pre-eminence of their order, but – like all their contemporaries – a series of material, moral and religious crises, in which they lost their footing, wondering who they were and indeed if they were. The duel was their means of expression and was addressed to everything that was beyond them and crushing them (whether they submitted or rebelled): it was their way of saying that they existed, that they were not objects and that they were responsible for their collective history and their individual destinies.

Their actions were in profound harmony with their tragic experience of their present. The coincidence between the vogue for single combat and that of regicide has been stressed already. The style of duels has been linked to that of pre-Cornelian tragedies. Other links could be made. The time of duels which was, elsewhere, the time of Quixote, was in France the 'baroque age' and the age of 'peasant frenzies', the era of the 'mystic invasion' and the era of diabolical possessions and witch trials.

All these more or less contemporary phenomena emanated from different social groups in the same society. They were all symbolic actions, 'cries repeated by a thousand sentinels', with nothing of the marginal or residual about them. Their authors, each in their own language, were giving the most authentic accounts of the profound essence of their period. In the 'autumn of the Renaissance', in the 'perennial shaker' of a material world which was beyond their grasp, in a Christendom cracked by the Reformation, within that reduced and reductive absolute of absolute monarchy, the individual and the group, could only exist for themselves and for others in the extreme experience of their mortality. But, in that experience, they existed absolutely.

The Time of Duellists

The relation between duellists and time is characterised by suddenness, haste and impatience. Neither appellant nor *appelé* could stand delay, waiting or duration. They could fulfil themselves only in the ephemeral instant, in a moment disconnected from all antecedents and any foresight of consequences.

Everything converges to give us an impression of instability and impatience. No 'regulated' code sets out the laws of honour, which remain essentially oral: 'each by his own authority changed and reformed it every day. The most sure and well-thought-of rule . . . lasted no more than five or six years.' Postponements, which were normal in the formal duel, as in any judicial procedure, were unbearable in the private duel: they were suspected of being procrastinations and proof of cowardice. Efforts to avoid a fight (attempts at reconciliation, or the sending in of guards) plunged the quarrellers into a kind of temporal limbo which they generally could not bear. The interval between the *démenti* and the armed encounter was reduced further and further. And the latter itself had to be brief: at any moment it could be interrupted (and therefore annulled) by the intervention of relatives or the authorities. If it unfolded without hindrance, but without a clear outcome, it had to end with the day or night in which it had begun, and any return to fighting the same duel was unthinkable; it was a kind of unity of time applied to the theatre of honour.

This fight which was seen in terms of chance and luck escaped any relations of causality, any temporal sequence: it was said that in it Satan had 'given all the power to fate'. The duellists 'risked their lives at the slightest thing' and death was the usual outcome for at least one of the combatants. The verb used for suicide in the vocabulary of the time, 'to rush' (*se précipiter*), wonderfully describes the 'kind of despair [in which] we are in such a hurry to remove and take out of the world this fine creature made in God's image'. If the winning duellist survived the ordeal, he had no lasting reward: he had to hide, to go into exile, as though struck down with 'civil death', and the honour he had so dearly won did not withstand the first subsequent challenge. The gentleman lived the life of honour only in intense and fleeting moments, separated by interminable expanses of uncertainty.

This conception of temporal destiny experienced through the ethics of the point of honour was well described by some moralists who tried to warn their contemporaries off duelling. Pont-Aymery wrote: 'Everything is changeable and uncertain ... and in such a great mixing and moving of human things, the only thing everyone can be sure of is death. He who fights a duel does neither more nor less than two gamblers.' Jean de Loyac entitled a chapter 'The belief of gentlemen of these times concerning the licence destiny has given them to fight duels'. In it he states, 'Many gentlemen in France let themselves be tied to the chain of fate and the wheels of fortune, which lead them like conscripts into discord, quarrels and single combat.... Pushed by sails of so-called destiny, they flounder in a sea of quarrels, thinking that they can hug the wind and contain the storms in the wineskin of their adventures to reach the port of the point of honour.' How illusory was this port, lacking both surface and thickness! It was an escape beyond time which did not lead into true eternity, vigorously summed up by Cyprien de la Nativité: the duellist 'prefers accidents to substance, the atom to the infinite, the creature to the Creator, *the moment to eternity*'.*

Perhaps time as experienced by French duellists around 1600 was just a particular example of the temporality experienced by any warrior. A temporality which the anthropologist Miller describes on the basis of examples taken from other periods and countries:

> The [warrior hero's] ego is caught and held at a stage where violence continuously breaks out like a proclamation of himself: a celebration of death which signifies immortality and eternity.... Death makes the first move and in the ideal chronology it is death which ends the career, while *youth* is still present. The final violence done by the hero to ordinary life thus consists in distorting the rhythm of that life, in the name of a powerful and isolated individuality.

This brings our duellist into a trans-historical human category, that of the warrior hero; but his vision of time is just as closely related to that of the non-combatants of his time and country. Georges Poulet's work on 'human time' and Jean Rousset's on baroque sensibility show a few generations of artists, poets and

* Italics FB.

thinkers, from Scève to Pascal, who were a prey to time as to a loss
of being. For the man of the period (at least the man who had the
means and desire to talk about himself), the only escape from this
incessant flux was 'the island of the moment which isolates him but
which he fills with his presence'. We see this in Montaigne's declaration: 'I want to stop the speed of its flight with the speed of my
grasp.' We see it in Corneille's hero who 'whatever he has lost, has
lost nothing, since he possesses himself: a self-possession locked in
the instant'. We see it in the Cartesian thinking subject whose only
(but how intoxicating!) certainty lies in the act of the *cogito*. We see it
in the Christian living with the notion of continuous creation, whose
'existence hangs, second by second, on an act that God may not
perform'. We see it in a more modest form in the heterodox
conventicles which flourished at the time 'with neither inherited
wealth nor guarantees for the future, reduced to this present which
from now on is married to death'.

The time that the French duellists of the sixteenth and seventeenth
centuries were experimenting with, that tragic and joyful impetuos-
ity, was a finished synthesis, a finely realised encounter at the point
of intersection of two manifestations of humanity, the ageless heroic
warrior and the baroque age.

Duels and Duellists Beyond Time?

The link we have just outlined between the baroque gentleman in
France and an ahistorical type of warrior hero requires some developing. Did the duel as defined here exist in other periods besides
this one? Is it a structure that endured over a very long period of
time, with or without centuries of latency? Is it even an invariable in
an 'immobile history'? We have no intention of using as an instrument of analysis the formal resemblances noted by duellists short of
exempla or by *scienza cavalleresca* in its search for precedents: the
artificial series of David and Goliath, Achilles and Hector, the Horatii
and the Curiatii and Bayart and Sotomayor, or that of the Lombard
laws, Philippe le Bel's decrees, the Duc de Guise's *pareri* and the rules
of the Marshals of France.

However, much light has been shed for us on this modern French
phenomenon by the 'pre-law' practices and their relics in pre-
classical and classical Greece described by Louis Gernet. This is not
to affirm the existence of an analogous process of juridical maturation going from the archaic, sacred or 'magic' phase through to a
rational, civic and lay practice; nor is it to presuppose that all history
is made up of developments which are not simultaneous, but unfold
in a perfectly similar way, a necessary path travelled by all human

development in society. It is not to accept the dogma of progress, nor to uphold a cyclical conception of time, nor to drain away the historical in the name of 'immobile history' (which is too often a shameful affirmation of a totally intemporal human nature).

Nor is it to side with this or that orthodoxy (rejecting the others). It is a kind of act of faith. If we set out to draw the map of a 'world that we have lost', it may be as useful to us to take along the charts of other worlds as the map of our own metro system. No one will deny that, as a learned discipline, history must be rigorous and meticulously methodical. But (at least when, as here, it is dealing with institutions whose value is essentially symbolic) it loses too much if, in trying to be a science, it forgets to be poetry. To recall the foundation of the Areopagus and the writing of the *Oresteia* in regard to royal edicts and the 'bloody theatre of our duels' is, in a sense, to use metaphors and correspondences. It is to think that one can only describe another space, that one can only bring it here to any extent, with the aid of other, different spaces. It is to affirm, with a mixture of lucidity and passion, that 'man infinitely surpasses man' and that 'nothing that is human is totally foreign' to another human being.

To write history is not to make a line-by-line translation of the past (such an attempt would give us only nonsensical mistranslations). To write history is to speak in parables.

Select Bibliography

This bibliography offers a selection of the more important or more general-ly available works to which François Billacois refers and provides details of the texts cited in epigraphs. (Ed.)

Works Written Before 1720

Alciat, André, *De duello*, Paris, J. Kervers, 1541.

Aubigné, Théodore Agrippa d', *Les Aventures du baron de Foeneste*, in *Oeuvres*, Paris, Gallimard, 1969.

Audiguier, Vital d', *Le Vray et ancien usage des duels*, Paris, P. Billaine, 1617.

Bodin, Charles, Sieur de Freteil, *Discours contre les duels*, Paris, T. du Bray, 1618.

Bousy, P. de, *Méléagre*, Caen, P. Le Chandelier, 1582.

Brantôme, Pierre de Bourdeille, Seigneur de, *Discours sur les duels* in *Oeuvres complètes*, ed. L. Lalanne, Paris, Société de l'Histoire de France, 1864–82.

Camus, Jean-Pierre, *Homélies des Etats Généraux (1614–1615)*, annotated text, ed. J. Descrains, Geneva, Droz, 1970.

Caussin, Nicolas, SJ, *La Cour saincte*, Paris, Chappelet, 1624.

Cabans, Louis de, Sieur de Maine, *Advis et moyens pour empescher le désordre des duels proposéz au Roy en l'assemblée des Etats Généraux*, Paris, D. Langlois, 1615.

Cheffontaines, F. Christophle, known as Penfentenyou, *Chrestienne confuta-tion du poinct d'honneur sur lequel la noblesse fonde aujourd'hui ses querelles et monomachies*, Paris, Fremy, 1568.

Chenel, Jean, Sieur de La Chapperonaye, *Les Révélations de l'hermite solitaire sur l'estat de la France*, Paris, T. du Bray, 1617.

Corneille, Pierre, *Théâtre Complet*, Paris, Gallimard, 1951.

Demont-Bourcher, Paul, Seigneur de La Rivaudière, *Advis au Roy touchant le restablissement du gage de bataille en champ clos, et du duel et combat libre entre la noblesse*, Paris, G. Marette, 1608.

Druy, Comte de, *Le Beauté de la valeur et la lascheté du duel, divisé en quatre parties*, Paris, J. Bessin, 1658.

Du Bellay, Jean (Cardinal), *Correspondance*, Paris, Klincksieck, 1969.

Du Bellay, Joachim, *La Monomachie de David et de Goliath*, annotated edition, ed. E. Caldarini, Geneva, Droz, 1981.

Dupleix, Scipion, *Les Lois militaires touchant le duel*, Paris, D. Salis, 1602.

Favyn, A., *Le Théâtre d'honneur et de chevalerie*, Paris, R. Fouet, 1620.

Joly, Guillaume, *Antiduel, ou Discours pour l'abolition des duels*, Paris, P. Chevalier, 1612.

La Béraudière, Marc de, Seigneur de Mauvoisin, *Le Combat de seul á seul en champ clos, avec plusieurs questions propres á ce sujet*, Paris, A. L'Angelier, 1608.

La Marche, Olivier de, Jean de Villiers, Seigneur de l'Isle-Adam, Hardouin de La Jaille et al, *Traitéz et advis de quelques gentilshommes françois sur les duels et gaiges de bataille. [. . .] et autres escrits sur le mesme sujet, non encore imprimêz*, Paris, J. Richer, 1586.

La Rochefoucauld, François, Duc de, *Mémoires*, in *Oeuvres complètes*, Paris, Gallimard, 1950.

La Taille, Jean de, Seigneur de Bondaroy, *Discours notable des duels*, Paris, C. Rigaud, 1607.

Loque, Bertrand de, *Deux traités, l'un de la guerre, l'autre du duel, auquel est vuidée la question de scavoir s'il est loisible aux chrestiens de dêmesler un différent par le combat singulier, où est aussi dêsmeslée la dispute du point d'honneur*, Lyons, 1589.

Malherbe, François de, *Lettres*, in *Oeuvres*, ed. L. Lalanne, Paris, Hachette, 1862–9.

Molière, *Oeuvres complètes*, Paris, Gallimard, 1959.

Montaigne, Michel de, *Les Essais*, Paris, Gallimard, 1950.

Montaigne, Michel de, *Essays*, trans. J. M. Cohen, London, Penguin, 1959.

Mutio, Justinopolitain [Girolamo Muzio], *Le Combat, avec les responses chevaleresques*, trans Antoine Chappuys, Lyons, G. Roville, 1561.

Pascal, Blaise, *Oeuvres*, ed. L Brunschvicg, Paris, Hachette, 1908–14.

Pascal, Blaise, *The Provincial Letters*, trans. A. J. Krailsheimer, London, Penguin, 1967.

Possevin, Jean-Baptiste [Giambattista Possevino], *Les Dialogues d'honneur esquels est complètement discouru et résolu de tous les pointz de l'honneur entre toutes personnes*, trans. C. Gruget, Paris, J. Longis, 1557.

Ronsard, Pierre de, *La Victoire de Guy de Chabot, seigneur de Jarnac* in *Oeuvres complètes*, vol 1, Paris, Gallimard, 1950.

Saint-Pierre, Abbé de, *Mémoire pour perfectionner la police contre les duels*, Paris, 1717.

Savaron, Jean, Sieur de Villars, *Traicté contre les duels avec l'édict de Philippes le Bel de MCCCVI non encore imprimé*, Paris, G. Chaudière, 1578.

Sorbin, Arnauld, *Exhortation á la noblesse pour la dissuader et détourner des duels et autres combats*, Paris, G. Chaudière, 1578.

Trelon, Gabriel de, *Advis sur la présentation de l'édit de Sa Majesté contre la damnable coustume des duels*, Paris, R. Fouet, 1603.

Urrea, Jeronimo Jimenes de, *Dialogues du vray honneur militaire traitans l'abus de la plupart de la noblesse comme l'honneur doit se conformer à la conscience; orné de plusieurs choses belles et plaisantes qui luy servent d'un esmail de diverses couleurs pour la récréation de lisans*, trans. G. Chappuys, Paris, T. Perrier, 1585.

Vulson de La Colombière, Marc de, *Le Vray théâtre d'honneur et de chevalerie, ou Le Miroir héroïque de la noblesse*, Paris, A. Courbe, 1648.

Works Written After 1720

Althusser, Louis, *Montesquieu, la politique et l'histoire*, Paris, Presses Universitaires de France, 1959.

Bachelard, Gaston, *La Terre et les rêveries de la volonté*, Paris, J Corti, 1948.

Baudrillard, Jean, *L'Echange symbolique et la mort*, Paris, Gallimard, 1976.

Bénichou, Paul, *Morales du grand siècle*, Paris, Gallimard, 1948.

Bennetton, Norman A, *Social Significance of the Duel in Seventeenth-Century French Drama*, Baltimore, John Hopkins Press, 1938.

Berque, J., *L'Egypte, impérialisme et révolution*, Paris, Gallimard, 1967.

Bremond, Henri, *Histoire littéraire du sentiment religieux en France depuis la fin des guerres de religion*, 7 vols, Paris, Bloud & Gay, 1929–38.

Caillois, Roger, *Man, Play and Games*, trans. Meyer Barash, London, Thames & Hudson, 1962.

Castan, Nicole, *Justice et répression en Languedoc á l'époque des Lumiéres*, Paris, Flammarion, 1980.

Chaunu, P., *La Mort á Paris: 16ᵉ, 17ᵉ, 18ᵉ siècles*, Paris, Fayard, 1978.

Clark, Sir George, *War and Society in the Seventeenth Century*, Cambridge, Cambridge University Press, 1958.

Coustard de Massi, *Histoire du duel en France*, London, P. Elmsly, 1768.

Cuenin, Micheline, *Le Duel sous l'Ancien Régime*, Paris, Presses de la Renaissance, 1982.

Davis, Nataly Z., *Society and Culture in Early Modern France*, Stanford, Cal., 1975.

Davy, Georges, *La Foi jurée. Etude sociologique du problème du contrat; la formation du lien contractuel*, Paris, Alcan, 1922.

Devyver, André, *Le Sang épuré. Les Préjugés de race chez les gentilshommes français de l'Ancien Régime (1560–1720)*, Brussels, Editions de l'Université de Bruxelles, 1973.

Doubrovsky, Serge, *Corneille et la dialectique du héros*, Paris, Gallimard, 1963.

Duby, Georges, *The Three Orders: Feudal Society Imagined*, trans. Arthur Goldhammer, Chicago, Chicago University Press, 1980.

Dumézil, Georges, *Horace et les Curiaces*, Paris, Gallimard, 1942.

Dumézil, Georges, *The Stakes of the Warrior*, ed. J. Puhvel, trans. D. Weeks, University of California Press, 1983.

Eliade, Mircéa, *The Forge and the Crucible: The Origins and Structures of Alchemy* 2nd ed., trans. S. Corrin, Chicago, University of Chicago Press, 1979.

Foucault, Michel, *Surveiller et punir: naissance de La prison*, Paris, Gallimard, 1975. Translated as *Discipline and Punish: The Birth of the Prison*, trans. A. Sheridan, New York, Random House, 1975 and London, Penguin, 1979.

Foucault, Michel, *The Order of Things*, trans. from the French, London, Tavistock, 1970.

Gernet, Louis, *The Anthropology of Ancient Greece*, trans. J. D. B. Hamilton and B. Nagy, Baltimore, John Hopkins Press, 1981.

Girard, Louis, *La Violence et le sacré*, Paris, Grasset 1972.

Huizinga, Johann, *The Waning of the Middle Ages*, trans. F. Hopman, London, Penguin, 1965.

Huppert, Georges, *Les Bourgeois gentilshommes: An Essay in the Definition of Élites in Renaissance France*, Chicago, University of Chicago Press, 1977.

Jones, Ernest, *Hamlet and Oedipus*, London, Gollancz, 1949.

Jouanna, Arlette, *L'Idée de race en France au XVIᵉ et au début du XVIIᵉ siècle (1498–1614)*, 2 vols, Paris, H. Champion, 1976.

Kossman, Ernest H., *La Fronde*, Leiden, Presses Universitaires, 1954.

Letainturier-Fradin, Gabriel, *Le Duel à travers les âges*, Paris, Flammarion, 1892.

Mandrou, Robert, *Introduction to Modern France (1500–1640): an Essay in Historical Psychology*, trans. R. E. Hallmark, London, Penguin, 1979.

Mauron, Charles, *Des Métaphores obsédantes au mythe personnel. Introduction á la psychocritique*, Paris, J Corti, 1962

Mauss, Marcel, *The Gift: Forms and Functions of Exchange in Archaic Societies*, trans.I. Cunnisson, London, Cohen & West, 1954, reprinted London, Routledge & Kegan Paul, 1974.

Michelet, J., *Histoire de France*, Paris, 1856.

Muyart de Vouglans, P. F., *Institutes*, Paris, 1757.

Perrault, Gilles, *Les Parachutistes*, Paris, Le Seuil, 1961.

Pintard, René, *Le Libertinage érudit dans la première moitié du XVIIᵉ siècle*, 2 vols, Paris, Boivin, 1943.

Poulet, Georges, *Studies in Human Time*, trans. E. Coleman, London, Greenwood, 1956.

Rousset, Jean, *La Litterature de l'âge baroque en France: Circé et le paon*, Paris, J Corti, 1954.

Saint Thomas, Duverger de, *Nouveau code du duel*, Paris, Dentu, 1887.

Stegman, André, *L'Héroïsme cornélien. Genèse et signification*, 2 vols, Paris, A. Colin, 1968.

Stone, Lawrence, *The Crisis of the Aristocracy (1558–1641)*, Oxford, Clarendon Press, 1965.

Wiley, William L, *The Gentlemen of Renaissance France*, Cambridge, Mass., Harvard University Press, 1954.

Index